Planning Sucessful Museum Building Projects

Planning Successful Museum Building Projects

WALTER L. CRIMM, MARTHA MORRIS,
AND L. CAROLE WHARTON

ALTAMIRA
PRESS

A Division of
ROWMAN & LITTLEFIELD PUBLISHERS, INC.
Lanham • New York • Toronto • Plymouth, UK

AltaMira Press
A division of Rowman & Littlefield Publishers, Inc.
A wholly owned subsidiary of The Rowman & Littlefield Publishing Group, Inc.
4501 Forbes Boulevard, Suite 200, Lanham, MD 20706
www.altamirapress.com

Estover Road, Plymouth PL6 7PY, United Kingdom

British Library Cataloguing in Publication Information Available

Library of Congress Cataloging-in-Publication Data

Crimm, Walter L.
  Planning successful museum building projects / Walter L. Crimm, Martha Morris, and L. Carole Wharton.
      p. cm.
  Includes bibliographical references and index.
  ISBN-13: 978-0-7591-1186-8 (cloth : alk. paper)
  ISBN-10: 0-7591-1186-3 (cloth : alk. paper)
  ISBN-13: 978-0-7591-1187-5 (pbk. : alk. paper)
  ISBN-10: 0-7591-1187-1 (pbk. : alk. paper)
  [etc.]
  1. Museum architecture. 2. Museums—Planning. I. Morris, Martha. II. Wharton, L. Carole. III. Title.

  NA6690.C75 2009
  069'.22—dc22   2008046401

069.22 CRI

Printed in the United States of America

♾ ™ The paper used in this publication meets the minimum requirements of American National Standard for Information Sciences—Permanence of Paper for Printed Library Materials, ANSI/NISO Z39.48-1992.

Contents

List of Figures

Preface

Museums today are facing many challenges, and one of the most critical is inadequate facilities. Whether renovating, expanding, or building a new facility, museums are investing time and funds to improve and enhance their buildings.

Since 2002, the authors have presented workshops on the topic of museum planning, design, and construction at various museum association meetings. These workshops were meant to share the best practices of the field as reflected in the professional experiences of the authors. Martha Morris served as deputy director of the National Museum of American History at the Smithsonian, a museum that has undergone several major renovations over its fifty-year history. Walter L. Crimm is a practicing architect with years of experience helping museums and other cultural organizations solve problems of renovation, expansion, and new building. L. Carole Wharton has several decades of experience in budgeting, facilities planning, and management at major universities, government facilities, and museums. In 2002 Martha Morris began her efforts to benchmark the best practices and catalog the lessons learned from a variety of museum building projects. This research resulted in an article in *Museum News* (July 2004) and was the catalyst for an annual symposium, Building Museums, sponsored by the Mid-Atlantic Association of Museums (MAAM). The conference has drawn hundreds of attendees from the United States and abroad, attracting some of the best minds in the field—museum directors, designers, collections managers, and board members, as well as architects, engineers, and planning consultants—to share lessons learned about this vital activity. Case studies on

new museums, historic preservation, and green design have been augmented by
workshops on project management and planning, financing and fund-raising,
marketing and earned income, and impact on collections and staff.

The response to Building Museums is a strong signal that the field needs
more tutorial materials for the board of trustees, staff, volunteers, funders,
and students. Given the recent litany of cost overruns and poorly planned
projects, it is clear that many museums are not well equipped to undertake
such complex projects. Few texts address the world of museum construction.
An annual conference is only one approach to this deep-seated need.   ·

The MAAM symposium is organized under three overarching themes: vision, implementation, and sustainability/life after opening. This comprehensive view is critical to understanding the drivers, the organization, funding,
and mission-based approach to success. The ratings for the symposium have
been extremely positive and many participants return to the conference each
year. The Building Museums conference has provided a rich source of information about museum building projects, including 125 case studies along
with supplementary materials regarding service providers, as well as biblio-
graphic resources. From its inception the symposium has featured a Nuts and
Bolts Workshop, on which this book is based.

Planning Successful Museum Building Projects is a practical handbook of
tested tools and techniques to assist museum boards, administrators, and staff
as they undertake construction projects. It is meant to educate funders,
donors, contractors, and other practitioners in the basic needs of museums
and what makes them unique. The text draws on the professional experience
and practices of the authors, their academic research on best practices and
trends, and from other sources, including the case studies featured in the
Building Museums symposia.

This book is organized to walk the reader through the building process starting with an overview of trends in museums (chapter 1), leading to chapters on
planning (chapter 2), roles and responsibilities (chapter 3), exhibitions and collections programs (chapter 4), hiring the team (chapter 5), project management
of the design and construction process (chapters 6), developing criteria and
documenting your building (chapter 7), financing and cost management (chapter 8), fund-raising and capital campaigns (chapter 9), communications (chapter 10), operations (chapter 11), and evaluation of project success (chapter 12).
The book includes do's and don'ts that offer summary steps to ensure success
and highlights the red flags that identify potential problems. The book provides

a practical how-to approach, illustrates case studies from the field, and includes an array of helpful references that include checklists, suggested readings, sources of professional guidelines, a glossary, and samples of working documents.

We would like to acknowledge the special assistance of the following persons. For technical review assistance: Jeff Hirsch, Jim Cranage, Bill Jarema, Bob Ghisu, Roger Rudy, Mary Alcaraz, Michael Brumberg, Gary Lockman, Don Barth, Gayle Lane, and Peter Levasseur of EwingCole and Steve Keller of Steven R. Keller & Associates. For graphic design of charts and diagrams: Chris Mayrides and Ashlee Carrulo. For administrative support: Anita Clark. For assistance with the glossary and bibliography: Diane Goldman, independent researcher. Dana Allen-Greil, project manager in the new media office, National Museum of American History, contributed her research to the chapters on communications and operations.

Special thanks go to Graham Hauck, executive director of MAAM who has worked tirelessly on Building Museums. We also wish to acknowledge John Suau, former executive director of MAAM, for his early encouragement of our efforts to create the annual symposium, and Mary Case, principal of QM2, who has worked closely with MAAM from the outset on the creation of Building Museums. The members of the MAAM board of directors have strongly supported the symposium, and we are grateful for the faith they have placed in us in developing this book for the field.

A special thanks goes to those who have supported and encouraged our efforts. Walt would like to thank his wife, Deenah Loeb, and children, Jonas and Emma Crimm, who have gone to museums around the world with him, but never to Orlando. Martha would like to thank her husband, Joe Shannon, for his enthusiasm and patience and his insights into the value of museums in our society. Carole would like to thank her husband, Yi Tsien, her most honest critic, who has dutifully and diligently read her prose, mercilessly chasing out jargon and fuzzy thinking for over thirty years.

Finally, we must say thank you to the many museum professionals who have mentored and worked alongside us with the hope that this book captures the collective wisdom of them all.

Walter L. Crimm
Martha Morris
L. Carole Wharton

1

Introduction

The museum field today faces many challenges. Because museums are recognized, respected, and supported by their communities in a significant way, they must have the highest levels of management and leadership skills to meet the expectations for quality services and engagement that the public demands. Yet many museum professionals, boards, and supporters lack the resources and programs to provide these skills. In today's highly competitive environment for the public's time and attention, museums struggle for relevance. That factor is often the impetus for a variety of bold endeavors.

Museum expansion and renovation is often seen as an imperative. Yet this most important trend requires extraordinary care in planning and implementation. Research and observation show that the museum building boom under way for more than a decade is likely to continue unabated. More than ever, museums need sound practical advice on how to successfully navigate what is probably the most expensive and time-consuming activity they will undertake.

TRENDS IN MUSEUM BUILDING

Museums of every type and size are engaged in facilities projects ranging from renovation of older historic structures to expansions to entirely new facilities. Billions of dollars are being invested in these projects, often the most visible component of a museum's program. Census data reveal that between 1993 and 2007 the investment in construction of privately funded museums grew at over 15 percent per year.[1]

In 2006 the American Association of Museums revealed that "almost one quarter of U.S. museums are engaged in a capital fund-raising campaign, with a median goal of $10 million. Half of museums have begun or completed building construction, renovation or expansion in the past three years."[2] Of these museums, 75 percent represented private museums. In all museums surveyed there were twice as many renovations as new buildings and expansions. Although there is often more press coverage about art museum projects, there was more building under way in zoos, children's museums, natural history, science centers, and history museums in that period of time. However, art museums and science centers were spending larger amounts.

The Association of Art Museum Directors tracks the progress of expansion projects for its member museums. In 2007, 66 percent of planned expansions were moving forward, while 18 percent were changing the time frame, 6 percent changing scope, and 7 percent revising plans. In addition, between 2004 and 2007 their member museums saw an average 41 percent increase in contributions to facilities growth.[3]

We also see a number of new museums being created. Museums are now being formed to memorialize historic events such as the Ground Zero site in New York City and the Holocaust museums in Washington, New York, and Houston to name a few; or to honor special communities such as the Arab American National Museum in Dearborn, Michigan; or to honor the history of African Americans in this country. Just about any topic is being covered, including museums devoted to artists (Andy Warhol), or broad topics (the Creation Museum or Museum of American Finance), or significant locations (American Revolution Center at Valley Forge). Not only U.S. museums are engaged in this boom, but Chinese, Canadian, Australian, French, Greek, German, Japanese, and Middle Eastern museums are building as well.

Museum building projects can consume anywhere from two to twenty years, including initial planning, through architectural design, fund-raising, construction, and opening. Although twenty years may sound extreme, there are reasons these projects can be seriously prolonged. Launching an idea can run into many hurdles, including finding the right building site, getting approval from government agencies, and testing feasibility. Many projects suffer from lack of strong planning, staff turnover (including executive directors), poor budgeting, rising costs due to the vagaries of the marketplace, and scope creep. Despite these realities, many museums are eager to engage in building projects.

WHAT ARE THE DRIVERS?

Why has expansion become a critical component of the strategic success of today's museum? We believe there are several factors that contribute to this phenomenon.

Mission

Museums and all nonprofits are being challenged to realize their mission, or reason for existing. If a museum is to stay in business, its relevance to society must be clear. Today museums are expected to ensure that all decisions and actions taken are in service to their mission. Are they good stewards of their assets? Do they serve the community? In the past decade the American Association of Museums developed a manifesto for museums and communities, calling on each museum to redefine its relationship with community to one of collaboration, mutual understanding, and public service. In response many museums have taken the bold step of reinventing themselves, including reexamining or even rewriting their mission statements. And what more obvious way is there to realize that new mission than through a highly visible building project? Museum planners need to stop at this stage and ask themselves, is a facilities or capital project the best approach?

Aging Facilities

As noted above, among museum construction projects there are more renovation projects than new buildings. Museums, like other organizations, have a life cycle. Twenty-five years is an industry standard. No wonder many museums face backlogs of facilities maintenance and replacement of worn infrastructure. In 2007 the Smithsonian Institution revealed a backlog in facilities maintenance of $2.5 billion.[4] How many museum buildings will eventually suffer from leaking roofs, deteriorating electrical or plumbing systems, or inefficient heating and cooling? Even newer buildings can be subject to roof leaks or the breakdown of infrastructure components. A landmark report on heritage health in this country revealed that the most pressing needs are environmental controls and improved collections storage.[5] ADA compliance is also a major concern for older structures and drives facility upgrades.

Historic preservation goals also drive renovation programs. Saving land-mark buildings is a moral and sometimes legal obligation. Historic buildings are constantly in need of renovation. Aging facilities also have other problems such as asbestos insulation or improper moisture barriers and leaky windows or negative air pressure. Advances in technology and in more energy efficient systems allow museums to save money and the environment. A sweeping movement to create buildings that are environmentally friendly has also led to new renovation approaches. LEED (leadership in energy and environmental design) certification, a sustainability benchmark, is a badge that many muse-ums now aspire to, and with that comes significant physical change. Finally, with a push for new technology in exhibitions and in managing operations there is need for more sophisticated information technology support systems.

Economic Impact

The modern museum is in the enviable position of being a catalyst for community change. This plays out in several ways. Richard Florida's writing on the creative class underscores this trend. Florida's theories relate to the value of creative individuals and organizations that attract new audiences. A highly educated workforce fosters economic development and a more vibrant economy. Noted museum architect Daniel Libeskind has stated that "the dif-ference between cities is their creative power and museums are manifestations of that."[6]

At the same time arts and cultural patrons are seeking new experiences. The museum is capable of and in some cases is becoming an entertainment venue. Much as a department store serves as an anchor in a shopping mall, the museum itself becomes the centerpiece of community revitalization efforts.

Clearly there are critics of this phenomenon, but museums are becoming more businesslike in their alliance with community revitalization efforts. An article in the *Wall Street Journal* questioned the ability of nonprofit museums to manage the demands of expansion: new audiences, high operational costs, the need to present a wide variety of blockbuster attractions, and so on. How many will fail?[7]

Visitor Experience and Competition for Leisure Time

Competition for audience attention and more sophisticated museum visitors are driving museums to overturn the old paradigms of design and interpretative

techniques. Partnering with for-profits or other nonprofits to create more pow-
erful learning experiences is a way of leveraging a successful business model.

Government and foundation leaders are strong proponents of the educational value of museums. They have crafted public policy objectives that will
help museums further define their relevance. Education underlies the significance of these policies. More sophisticated boards and staff understand that to
deal with the realities of competition the museum must use creative marketing approaches to sustain old and attract new audiences.

Boards or Major Donors

Increasingly board members and major donors are investing in new buildings. In some eyes it is a competitive drive to stay current with other museums. In other instances these individuals may desire to create legacies and
obtain personal recognition. Today's boards and major donors are often per-
sonally involved as well as invested in their museums. In addition, corporations are invested in museums as marketing vehicles or through philanthropic
gifts, while foundations support museums as platforms for improving society.
This is good news for museums. Major donors are extremely important to the
financial success of building projects, but there is still great value in seeking
grassroots funding.

Collections

Collections are at the heart of most museums. They continue to grow and
create enormous demands. Many museums are opting to move collections to
off-site facilities for storage and research. Appropriate space for storage, exhibitions, research, and conservation treatment is a critical need. These needs
are unfortunately never perfectly answered in museum facilities and drive responsible board and staff to seek increased space as well as special conditions
such as climate control, lighting, and security. Most museums consider this a
top priority and seek a solution through building renovations and expansions.

WHAT ARE THE RISKS?

As compelling as the drivers are, many risks are inherent in undertaking a
building project. Can new buildings stimulate needed change? The building
project is often seen as the "easy answer" to implementing dramatic change.
Working with a star architect is considered by some a guarantee of success in

ensuring a prime leadership position among cultural attractions in the community or even in the country. Jim Collins in his landmark book *Built to Last* defines the BHAG (big hairy audacious goal) as a prime measure of success in organizations. Yet these larger-than-life goals end up being major risks in times of uncertainty marked by wars, economic instability, global warming, and so on. Museums that move into the long-term BHAG of an expansion or a new building need to be clearly armed for all risks.[8]

Studies have shown that, after the first year or so, attendance often dips at newly opened or renovated museums, but that is only one risk. A few examples of the challenges of new museum construction follow. In 2006 the Denver Museum of Art opened a $110 million, 146,000-square-foot addition designed by Daniel Libeskind. Within the first six months, the museum announced staff layoffs, noticeable repairs were being made to a leaking roof, and attendance numbers were not as high as expected due to a severe winter. These circumstances highlight the types of unexpected risks associated with such ambitious projects. Less positive cases include Cleveland's HealthSpace museum, which closed after three years of operation due to its inability to cover construction debt. Poor attendance at the new City Museum of Washington, D.C., forced it to close in 2004 after eighteen months of operation. Cincinnati's National Underground Museum and Freedom Center opened in 2004 and within eighteen months was suffering significant operating deficits. Washington's Corcoran Gallery of Art developed an ambitious expansion plan designed by Frank Gehry in the late 1990s, and pledges were made by major donors and the city government. Yet fund-raising stalled in 2005 and the project was canceled.[9]

The risks that museums face in embarking on building projects include unrealistic expectations, lack of successful planning, poor definition of scope, underprepared board and staff, and poor synchronization of physical and program plans. Museum building projects are ambitious and often need to be implemented in phases that can stretch out for many years. At the same time the museum usually faces the need to work with multiple funding streams. Many building projects require the talents and input of a variety of specialized contractors, community members, and staff and board members. These projects are a balancing act to say the least.

Many new museums are launched to build community pride, reflect aspirations, memorialize important events in history, preserve artifacts, works of art, and historic sites, and respond to changing demographics and public interests. Museums provide legitimacy, and this is the good news. Yet many well-meaning boards of trustees seem unprepared to take on a building program *and* the ongoing operations of the new museum. Perhaps new museums risk the most because they have little institutional history, unformed collections, few established organizations with which to collaborate on programming, and they lack well-developed audience and donor bases.

However, many museums have fared well in the process of new building programs. The Strong National Museum of Play in Rochester, New York, the Museum of Modern Art in New York City, and the California Academy of Sciences in San Francisco are just a few of the institutions that have produced successful expansions in recent years. Most of these museums have a strong and diversified donor base, community support, experienced leadership and, in many cases, substantial endowments.

To weigh risks, museums often use feasibility studies to predict the success of new facilities projects. There is much value in this approach, which will be discussed in greater detail in chapter 2 on planning. Some, however, believe that relying on feasibility studies is a flawed model and prefer to simply move forward on a "build it and they will come" approach. What can mitigate risk in a case such as this? A strong brand name, for one thing. Museums such as the Metropolitan or the Smithsonian can count on a stream of visitors, and expansions are less likely to fail in these cases. However, what is the impact of oversaturation of the museum market itself? A small but potentially disruptive trend is occurring in the art museum field: major collectors are building their own museums. Are they looking for immortality and independence? Do they compete with existing museums? If every city, university, private collector, or special interest group succeeds in building a new museum, what will be the impact on the established institutions in their market?

DESIGN TRENDS FOR MUSEUMS

Art versus Container

Museums need to consider the dilemma of whether the building is a work of art in itself or whether it serves to contain collections, exhibitions, and programs. Often this choice is based on marketing issues or the pressures of the community or the desires of the board. A container approach focuses on the content—the collections and programs. The art approach sees the building as an attraction in itself.

Green Design

There is a clear emphasis on sustainable design today. Museums feel the imperative to go green for several reasons: to lower operating costs in the long run, to benefit the environment, and to attract the support of funders and other stakeholders. Many museums also see the green aspects as a way of educating the public about this most compelling need. There is of course the issue of payback: how long before you break even on what is often a more expensive investment up front?

Signature Architects

Not all museum projects are designed by internationally known architects, but clearly there is a desire to work with the best. Doing so can add a premium to the cost.

Open Collections

Museums need to share collections with the public as widely as possible. Often this is done through open storage, where a systematic display of objects is accompanied by in-depth information on the collections to offer a more contemplative experience.

Off-site Facilities

Museums will choose off-site facilities either for storage and other back of house functions or as satellite museums open to the public. The Smithsonian's Air and Space and American Indian museums have both opened satellite facilities, as has the Museum of Modern Art in New York. The Guggenheim is the leader in this regard with off-site museums in Spain, Italy, Germany, Nevada, and the Middle East.

Not only are museums moving collections to off-site locations for storage, they are also setting up off-site exhibition spaces. The Bilbao effect made famous by the Guggenheim Museum has been replicated by other museums seeking the opportunity to share collections and reach new audiences. The rationale is clear, but often the cost of building and operations is overwhelming.

Visitor Amenities

Emphasizing spaces that will make visitors feel comfortable and prolong their visit is a widespread trend. Orientation spaces, parking, dining options, gift shops, hands-on learning centers, theaters, gardens, collections study space, and lounges all add to the improved experience. Accessibility and accommodation of a wide variety of visitors is also an important factor in building projects.

Museums also seek larger and more flexible spaces for hosting special events, changing exhibitions including large traveling shows, and improved circulation to facilitate crowd control.

DOES YOUR SIZE MATTER?

All sizes and all types of museums can be candidates for a building program. Aside from time and cost issues, many of the problems encountered will be the same no matter what the size of your programs, collections, and staff. Trade-offs will always be needed in order to match visions with the reality of the budget.

WHERE DO YOU BEGIN?

The following chapters will outline the logical steps necessary for a successful building project. Clearly the best advice is to start with a strong planning effort. The diagram in figure 1.1 is a high-level view of the steps. At the outset, a museum must develop a strategic plan with clear vision and goals, followed by an implementation planning phase where a more specific scope of the project can take shape. As ideas are honed, an iterative process takes place that marries design ideas with strategic vision and the all-important budget feasibility. Scope definition is critical and must be detailed in the early phases. Selecting the best team of experts to work with the museum's board and staff is crucial for success. Determining the phasing and making decisions about closing the facility during construction are major issues. Construction itself is a complex phase that can create further challenges for the museum, its staff, board, and community. Selecting the best firms, managing expectations, and understanding the operational details of construction require extraordinary communications. Developing financing plans, conducting capital campaigns, and working effectively with donors can be challenging. Finally, at the point of occupancy and operations the museum has the obligation and opportunity to test its assumptions and measure its success through audience studies, effective commissioning systems, and gauging public pride and staff morale. The process is exhilarating and the end product something that promises to be continually enjoyed by all.

FIGURE 1.1
Life of Project Process

NOTES

1. U.S. Census Bureau, www.census.gov/const/C30/private.xls (accessed April 6, 2008).

2. American Association of Museums, *Museum Financial Information* (Washington, D.C.: American Association of Museums, 2006), 92–96.

3. Association of Art Museum Directors, *2007 State of North America's Art Museums Survey,* www.aamd.org/newroom/documents/2007SNAAMReleaseData_final.pdf (accessed April 6, 2008).

4. Jenny Mandel, "Smithsonian Problems Include $2.5 Billion Maintenance, Repair List," April 11, 2007, www.govexec.com/story_page.cfm?articleid=36583 (accessed April 11, 2007).

5. *Heritage Health Survey Report,* 2005, www.heritagepreservation.org/HHI/execsummary.html (accessed March 18, 2008).

6. Daniel Libeskind, "Designing Soul," *Museum News,* March-April 2005, 45.

7. Douglas McLennan, "Culture Clash: Has the Business Model for Arts Institutions Outlived Its Usefulness?" *Wall Street Journal,* October 8, 2005, 11.

8. Jim Collins and Jerry Porras, *Built to Last* (New York: Harper Business, 1994), 94.

9. Martha Morris, "Building Boom or Bust?" *Journal of Museum Management and Curatorship* 22, no. 2 (June 2007): 102–3.

Planning and Organizing for Success

Few museum staffs build more than one building during their professional lifetimes, and now we know why.

—*Redmond Barnett, Washington State Historical Society*

GETTING STARTED

Is your museum a start-up? An established museum? It's important to understand that museums have a life cycle. Knowing your stage of development will help determine the way you need to approach a building program. What is a life cycle curve? Literature on this topic points to the varied stages of growth of the organization starting from infancy and stretching out to senility. Typically in the start-up phase a founding individual or group has a great deal of enthusiasm and drive but few or no resources or structure. As the organization begins to grow, it attracts new resources, including staff, collections, and a facility in which to operate. Organizations in their prime are challenged by new ideas and are constantly improving. Older organizations can be plagued by bureaucracy. A senile museum is often characterized by lack of resonance with the public, dwindling finances, decaying facilities, and poor morale. A museum seeking to stay in its prime must recognize the challenges to its facilities and seek to improve them.[1]

How to Start a Museum

Starting a new museum is a daunting endeavor. If you are a start-up, there are several things you must do before planning a building program. In the United States museums exist primarily as part of the nonprofit sector. Museums established as nonprofit charitable corporations typically file for status as a 501c(3) seeking federal and state tax exemptions. The Internal Revenue Service has specific requirements along with information to guide you on its website (www.irs.gov). Obtaining this status will spare you from paying taxes (with exceptions) and will allow you to receive tax-deductible contributions. Instructions for creating a charitable corporation are regulated by each state. You will be required to write and file articles of incorporation, develop a purpose statement or mission, and select a name for your museum along with naming a founding board of directors. Your board will need to understand its fiduciary duties as it develops operating bylaws and early plans for the museum. Nonprofits are required to receive a substantial amount of their support from public sources including governmental units or the general public. Foundations, corporations, and individuals can start museums as well, but they may not have the full range of exemptions and benefits. In any case, an attorney should be your guide as you form a new museum.[2]

If you are a new museum within a parent organization such as a university, corporation, or government entity, the steps necessary will be dictated by local and state laws and policies and procedures established by the parent organization.

THE NEED FOR PLANNING

Long before construction, museums embarking on a building project must engage in careful planning. Why? Because without a strong and well developed plan the museum is at risk for failure. *Indeed planning is the best predictor of success.* We are happy to report that the majority of museums we have surveyed in recent years have done strategic planning. However, without additional planning museums that embark on building projects can experience cost overruns, public criticism, and staff morale issues. These problems can be avoided or greatly reduced by a strong planning process. As an example, a museum in the Midwest was the recipient of a generous pledge by a well-known arts philanthropist. In its excitement to quickly move forward on a building program, the museum administration and board selected a star architect.

Once the selection was made, the museum crafted a project budget which quickly spiraled well beyond the original donor's pledge. Planners were forced to drastically scale back their program ideas. This was unsettling to many of the participants in the planning.

Unfortunately, this story is not unusual. There are many unknowns in a building project that the museum board, staff, and community may overlook in their excitement and enthusiasm until it is too late and they are facing potential disaster. Every part of the process carries risk—site selection, mission statement and vision, selection of the planning team, the building design, and the cost of construction and operations. What should a museum do when the external world changes suddenly and new demands, such as increasing security after September 11 or more stringent building codes in reaction to natural disasters such as floods or earthquakes, are placed on museums? Managing expectations becomes a critical factor. Planning is therefore the best recourse to avoid reactive situations.

One major factor that your museum must remember about planning is that funders expect a strong planning effort in advance of making a grant. In addition, accreditation through the American Association of Museums requires evidence of a strategic plan. It is no longer an optional effort, but a requirement for success.

What is planning? It is organizing ideas and resources for optimum results. It is a process that results in a product. It is a system of assuring the best decisions of staff and board and other key stakeholders involved in your building project.

Planning begins early. Without early planning and decision making, the ability to influence change diminishes over time. Once key decisions are made, especially about a building project, the museum has reduced leeway in making changes without increasing costs (figure 2.1).

What Type of Plan?

Museum building projects rest on many types of plans. The initial plan that a museum must engage in is an overarching strategic plan. However, many associated plans will create the blueprint for success in your building project:

- Facilities master plans
- Site plans

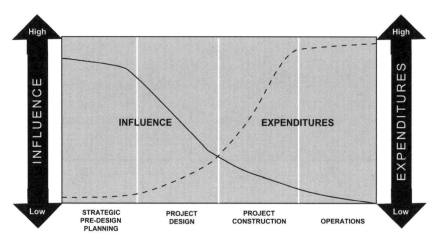

FIGURE 2.1
Early Planning Reduces Risk

- Collecting plans
- Visitor experience or interpretive plans
- Staffing plans
- Fund-raising plans
- Business plans
- Marketing plans
- Communications plans
- Operations plans

This chapter will focus on the strategic plan while subsequent chapters will address other types of plans.

STRATEGIC PLANNING: INTRODUCTION AND OVERVIEW

What is involved in strategic planning? It is a process that involves many players, data gathering, decision making, and strong commitment from your museum leadership. The effort involves several critical steps, as outlined in figure 2.2. Preparing for strategic planning is critical. Your museum will need to identify the key players, communications systems, and information sources in advance of launching the planning work. You may spend months or even years in creating your plan, so the process needs to be carefully designed up front

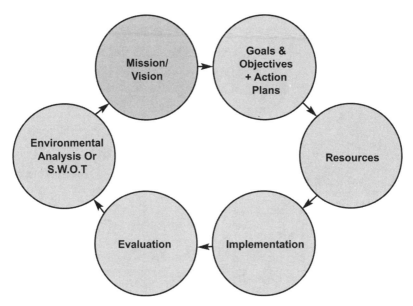

FIGURE 2.2
The Strategic Planning Process

and monitored throughout. The planning team must schedule regular meetings, maintain minutes, and document and share key decisions. At the outset a great deal of data gathering will occur. This information, along with all the key decisions, needs to be cataloged in such a way as to be easily understood by all players. Your museum should assign a staff member to oversee this function. Use of outside consultants in this process can be very helpful, but a permanent staff member should have primary responsibility for managing the process and maintaining the documentation.

As a circular process, strategic planning begins with an *environmental analysis* to determine the context of the organization, its assets and liabilities and the needs of the community and stakeholders. It ends with the *evaluation* of its success or failure in meeting its *mission and vision*. Even before the museum embarks on this process there is a preliminary step: the formation of a *planning team* or steering committee and operating structure. Participants will include board, staff, and other stakeholders and outside experts. It is the board's fiduciary responsibility to lead this process, although the actual planning work can be managed by staff and even outside consultants. The important factor is to create the best team at the outset. The core group for planning should not be too large, perhaps numbering no more than eight to ten individuals. Advisory task forces will be formed to bring input from the community, such as other museums, the public, school systems, and other key stakeholders.

Once your planning team and operating structure are in place, the initial phase of strategic planning involves an environmental analysis. Planning is a data-rich effort and requires the collection of facts and opinions that will support sound decision making. The four elements that are typically identified in this phase are strengths, weaknesses, opportunities, and threats, often called a SWOT analysis. They are further defined as internal strengths and weaknesses and external opportunities and threats. For example, as illustrated in figure 2.3, a typical approach to the *internal strengths or weaknesses* task is an assessment of the following: collections, programs, staffing, reputation, funding, facilities, location, visitation, and leadership. Some of the latter could be considered strengths while others could be weaknesses. For example, a museum may have a fine collection, but it may not be accessible due to deteriorating and cramped facilities. A typical planning process will examine the existing status of all the major internal operations from the board to staff to collections, programs, facilities, finances, and public perceptions.

External threats and opportunities can be factors such as the economic health of the region or nation, competition from other leisure activities (including museums that serve the same community), regional or even national demographic makeup and trends, audiences who don't visit your museum,

INTERNAL FORCES	EXTERNAL FORCES
• Culture & Values • Membership • Staff • Collections • Organizational Structure • Reputation	• Economy • Legal Constraints • Location • Demographics • Cultural Trends • Political Factors • Competitors

FIGURE 2.3
Environmental Analysis, or SWOT

public policy regarding arts and cultural funding, professional standards of conduct, donor preferences, and legal requirements. A typical SWOT process is conducted by the planning team with the help of special task forces of staff, board, opinion leaders, audience members, and outside consultants. It includes an intensive review of all the key factors affecting the museum. An example of such a process is that conducted by the National Museum of American History at the Smithsonian Institution in the 1990s.[3] Its environmental analysis involved creating sixteen staff-led task forces to study a variety of key internal functions from educational programs to the use of new media, as well as external issues such as trends in visitor services, exhibition development, and collections management. The museum spent close to a year on this phase of the planning alone.

Benchmarking, or examining best practices of similar organizations, is a key tool in the SWOT phase. What makes those organizations successful? In the case of museums, benchmarking can be done by surveying peer museums and learning about their approaches to mission development, collecting, educational outreach, funding, and facilities, for example. It is typical to study the practices of several other museums, even taking the time to visit them and talk with staff and board about their approaches. This phase is most critical in the building project. Benchmarking contributes critical information to determining feasibility of a building program, selecting architects and other contractors, and planning for funding. Benchmarking involves identifying best practices in building design, site planning, solutions for collections preservation, or achieving LEED (leadership in energy and environmental design) certification, and financing options, for example. A questionnaire is developed by the steering committee working on the building project. Peer organizations are selected and invited to share data with your museum. If you are a science museum, you will be seeking to benchmark other science museums, or other science-based educational programs. You may want to benchmark museums that are similar to your museum in size of collections or in the type of audiences served. You will be looking at museums in your community and in other parts of the country or the world. On-site visits that allow firsthand experience of the facility and face-to-face discussion with staff and board are very helpful to augment the benchmark survey data. Some of this information may be gathered during a market feasibility study. It is critical that your board and senior staff be thoroughly familiar with this information.

How is SWOT and benchmarking information used in the strategic planning process? You should be able to define what makes you a viable organization, where you need to improve. You will be clear about the external constraints that affect the museum and how you can take advantage of opportunities. These data guide the formation of a vision for change and the specifics of the planning goals, objectives, and strategies. Based on the needs of the community stakeholders, the internal areas needing improvement, and the opportunities for long-term service to the public, more specific ideas for change can be developed. If your museum collection is not being seen due to cramped space or inadequate conservation, or the nature of your visitors' needs and expectations have radically changed, while new funders and potential partners are materializing, then you are in a position to create a vision for change.

Mission/Vision/Values

This phase of the planning cycle is the most critical. Although months may be invested in the environmental analysis, the visioning phase is probably the one that most planning team members will want to spend their time on. There is really no reason to invest time in planning if a significant positive change is not contemplated. Therefore, no matter what the museum's ultimate vehicle to realize its mission, a strong vision with unanimous buy-in is fundamental. Most museums as nonprofits have established mission statements. However, during a strategic planning process there is always an opportunity to revisit the mission. Is it responsive to the internal strengths and external opportunities? Does it resonate with the public? Is it worded in such as way as to define the purpose of the museum, who it serves, and how that service makes a difference? Is it worded in such a way as to be easily understood and remembered by board and staff?

Vision. A vision statement is unique to each museum, yet several questions should be addressed.

- How will your museum look in ten or twenty years?
- Who will be visiting?
- What will visitors learn?
- How will the museum be managed?
- What assets will be acquired?

Although the leadership of the museum (board, CEO/director) will articulate the vision statement, it must be collectively developed by as many stakeholders as possible, widely shared, and endorsed unanimously. A vision statement pushes the organization to a higher level of service and operation. It is expansive and ambitious. It emphasizes that the museum is a dynamic and engaging center for a variety of audiences, accessible to all, and providing meaningful learning experiences, for example. Some vision statements are short, but the more fruitful approach is to outline the elements of your transformation in some detail.

Values. Many strategic plans include a values statement. Values are words and phrases that guide the operations of the organization. In a sense they are linked to the vision by the inspiring tenets they describe. For example, a values statement for a museum might include the following:

Our museum will display *respect* for the public and fellow staff members.

We will create opportunities for *creativity* in all programs.

We will promote *stewardship* through sustainable practices.

Values set a tone for the internal culture of the organization and the behavior of the museum staff, board, and volunteers, and they establish guideposts for communication with the external world about what is fundamentally important.

Vision and values work together to serve as a foundation for the unfolding building project. Decisions about design and construction, staffing and operations, funding and communications, should always refer to the vision and shared values developed during this phase of planning.

Goals and Objectives/Action Plans

The articulation of a framework of *goals and objectives* allows your museum to specify how you will achieve the mission and vision. This is the point at which a planning team will develop a list of ways to meet the vision through a variety of projects. Knowledgeable staff needs to participate intensively at this phase to develop a balanced set of goals and objectives for collecting, exhibitions, educational programs, staffing and organizational structure, funding, and infrastructure. In the end all the goal areas will form a balanced approach among external and internal activities.

Decision making. One of the key activities in this phase of planning is selecting priorities. How will decisions be made among the many competing and attractive ideas that the planning team has developed? A set of decision criteria must be developed and should include the following:

- Relevance to mission
- Responsiveness to audiences
- Funding feasibility
- Leveraging internal strengths and external partners
- Adherence to legal and ethical guidelines

To build or not to build? Here the museum needs to consider the reality of building construction as a major component of its vision. What is the opportunity cost of investing time and money in a new building, an expansion, or a renovation versus other worthy needs of the organization? Which is the best approach? What is the opportunity lost when investing in the facilities solution instead of collections, programs, or staffing?[4]

If the museum decides to build or renovate, a program plan will be developed at this phase that outlines in some detail your collections, exhibitions, and educational outreach goals along with associated space needs.

Resource Analysis and Acquisition

Each objective that is developed by your museum needs to be carefully analyzed to determine how it will be realized. What resources are needed in regards to staff time, outside services, space utilization, or collections availability? Each major objective needs some realistic level of feasibility in order to make sound decisions.

Feasibility study. One of the most important activities for the museum to undertake at this juncture is a feasibility study. There are different types of feasibility studies that need to be undertaken in regard to building projects. The two favored approaches are studies that assess the market for a new facility and those that assess the donor interest in the project and its associated capital campaign. In undertaking a study to gauge market feasibility, many museums work with external firms to develop the necessary financials and visitation projections. These studies will include the level of interest in the community, who will visit the new facility, interest of members in supporting this new vision, the competition, and their operations and future plans. The feasibility phase also helps to define space assumptions: visitor projections will likely impact size of public areas, food service and other amenities, location of key activities such as shops, theaters, and the like.

A checklist of variables that might be included in these studies covers the following:

- Internally, how will the new facility operate?
- What are the staffing needs?
- What about facilities requirements for collections care?
- How will the museum maintain new mechanical systems and exhibit components?
- How much security is needed to manage increasing visitation?
- Will retail functions net new income?
- What are the demographics and psychographics of your region, including tourism patterns?
- What is current attendance and what are visitor data about your existing facility?
- What are the reasons that people do *not* visit your museum?
- What is your competition?
- Are you interested in targeting certain audiences?
- What is the economic benefit to the museum's community in dollars per visitor?

Often a museum will undertake an economic impact study. For example, the Museum of Modern Art in New York determined that its impact on the city's economy was $2 billion over its first few years after opening in 2004.[5] Feasibility studies need to be evaluated with the proverbial grain of salt. A few museums that relied on marketing studies failed soon after opening. The City Museum of Washington, D.C., estimated 300,000 persons would visit after opening in 2003. The reality of post 9/11 Washington left the number closer to 30,000. One might ask are feasibility studies reliable? In many cases they will be, but your museum must approach numbers in the most cautious and conservative fashion. Of great importance is ensuring that the museum has a strong and well-diversified financial base to absorb fluctuations in attendance. Effective marketing also plays a factor.

"What if" scenarios are critical to build into your feasibility phase and budgeting: What if a major donor dies? What if a key contractor goes out of business? What if there is fraud? What if there is opposition from community members? What if there are environmental hazards, for example, asbestos, archaeological materials, toxic waste, flooding, or skyrocketing cost of materials? Finally, be sure to select consultants with strong track records especially in the museum field.[6]

Funding is critical to the resource analysis phase. Obviously major amounts of funding will be needed to advance a new vision and associated projects. The status quo will not move the museum forward. At this phase it is important to answer several questions, many of which can be incorporated into a strong business plan that will support the case for major funding.

- What internal resources can be applied to the museum's priority projects? (In most cases those resources will be staff time and collections.)
- What matching funds are available from the museum as it seeks external grants?
- Are major gifts a possibility?
- Are board members making leadership gifts?
- What earned income can be anticipated from a future new facility?

Implementation of Projects

Once resources are in hand, the museum needs project management systems to create a sequenced set of activities to implement major project elements. All projects can benefit from this approach, especially the building project and its major components including program activities such as exhibitions. Project management tools allow the museum's management and board to chart the work to be done and measure progress, including major goals and objectives, strategies and target dates, assigned responsible staff and resources allocated. Charts can be created in readily updateable software programs including word processing, spreadsheet, or project management software. (See appendix A for an example.)

Evaluation

All planning efforts must contain a strong evaluation component. You will want to identify project success criteria and ways to measure them. Unfortunately, many museums are so exhausted by the process of implementing projects and moving on to the next phase of their planning that they have little time or enthusiasm for assessment. So it is essential to think ahead to how you will evaluate your plan prior to implementation. Don't make it an afterthought. Targets and measurements serve as touchstones throughout the project for each stakeholder to answer the questions, How am I doing? How are we doing? They also become useful communications tools to engage the public in tracking the project's progress. Practically speaking, at project completion, a good evaluation process ensures that lessons learned are catalogued, that systems are working properly, that staff understand their roles and responsibilities, and that the museum knows how effectively it has used its resources. At the same time the impact on the public is paramount. Did we meet our vision for change in the eyes of the public? What impact have we made on our audiences?

Measurement of effectiveness can be both qualitative and quantitative. Were audiences delighted by the visitor experience? Did new education programs result in learning advances among school children? Did membership and visitation increase? How did the press react to the new building and the museum exhibitions? Are funders satisfied and new donors lining up? Are staff aware of the plan and how they make a contribution? The evaluation of the major components of the strategic plan allows the museum to learn about their successes and failures and to feed that information into the next planning cycle.

Evaluation requires a systematic approach to measuring success. The museum should start with a baseline of data that it can then compare itself to in future years. Items that you might include in that baseline are attendance, costs per visitor, visitor ratings of facilities and programs, membership numbers, contributions by type of funder, percentage of collections exhibited, rates of new collection gifts, amount of space devoted to state-of-the-art storage, and so on. Staff and board should be sure these measures relate to the vision for change that has been developed in the strategic plan. The baseline benchmarks help the museum measure its progress. As the data are compared over time your board, director, and staff will have important information about the impact of the strategic vision on the public and on internal operations.

IMPLEMENTING AND ENSURING A SUCCESSFUL PLANNING PROCESS

Strategic planning is a lot of work. The time involved can be anywhere from a few months to several years. Typically strategic plans are meant to cover an implementation period of three to five years. However, if a building program is involved, the time involved could stretch to a decade or more. In reality the plan is a living document that continues to guide the work of the museum. It can also be changed as internal and external circumstances warrant. For example, a museum on the East Coast invested several years and millions of dollars in planning a new facility that included a name architect and a local developer. In the midst of a successful capital campaign the developer pulled out, causing the museum to spend a year securing a new site. Without a strong strategic plan and dedicated board and staff, this might have been a failed initiative. They were flexible enough to make the change, and the museum's basic vision and plan components are stronger than ever.

Once your museum has reached the point of defining a vision and selecting goals and objectives, many other related plans will need to be developed. These will include at a minimum a facilities master plan for building projects, collecting plans, visitor experience or interpretive plans, and business plans. Each of these plans will draw heavily on the groundwork of the strategic plan. Each of these plans guides the ongoing phases of your museum building project.

The planning process needs to be inclusive of key staff, board, community members, outside experts, and funders. The board is ultimately responsible for leading the process and for assuring buy-in. Creating a plan takes time and money. Conducting feasibility studies, working with outside experts, and others require substantial investments of both. The experts you may include in your planning phase range from architects to marketing specialists to academics and exhibition designers. Planning grants are often sought from funding agencies or board members.

Communications systems are fundamental during the process. Keeping the staff, volunteers, and community members aware of the unfolding decisions is important. Reporting and tracking progress in a visible way through published minutes or websites helps to ensure everyone is up to date. Sharing data widely assists enormously in achieving buy-in. In fact as key decisions are made, they should be documented and archived. The planning process will evolve over time and decisions will often be made in an iterative process. A full record of decisions is needed for future reference.

How do we move from the strategic plan to the building project? Much effort has been expended on planning and now you are strongly considering a building project as a key component of your vision. Whether a renovation, an expansion, or a new building, several factors are crucial in making the decision to proceed. Now is the time to test the feasibility by creating an early snapshot of your building project. Figure 2.4 highlights the factors that will go into that decision. The questions you will ask yourself are

- Do we have the staff, collections, and finances to do this?
- How much will it cost and is the funding capability there?

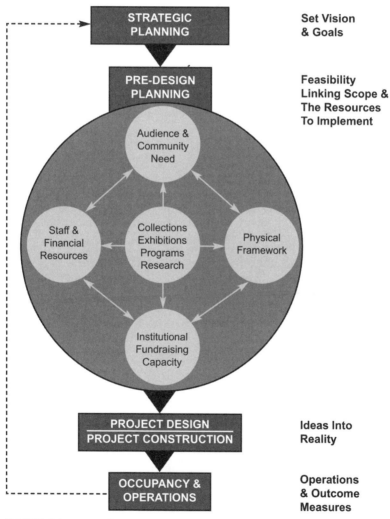

FIGURE 2.4
Predesign Planning: Linking Strategic Plan to Project Design

- What does our audience and community expect?
- Are sound plans in place for collections, visitor experience, and outreach?
- Have we assessed our physical framework and space needs?
- Can the board make a unanimous commitment to this project?

IN SUMMARY

Do's and Don'ts

- Choose the right planning teams.
- Involve leadership in planning and decision making.
- Prepare the board in advance.
- Ensure a compelling vision.
- Incorporate internal and external viewpoints.
- Assign responsibility for implementation and oversight of planning.
- Complete a thorough feasibility study allowing sufficient time to fully understand the options.
- Know where your museum is in its life cycle.

Red Flags

- Lack of ownership of the plan: "It's what the board wants, not me"
- Staff or board are "too busy" for planning
- Inability to gain donor support
- Apathy on the part of the public
- Unrealistic expectations on the part of board or staff
- Poor alignment with goals of the plan
- Resistance to change

FRAMEWORK FOR SUCCESS

As the museum moves forward toward realizing the new vision for its future through a building project several steps are critical for success. The following will be detailed in the ensuing chapters:

- Roles, responsibilities, and building the team: Who will do what?
- The heart of the museum: What is the content?
- Hiring your design and construction teams: What is the process for bringing on outside experts?
- Project management tools: How do we get from predesign to opening?

- Physical framework: What will you build?
- Financial planning and cost management: What are the costs and how can they be controlled?
- The capital campaign: Where are the financial resources?
- Communications strategies: Who should know what and when?
- Operations: How will it work?
- Evaluation: What is success?

NOTES

Quote by Redmond Barnett included in benchmarking survey conducted by Martha Morris, 2002.

1. Ichak Adizes, *Managing Corporate Life Cycles* (Paramus, NJ: Prentice Hall, 1999).

2. Hugh Genoways and Lynne Ireland, *Museum Administration: An Introduction* (Lanham, MD: AltaMira, 2003), 21–35.

3. Discussion of the strategic planning process is drawn from the author's experiences as manager of the process at the National Museum of American History from 1993 to 2001. See bibliography for relevant publications on this topic.

4. Franklin Robinson, "No More Buildings," *Museum News* 81, no. 6 (November– December 2002): 28–29. Robinson discusses the trade-offs of deciding to build versus investing in the museum's core programming, such as collection building.

5. Kevin Hassett and P. Swagel, "Creative Accounting: MoMA's Economic Impact Study," *Wall Street Journal,* August 30, 2006.

6. Gail Lord and Barry Lord, *The Manual of Museum Planning*, 2nd ed. (Lanham, MD: AltaMira, 2000), 85–105.

Roles, Responsibilities, and Building the Team

The purpose of this chapter is twofold: to define the roles and responsibilities of the individuals engaged in the development and execution of a museum construction project and to suggest how they can be structured to form an effective team.

From the time a museum construction project is a gleam in someone's eye to completion and full operation, many hands will have shaped and guided it. While players filling roles large and small may come and go throughout the process, successful planning and completion of a building renovation and/or expansion project requires the coordinated and cooperative efforts of a host of individuals: the board of trustees; the museum's senior leadership, program and administrative staff; outside consultants, architects and their design teams, exhibit designers and their team, and the construction team. In addition public officials and donors, community and corporate partners, and other interested stakeholders may also fill specific roles. Although players in small museums may wear many hats, no one person will be able to manage the complexity of such an endeavor alone.

The board of trustees and any authorizing bodies of publicly financed museums make the first decisions that set a museum's construction project process into motion. Once the decision to undertake a project has been made, the board and the museum's senior leadership must establish a structure to guide the project, including appointment of a steering committee who are a

core team of board members and senior museum managers with clearly defined roles and accountabilities. Staff and stakeholders must also be organized
into working groups to ensure their input informs the process and generates
buy-in of the players.

BOARD READINESS: MORPHING FROM BUSINESS AS USUAL
TO FULL BATTLE MODE

At the heart of the board's role and its engagement in a building project is its
fiduciary responsibility to the museum and its community. For that reason
alone boards must assume an active role in any major building project the
museum undertakes. Undertaking an expansion project, often a once in a lifetime event for board members and museum staff, is a daunting task overlaying an already heavy workload. It is not to be undertaken lightly, nor driven
by unrealistic visions or schemes. A detailed discussion of the board's responsibilities follows.

The structure of the governing board for oversight of the project will vary
depending on the board's historical degree of engagement in museum operations, its size, the scale of the proposed project, and its capacity to oversee a
major initiative. Board roles will be discussed here and will be referenced at
different steps of the process as appropriate.

A typical midsize museum board would have an executive committee and
standing committees responsible for finances, programs, collections, development, and buildings. Depending on the size of a museum, each of these standing committees is staffed and supported by a member of the museum's
management staff; for example, the finance committee by the chief financial
officer, the programs committee by the chief curator and/or educator, the
fund-raising committee by the development officer, and the building committee, by the deputy director or the chief operating officer, an assistant director for administration or the chief financial officer. In a small museum, the
museum director and/or the deputy director may have to assume all of these
support roles. In very small museums, the financial responsibility may rest
with a board member.

Whatever the size, boards undertaking a building project must recognize that
their task is no longer business as usual. Boards of large museums may divide responsibilities for an expansion project among existing standing committees, create a separate steering committee to guide the planning, design, and construction

of the project, or appoint a steering committee made up of chairs of key standing committees. Boards of smaller museums may create a single project committee of key members with strong interest and capacity to undertake the
project. Whatever the structure, creation of a streamlined decision process is critical and depends on a commitment to openness, clear lines of communication,
and trust among the parties. Ideally, and for the sake of efficiency and smooth,
rapid communication, the board will likely vest a single committee, hereafter
called the steering committee, with the responsibility for project oversight. The
board may assign that role to its existing building committee, or create a broader
committee whose membership will be drawn from existing executive, planning,
finance, fund-raising, and building committees; or with smaller boards, from individuals with knowledge and/or expertise in those areas.

THE PROJECT STEERING COMMITTEE

Steering Committee Structure

The board chair is the most likely individual to assume the lead role in
steering the project. However, another board member may fill this role, particularly if the chair cannot commit a significant block of time to the effort.
In such cases, another member of the board, someone with special expertise
or a deep commitment to the project or a longtime museum supporter could
fill that role. If necessary, the board may go outside its own membership or
contract for services to find the full range of expertise on the steering committee. The board will also need legal advice throughout the process for assistance in hiring consultants and staff, contracting for construction and
services, borrowing to finance the project, and in crafting agreements between
the museum and donors and sponsors.

If the project's financing depends on a capital campaign, a separate board
committee with overlapping membership or a subcommittee of the steering
committee may assume responsibility for campaign activities, and should maintain strong lines of communication with the steering committee. Staff joining
the steering committee would include the director, the deputy director/chief
operating officer, the chief financial officer/business manager, the director of facilities, and the museum's project manager. From time to time key program directors and the development officer may sit with the steering committee as well.
The development officer will be the lead staff to the campaign committee or

subcommittee. The board will also develop a charge to the committee or a charter outlining its authority and responsibilities. Ultimate decision-making authority for the scope, design, schedule, and financing of the project rests with this committee. However constituted, the steering committee must be able to meet frequently, often on short notice, and its members must stay abreast of key project issues, trust one another, and communicate often and openly with the remainder of the board and the museums' constituencies. This level of engagement, a marked departure from the board's normal oversight role, requires a significantly higher level of commitment and unity for the duration of the project.

The steering committee should be large enough to have regular input from key stakeholders and small enough to meet frequently and dispense with cumbersome meeting protocols. Museums will need to examine their meeting management history and skills to determine the best number: more than five and fewer than fifteen would be a good starting point. The steering committee should create a supporting structure of stakeholder working groups to focus on various aspects of the overall project—development, community, exhibitions, collections, operations, and visitor experience. Each group should be directly linked to the steering committee through the project manager and/or through a member of the steering committee. In addition, each working group should be chartered with its purpose, membership, structure, and duration clearly defined. Some stakeholders may be members of more than one working group. The steering committee should also create numerous opportunities for review and input from staff and other stakeholders during the project and leading up to the opening.

Steering Committee Role: Policy Setting, Oversight, and Champion of the Project

At the outset, the steering committee must establish policies defining authorities, policies, and procedures for acquiring property, goods, and services, including

- Leasing or purchasing property if necessary
- Selecting and hiring consultants, including the architect/design team, the exhibit design team, campaign consultants
- Selecting the building construction team and awarding the contract for construction

- Purchasing goods and services associated with the project, such as major equipment or systems not part of the construction contract, marketing assistance, or catering contracts for opening events
- Partner agreements

In addition, it will

- Establish policies and procedures associated primarily with the capital campaign to guide trustee, staff, volunteer, and consultant conduct during the campaign with respect to donor rights and the appropriate receipt, recording, and acknowledgment of gifts.
- Define relationships with individual, corporate, and foundation donors and public officials relevant to the project oversight.
- Establish naming rights to the building or portions of the building and attendant donor benefits.

Throughout the life of the project, the steering committee will oversee all major hiring, selection of consultants, review of designs, contracting, and contact and agreements with donors, as well as of the project schedule, planning of major opening events, and project budgets. In some cases, particularly those that require major financial commitment, the steering committee should seek approval, preferably unanimous, of the full board.

Last, and in many ways most important, the steering committee serves as the public champion of the project, communicating to a waiting audience on the project's progress, working with potential donors to secure the project's funding, appeasing the impatient, coordinating and holding tired and fragile teams together throughout with calm, wise counsel, a steady hand, and support in the form of time, additional funding, and advice.

Steering Committee Members

Organizing your internal museum stakeholders to be prepared for all that comes over the life of the project requires extensive planning and communication. Project schedules become the control mechanisms for all museum activities until well after building occupancy. Regardless of whether the museum remains open, partially open, or closed, every member of the staff will feel the impact of the change from business as usual. All staff will have to gear up for uncertainty, rapid change, disruptions, heavier workloads, new faces, new responsibilities, and higher stress levels. During construction, important daily tasks will often be subordinated to the demands of the project: museum personnel must be prepared to prioritize and choose among tasks. Many will be asked to work outside their normal functional areas as well as their comfort zones. The museum leadership must prepare adequately with extensive discussions about how to cope with change, inviting staff participation in planning the project to give them a better understanding of how the project will affect them and a say in how the impact can be mitigated, and by clearly defining expectations of their roles for the duration of the project. Concurrently, the museum leadership and managers should conduct ongoing discussions about changes in the workplace after project completion. Staff will be called on to participate in the project's planning and implementation at various levels: some on the steering committee and some as members of working groups. Staff members of the steering committee are discussed below.

The director or chief executive officer. Although the board has ultimate responsibility for the project, the day-to-day burden of ensuring realization of the museum's vision for the project rests with the museum director, including accountability for achieving the fund-raising goals and for successful project execution. The director will be the daily public face of the project, ensuring the museum's ongoing operations during construction, keeping the museum in the public eye, wooing donors, and maintaining staff morale.

The deputy director or chief operating officer. Most large museums have deputy directors who focus on internal activities, freeing the director to work directly with the board, major donors, and key public figures and constituencies. If possible, during a construction project the director should turn over internal operations to the deputy director or a trusted senior administrator in the case of a smaller museum to free up time to be the public face of the museum and the project. A solid, trusting relationship between the director and the deputy director is critical to the project's success of ongoing operations. You may select the deputy director to take the lead role to become the project manager for the project, but if not, he or she will concentrate on maintaining smooth museum operations.

The chief financial officer or business manager. While the director and development officer may take lead roles in fund-raising, the business manager or chief financial officer plays a critical role in determining when or whether the project has sufficient funds promised or in hand to go forward, the mix and reliability of revenue sources, how funds are allocated, how funds are flowing into and out of the museum and the project, and whether the museum is sufficiently creditworthy to borrow funds. The chief financial officer must also ensure smooth financial operations and management controls throughout the process, as well as work with lenders if the museum borrows funds. This role is discussed in more detail in chapter 8.

The development officer or fund-raiser. Along with the director, the development officer plays a key role in leading a capital campaign, working with donors, including public officials, foundation officers, key individuals, and partners. Developing and nurturing a strong membership program is a major responsibility, as well as engaging members throughout the life of the project through special fund-raising events and in developing the case for the project for presentation to foundations and major donors. In museums with small staffs, the museum may choose to hire a consultant or consulting firm to lead the campaign and/or assist in identifying donor pools, assessing feasibility, developing a case statement, planning the strategy, and training and mobilizing the staff into full campaign mode. This role is discussed in more detail in chapter 9.

Facilities or plant operations manager. If a museum is small or housed in a multiuse facility, it may not have its own facilities manager. In the case of a publicly supported museum, the general services department of a state or local government or university facilities department may fill this role. In any case, before, during, and after construction, the on-site facilities manager has a special responsibility to ensure the safety and security of staff and collections during ongoing operations, to understand the impact of project design decisions on operations after project completion, to inform the design process as necessary, and to ready the staff, museum or contract, to care for and operate the new space.

The project manager. The term "project manager" refers to the individual selected by the museum to manage the project on behalf of the museum and to serve as liaison between the steering committee and the museum project working groups. The architect's design team, as well as other consulting teams, and the contractor may also have individuals called project managers. In this book, we will use the terms museum project manager, design team project manager, and construction team project manager where needed to maintain clarity.

The success of the project lies in the museum's ability to link its internal stakeholders at all levels (trustees, steering committee, and museum staff) with the consultants, building and exhibit design teams, and the construction team. The critical link between the museum (the steering committee and the museum working groups and staff) and the various design teams and the construction team is your museum project manager.

The person selected as museum project manager must show equal skills as a communicator, facilitator, expert in organizational dynamics, and therapist: his or her knowledge of the planning, design, and construction processes and an understanding of the culture of a museum are key criteria to be used in selecting the right person. The best project managers understand and share the values of the museum. Frequently the project manager comes from the museum staff—often the deputy director or a trusted senior staff member who understands all facets of the museum's operations and is fully committed to the mission of the museum. It is important to select the individual to fill this role carefully. Those lacking understanding and common purpose become intermediaries who may hinder the creative process and inhibit free flow of information.

Program staff and others. Depending on the individual museum circumstances, other museum staff or outside individuals may serve on the steering committee. Each museum will need to assess its own requirements for input at different levels. For example, given the importance of the exhibitions and collections programs in the museum, the chief curator, education director, and/or registrar may sit on the steering committee. If the project includes new or renovated collections storage space, staff from collections management may be added to the steering committee. If the project receives all or a substantial portion of its funding from public sources, a public official may be included.

Figure 3.1 depicts the relationship among the key players and other stakeholders engaged in a museum construction project.

WORKING GROUPS OF THE STEERING COMMITTEE

Each project will require input during the planning and design process from a variety of individuals representing programs and activities inside the museum as well as interests and activities outside the museum. The steering committee should charter a series of working groups to focus on areas requiring

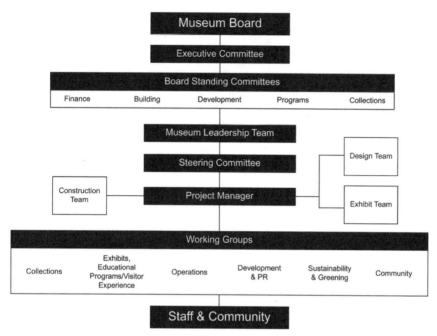

FIGURE 3.1
Project Organization Chart

the attention of the many stakeholders. Each working group will also need a position description for each of its members with clearly articulated expectations for each role. The number of working groups and the focus of each will depend on individual museum circumstances. For convenience and illustrative purposes, we have identified six working groups reflecting the array of stakeholders and the nature of input required from them. Note from the graphic (figure 3.1) that the critical link is the museum project manager.

Collections Working Group

This working group includes curators, conservators, researchers, and registrars. It is charged with ensuring proper care of the collections during construction, including relocation to off-site storage and return to the newly constructed space if appropriate; access during construction to collections for travel, exhibit development, conservation or research; and with the design of safe, accessible, secure, and properly conditioned space; as well as sufficient room for registration, collections research, and conservation-related activities in the new facility.

Educational Programs/Visitor Experience, and Exhibitions Working Group

Members of this working group will include exhibit design staff, curators, educators, docents, and other volunteers. Each of these program areas must have input in development of the project's plan, and in initial design discussions. Members of this working group will pay particular attention to space for educational programs to ensure sufficient gathering and support spaces for the types of educational programming the museum intends to offer; amenities for visitors, ease of way finding among galleries, educational spaces, and amenities; and considerations for special audiences, such as young children or individuals with handicaps. This working group will also be responsible for ensuring the spaces for exhibits and exhibit support will be appropriate for the museum's intended offerings with adequate infrastructure, such as for lighting, IT, and climate control, as well as adjacent exhibit construction/staging areas; and secure loading docks, elevators, and passageways sufficient to accommodate objects, containers, and structures the museum would be likely to use in its exhibits. Since docents and other volunteers are often the first line of contact with the public in the museum, on this working group they can offer input on visitor habits and concerns, particularly about amenities such as seating areas, check rooms, food services, and restrooms to accommodate large numbers of children and/or older adults. Volunteers, both members of the community and an important link to the community, can also play an added vital role in articulating the project's objectives to neighbors and colleagues.

Operations Working Group

This working group must pay attention to an array of behind the scenes functions including security, information technologies and systems, facilities management, retail activities, and administrative functions such as accounting, human resources, and purchasing. Membership on this working group will include the heads of security and IT services, and managers of food services and shops. Not only is this working group charged with considering future space, but it must also be attentive to the needs of staff, visitors, and collections during the construction project. Whether the museum remains open or is closed during the construction project, the individual responsible for security must prepare the security staff for disruption, staff morale problems, and confusion during the construction project.

Similar to docents, often the security staff is the first line of information for the public. For that reason they should be informed about the scope and progress of the project, and alert to the safety of staff, the public, and the collections near construction zones. Similar to the facilities manager who has a seat on the steering committee, the security manager must be engaged in the design process to ensure that the project will include adequate protection of people and collections and to ready the security staff to assume responsibility for the new space.

With the increasingly sophisticated technologies available for exhibits and other programs and for administrative functions, the role of the person responsible for information technology before, during, and after a construction project is one that is emerging and evolving at a rapid rate. This information technology representative on this working group is responsible for ensuring the museum's technology objectives are articulated clearly well before design begins in order to secure and work with a design team with expertise to provide the vision and the information technology infrastructure to see the museum well into the future. The staff and contractors responsible for information technology must be actively engaged in the planning and design processes, both to support the vision and to bring reality to the discussion, to decide what elements are core to meet the museum's program objectives and what elements are mere whistles and bells that add only to price.

Increasingly museums are contracting with outside vendors to operate their retail activities, and food services. When food, beverage, and retail areas are part of the construction project, vendor input (and often their funding of build-out of the retail and food and beverage areas), is critical. Experienced vendors bring marketing expertise and can offer the design team insights with respect to location, offerings, traffic flow, support requirements, and layout of retail spaces to maximize revenues. It is also important for the museum to work with them to customize their offerings to the museum and the community. For example, the Smithsonian Institution's National Museum of the American Indian, working with its food vendor, customized its food service menu to feature Native American foods by region, created a rich dining experience that has become an attraction in its own right.

Last, staff of administrative functions need to give their input with respect to location, adjacencies, and office layouts; conference areas and employee amenities, administrative systems, and access to loading docks for deliveries.

The deputy director and/or the chief financial officer, with a seat on the steering committee, should contribute input for these areas as well.

Development and Public Relations Working Group

This working group includes the development officer, discussed earlier, and individuals responsible for public relations, government relations, marketing, and membership development. This group must maintain an outward focus, keeping the world beyond the museum abreast of the capital campaign and progress of the project. Communications planning is an important part of its charge. This working group will coordinate, guide, and be responsible for keeping public officials, the press, key supporters, and the general public apprised of the project's progress, presenting inviting and compelling pictures of the museum's ongoing activities during a period of shutdown or disruption, and publicizing special fund-raising events during the construction period and leading up to the opening, as well as maintaining member and donor engagement and momentum after opening.

A Special Word about Major Donors

Typically a major individual donor or donors are members of the board or have close connections with members of the board. In their trustee capacity, they may serve on the steering committee or the campaign committee. However, the board must recognize the delicacy of allowing a major donor undue influence during the planning or design process and take care at the outset to define relationships between major donors and project decision making. If a major donor serves on a working group, development would be the logical choice. If a major donor does not have an official capacity, he or she may be given special briefings on planning and design processes, including private briefings on plans, design, progress of the project, plans for opening events, and donor recognition. The gift or gifts may provide naming opportunities for the facility or a portion of the facility, such as a learning center, auditorium, or special collections area. Thus there would be an expectation that the donor might have some, but not the final, say in the design of the named space. Whatever the role allowed for donors, the board must have an established policy on naming rights that must be clearly spelled out in advance by the steering committee and fully understood by every individual with donor contact. Naming of spaces will be discussed in more detail in chapter 9.

Sustainability Working Group

Increasingly, sustainability, including sustainable design, purchasing, and practices, is emerging as an active concern and a virtual imperative. At this time, it is a sufficiently new concept to be given voice independent of other working groups. While the overlap with other working groups is obvious, over time as sustainability becomes more mainstream, an independent working group will no longer be necessary.

Community Working Group

For a variety of reasons the museum may need input from stakeholders outside the museum family. A fluid working group can oversee engagement with various groups during the project, with particular attention to scheduling of input at appropriate times throughout the process; for example, engaging the neighbors before the construction crew arrives on site. Members of this working group may include public officials, state historic preservation officers, educators from local school systems, donors, business partners, discipline specialists/ researchers, neighbors, visitors, and community representatives. The nature of their input is described as follows:

Public or university/college officials. If the project includes public funds from a state or local government, a public official may have oversight on use of these funds and participate in the planning process and in some instances, the design review process. If the museum receives most of its operating support from a university, state, county, or city government, that entity, not the board of trustees, is likely to be the owner of the facility. For that reason it may manage the design and construction process. The museum will likely be termed the user but not the owner, and will have seats on a steering committee led by the owner. The museum would have its own steering committee to provide input to the owner's steering committee, where ultimate authority would rest. Similarly, if the museum is part of a larger multiuse complex of museums, performing arts facilities, science centers, and the like, the governing entity will have major input, if not full responsibility, for the design and construction process. In cases in which the museum is not the owner of the facility, all parties must agreed to and document their roles and responsibilities well in advance of undertaking the project.

State historic preservation officer (SHPO). If the project is a renovation or an addition to a historic structure or is located in a historic district, the state historic preservation officer will be included in the planning and design review processes to ensure adherence to preservation requirements for heritage properties.

Local school administrators. Local school systems are major consumers of the museum's educational programming. Input from teachers and system liaisons with the museum during the planning stages can provide valuable information about school system curricular plans for the future and its expectations from the museum, as well as any emerging methodologies addressing different learning styles or special populations. Their participation can also strengthen ties with the community.

Discipline specialists/researchers. Often in the development of exhibitions a museum will engage specialists to assist with scripts as well as physical designs. If a museum has specialized collections (e.g., living collections), it may seek input in the planning and design processes from specialists to ensure appropriate environmental conditions or unique display requirements for those collections are met.

Other donors. Major donors have been discussed earlier. However, every member or visitor is a potential major donor and those who have given to the museum, however modest the gifts, should not be ignored. Special events that include previews of the concept and of the finished project not only provide opportunity for their input, but also occasions to build excitement and encourage additional financial support for the project.

Neighbors, visitors, and community. Museums are wise to engage neighbors in the immediate vicinity in discussions early in the planning stages to consider matters of concern to them; for example, duration of construction schedule, hours of construction operation, construction noise, dust and debris, changing traffic patterns, fencing and barricades, and the need for parking and staging areas. While not likely to be members of the Steering Committee, neighbors who will be affected need a channel to voice their concerns and to keep abreast of construction activity. In addition, museums routinely gather comments from their visitors and undertake community surveys. As the planning and design processes proceed, museums would be wise to keep their publics aware of the project plans, through an array of communications vehicles, covered extensively in chapter 10.

SELECTING PROJECT TEAM MEMBERS

The Museum Project Manager

The first person the museum should select to work directly on the project is the project manager, who will be the critical link between the museum (the board, steering committee, working groups, and the museum staff), design team, and construction team. Where can you find the right person? If the museum is part of a university or a local or state government, the owner of the museum, the university or the government entity, may supply the project manager. In such cases, project managers tend to be excellent guides since they are experienced in working with a variety of university or public sector stakeholders.

Most of the time, particularly in small to midsize museums, the project manager comes from the museum staff—often a trusted senior staff member who understands all facets of the museum's operations and is fully committed to the mission of the museum. Options include the deputy director, high-level executive assistant to the director, or a senior staff member who will take this on and get extra support for his or her normal responsibilities. This can also be an opportune time to bring forward promising staff. Outside hires may include a retired museum professional, a design/construction professional, or someone hired from a firm that provides owner's representation. Outside firms tend to use the title "owner's representative" or "program manager," and may or may not have specialists in museums on staff. Whatever the choice, the steering committee should insist on meeting the day-to-day individual and get personal references on his or her skills and working styles from other museums and organizations for whom he or she has worked. Occasionally a board member who is a developer or in private industry will offer a project manager. This can be a success or a disaster, depending on whether the project manager is reporting to the person who pays or to the museum, and whether her or she understands that a museum's process does not mirror that of a private business.

Each choice has its benefits and challenges: someone with prior design and construction experience may not understand the museum's organizational structure or management culture, while a museum person may be too internally focused to be open to new design ideas or be a fair arbiter. Successful project coordination rests on finding the right person with the right skills to fill in the gaps in the museum's internal expertise to manage the project. The steering committee must take the time to give a project manager from outside the museum an "inside tour'" of the personalities and organizational dynamics of the museum to point out the pitfalls so that they can become adept navigators of the process. Conversely, the insider project manager must either have or receive project management training and time to master the language and processes of the design and construction milieu.

The Design Teams for the Building, Exhibits, and Construction

The balance of the steering committee consists of the design, exhibit, and construction teams. See chapter 5 for a more detailed description of their roles and processes for selection of each.

IN SUMMARY

We have discussed the roles and responsibilities of the board of trustees and key staff in overseeing a construction project, as well as working groups and other interested individuals whose input may be desirable and helpful to the project. In addition, we have discussed how the board of trustees and the museum must organize itself in order to become an effective team to deliver a successful project.

Do's and Don'ts

- Begin with a good foundation plan for the project.
- Vest full authority for decision making in the steering committee.
- Use charters for the steering committee and its subcommittees to make purpose, tasks, and timelines clear.
- Use a variety of mechanisms and avenues for obtaining input from multiple constituencies.
- Don't overlook staff expertise during the planning process.
- Don't begin the architectural selection process until the steering committee is in accord on the project vision.
- Don't underestimate the value of keeping channels of communications open and clear between staff and the project team, the museum and its publics.

Red Flags

- Overstepping boundaries
- Donor dominance
- Dropped balls
- Going on the cheap when contracting for expertise
- Miscommunications among any working groups or steering committee and working groups

4

The Heart of the Museum

Exhibits, Collections, and Educational Programs

How does the museum achieve its mission and vision? At the heart of the museum is the intellectual content—the collections and scholarship that drive the mission-based programs of the museum. This chapter is about developing an intellectual program that will shape the museum's physical plan. Your museum building should be responsive to collections, exhibitions, and educational activities. The strategic plan sets out goals for the achievement of the mission and vision, and the critical next step is to create specific plans that define the visitor experience. Closely linked to this step will be a discussion of collecting plans and factors that influence the space plan. This phase is so important because the decisions made here will in large part dictate the physical designs of the museum renovation, expansion, or new facility.

The essential programs in the museum are acquiring, researching, and managing artifacts, artworks, archives, libraries, and living collections. Scholarly research and the collections are incorporated into interpretive products such as exhibitions and educational outreach. For museums that are not collections based, there are intellectual themes that underlie the museum's programs. For example, science museums and children's museums may rely on the use of reproductions of artifacts, computer interactives, hands-on experimental laboratories, or films and other media to teach the visitor.

What kind of museum are you? This will drive the type of programming that you develop. Museums can be driven by objects (e.g., textiles, glass, living specimens); they can be driven by themes (e.g., art, history, and technology); and they can be driven by constituencies (e.g., African Americans, children, Native Americans, war veterans). These guiding drivers will help to define the scope of collections, types of exhibitions, and other educational programs at the heart of the museum. Museums are varied and idiosyncratic, reflecting the myriad ways we look at our society. Overarching themes may range from historical narratives to aesthetic styles to scientific innovation to environmental sustainability or humanitarian causes. Museums can be classified in many ways, some according to type: art, history, natural history, science, historic homes, zoos, gardens, and aquariums. Many museums are multidisciplinary or general in scope. Some may be focused on the history or art of the community or region. Some may be focused on topics such as the economy, military conflict, popular culture, decorative arts, or historic figures. Others may memorialize events or represent the cultural history of ethnic or special communities. At least 17,000 museums exist in the United States alone, and their variety in subject and size is vast.[1]

No matter what the type of museum careful planning is needed to create opportunities for learning by the public, known as the *visitor experience.* Visitors can be defined as individuals who physically come to the museum to see the exhibitions or educational programs, or individuals who experience the museum through outreach activities such as traveling exhibitions, or through web-based access. A visitor experience begins with the first impressions from marketing and learning about the museum before a visit, to convenience in getting to the museum, responding to the site, proper orientation to the public spaces and the exhibitions, to learning from specific exhibitions or programs, to the amenities that provide for a comfortable visit.

INTELLECTUAL FRAMEWORK

The visitor experience depends on the creation of an intellectual framework which builds on the core strengths and assets of the museum: the collections, exhibits, research, and education and outreach programs.

Who Is Involved?

Creating these programs is the responsibility of museum staff, supported by the board, and with meaningful input from community stakeholders and outside experts. Staff involved should include curators, collections managers, educators, and other program specialists. Curators most often take the lead in developing intellectual themes. Yet they do not work in isolation. The best museums will form a planning team or working group to develop themes or overarching educational messages. It is not unusual for the planning team to be augmented by outside consultants. Historians and exhibit designers, if not on staff, can be brought on to work with the museum team to develop the story line for exhibitions. Scriptwriters, filmmakers, and interactive media specialists will also be engaged in planning and developing the exhibitions and educational programs. The value of a team-based approach is in bringing varied skills to the planning. And at this point in your planning there is value in considering many options and weighing diverse points of view. It will take your museum a considerable amount of time to define the intellectual framework; many ideas will be debated and explored; and in the end you will have a strong product reflective of various stakeholders.

What Is the Product?

Intellectual themes take shape through collections and exhibitions, educational programs, and especially through the visual look of the museum. Themes are often quite broad, such as defining the essence of the American Dream, or connecting nature and people, or maritime art in the nineteenth century. From a broad base the museum creates a set of specific objectives to realize the intellectual goals. Typically you will end up with a document that outlines the goals for specific collections; for various exhibitions over a period of time; and for educational activities both within the museum and off-site. The document builds on the core strengths of the museum (collections and scholarly research) and proposes a storyline for public understanding. This intellectual framework is shared with exhibit designers and architects to begin the process of visualizing the program. Curators, registrars, and educators work closely with designers, architects, and other outside consultants to ensure the themes are properly interpreted and spaces are responsive to those needs. The final program plan will incorporate architectural and aesthetic improvements, visitor orientation to the museum, an overall narrative outlining the content of exhibitions, recognition of the key role of outreach, and assumptions regarding effective management of the plan's implementation.

VISITOR EXPERIENCE AND AUDIENCES

A successful museum in the twenty-first century serves as an advocate for the visitor. It is sensitive to visitor concerns, needs, and learning styles and in particular to an obligation to educate the public. Museums are no longer only institutions that preserve heritage; they are engaged with communities in a proactive effort to improve society. This mandate has been endorsed by the museum profession for at least twenty years. Museums seek to be relevant in this world with a focus on service to and active engagement with the community.

Therefore, it is not usual to find a museum that describes a future vision of itself as a "bright, exciting, and welcoming place for learning, socializing, and public gathering. One that assures orientation with easy access to offerings, and a coherent relationship among exhibitions."[2] Visitor research shows that today's museum needs to focus on providing multiple viewpoints, connecting the present to the past, and ensuring accuracy of information. Exhibitions and other interpretive programs use collections and the stories associated with them to teach the public. Goals can include improving critical thinking, elaborating on public debates, and providing opportunities for visitors to personalize their experience with the museum. Museums increasingly need to respond to the diversity of audience demographics, to provide visual, interactive, and text-based learning formats. The goal is to create a society of lifelong learners. Today's visitors expect to be educated and entertained. They come to museums mostly in groups and see the visit as a social experience. They also need to be encouraged to return to the museum and often that is done through changing exhibitions. Successful museums complement long-term exhibitions with special exhibitions that keep the museum vital, showcase new scholarship, and respond to new audience needs.

Visitor studies are critical at this juncture. Your museum educator should make a point of gathering data about existing and potential audiences to determine their interests, considering many options to delivering the educational message, and ensuring that the visitor will be satisfied with their experience. Engaging the visitor in dialogue before, during, and after visiting the museum is one key activity.

Visitor Expectations

Numerous studies have shown that museum visitors today are largely well-educated adults who visit in groups with friends or family. Visitor motivations are varied. The visitor is an explorer learning new information, or the visitor may facilitate the experience of family or friends, or as a professional/expert in a particular subject area. Visitors may also come to the museum to experience something special, through recommendation of another person, or to have a pilgrimage or special connection with the museum's exhibitions, objects, or spaces.[3] These factors help to define the types of exhibitions as well as the physical design requirements for space planning a museum should consider. Elements that shape the visitor experience include signage, exterior landscaping, parking, entrances, decompression and orientation spaces, welcome desks, public gathering spaces, interior way finding aids, color and lighting, landmark objects, and vistas to the outside. Amenities include rest areas, bathrooms, coat checks, information kiosks, food service, retail stores, special events spaces, and service areas.

EXHIBITION PLANNING

Planning for visitors involves translating intellectual themes into physical realities. It also requires a decision process that considers factors such as

- Collections
- Space
- Staff
- Outside expertise
- Audience needs
- Funding

Each of these factors will contribute to the final decisions to go forward with a particular exhibition project. Collections strengths, size of exhibition space to accommodate audiences, requirements for traveling exhibitions, and retail operations can all have an impact on the decision process. Formative studies of audiences and their needs will be critical in the development of exhibitions. Do they comply with state standards of learning for education? Are the themes appropriate? Are the design solutions accessible and well understood? Does the traffic flow through the exhibition facilitate learning and allow for a comfortable experience? Frequent interaction with audiences during and after an exhibition visit will help to assess their actual learning from exhibitions and lead to improvements in the future.

Types of Exhibitions

Exhibitions can take many forms. They include introductory or orientation exhibitions, special thematic shows, treasures or highlights of the collections, and special changing exhibitions. In particular many museums rely heavily on traveling exhibitions, including blockbuster shows meant to draw audiences. Because it is important to provide variety and to encourage repeat visitation, museums often use a mix of long-term and short-term exhibitions. In considering the intellectual framework museums often use a storyline that creates a narrative and links a set of exhibitions. Organization by time period, by major themes, or by physical types may be needed. A general museum may want to organize exhibitions by types of collections. A children's museum may want to organize the experience by social issues. A natural history museum, zoo, or aquarium may organize exhibitions by geography or other systematic or taxonomic classification. A history museum may want to organize by eras, by general themes such as transportation or politics, or by interdisciplinary approaches. Other museums may be motivated by overarching values such as redemption and reconciliation which influenced the exhibitions at the National Museum of the American Indian.[4]

What is the process? Based on the intellectual framework, the museum decides on themes and messages and moves through steps involving research, object selection, script writing, design, production, operation, and evaluation. Exhibitions include related products such as educational programs, publications, films, and web-based versions. Exhibits are planned and executed in line with project management systems that allow for a team-based approach. Internal committees are often involved in the approval and review process. Creating the exhibition program is the responsibility of a team of curators, educators, designers, and collections managers. These staff form the core team responsible for developing and implementing exhibitions that have the in-depth knowledge of the collections and their care, how they can be interpreted, and what the audience needs are in relation to the exhibition design and message. Other staff in the museum who are players in the exhibition planning effort include finance and human resources, development, facilities, and marketing staff.

Timing in regard to museum construction. Although it is ideal to have developed an intellectual framework and associated interpretive plans in advance of designing new or renovating existing spaces, many museums find themselves developing these themes and plans in tandem with the architectural design team. Even if the intellectual framework has been well developed before the architect is selected, there is still an expectation of collaboration during space planning. There should be a synergy between the architect and exhibition planners in regard to the design specifications for public spaces. In the best possible scenario there is a positive and iterative collaboration between space planners and programs specialists that may lead to more creative and possibly less expensive designs.

Timing is critical also in that there are issues in lead time for planning exhibitions and programs. It is not unusual for a museum to spend a year or more planning exhibitions, and large shows can take several years to produce. Some museums begin planning as much as five years before opening a major new exhibition. Thus there is a need to synchronize carefully with aspects of the building project. Your museum should be sure that design and construction teams fully understand the goals, vision, and values associated with the intellectual framework. Curators, registrars, and educators will need to be actively engaged in working closely with building project teams to ensure that museum standards are adhered to throughout the design and construction phases.

COLLECTIONS PLANNING

The goal is to produce a guideline which outlines what objects the museum will maintain in its permanent collection and where additions or deletions are needed over a period of time. Here the working group of curators, collections managers, registrars, and conservators will have a major role to play in developing a plan that links directly to the intellectual framework for development of visitor experiences. Collections reflect the scholarly themes of the museum, are often the centerpiece of the exhibition program, and are closely linked to research efforts by staff and the public. What collections will you want to own versus borrow? What is available? What existing collections fill the need? What staff is needed to both acquire and care for the collections? Who will be responsible for planning for collections? The plan not only includes what objects will be owned by the museum, but how they will be accessed. Some museums may seek to collaborate with others in their field or in the community and thus share use of objects rather than make the commitment to long-term acquisition. The plan itself will reference the history of the collections in the museum and the rationale for any new directions as well as outline the roles and responsibilities of board and staff in its implementation.[5]

What is the relation to space planning? Museums may wish to have flexible spaces for changing exhibitions, permanent exhibitions of key artifacts, and in-depth study galleries or open storage. Automated catalogs of collections can be made publicly available on site as well as on the web. In addition the plans must include current and future storage, receiving and shipping, loading docks, photography studios, exhibition staging, conservation treatment labs, lighting, security, environmental needs, materials storage, and staffing in support of the collections. In considering future space planning, a twenty-year time frame is not unusual.

EDUCATION PROGRAM

Closely aligned with exhibitions and collections planning is the articulation of educational goals and programs. Education is a key driver of all the core public activities of the museum. To assist in the interpretation of collections and special exhibitions there may be a need to create spaces for classrooms and workshops, hands-on galleries, experimental labs, musical performances, lectures and films, library, archive and research centers. Educational activities typically include multiple learning approaches such as first-person interpretation, brochures, audio guides, docent-led tours, lectures, symposiums, interactive games, and study galleries. Teacher training programs are often a central part of the program and classroom learning opportunities on site are often provided. Hands-on exhibitions such as science experiments or machine operations or other immersive learning can augment a traditional exhibition of collections. Films and theater experiences are often included in the program. Museum staff involved in this planning will include educators and curators as well as designers and technology specialists.

It is increasingly important that museums respond to the world they live in with new approaches beyond bricks and mortar. The kinds of programs that may be developed include an online presence, a website, or a My Space page or a Second Life version of the museum. Much of what the museum presents in the physical world can be replicated on the Internet.

Off-site Activities

It has been noted that many museums are offering programming in more than one site. Traditionally, many programs such as lectures, traveling exhibitions, school programs, walking tours, and various publications allow for this. Partnerships with other nonprofits allow for collections sharing, development of scholarly programs, and opportunities for working more closely with community groups. Beyond this the museum may decide to create satellite operations in order to serve new audiences. This trend has major ramifications for the building program and museum operations.

LINKING PROGRAMS TO BUILDING PLANNING

Having developed the museum's intellectual framework and related collecting, exhibition, and educational plans, planners will move on to develop a physical framework for their realization. Figure 4.1 illustrates the relationship

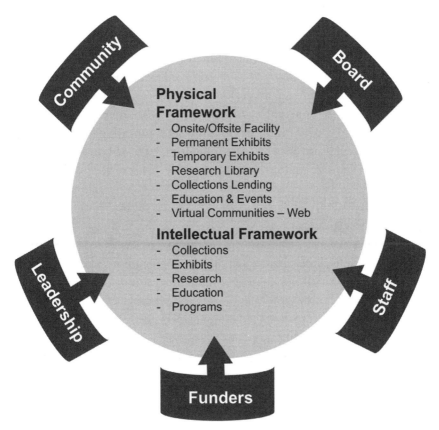

FIGURE 4.1
Marriage of Physical and Intellectual Frameworks

between stakeholders and the creation of programs and spaces. Some examples of important spaces include

- Collections: display, storage, research, and study
- Visitor amenities
- Orientation spaces
- Exhibitions: permanent, temporary, and changing
- Educational: theaters, classrooms
- Special events
- Nonpublic areas: offices, collections management, IT centers
- Off-site storage or satellite facilities

The end result of your program planning will be to meld these initiatives with the basis of design report (a document that may be entitled an "architectural space program plan" or a "master facilities plan") during the pre-design phase which includes a series of documents from your criteria to space program for your entire museum. This document will include a description of the collections, exhibitions, and educational programs, as well as the circulation spaces, visitor amenities, back of house support areas, facilities and technology infrastructure to achieve the overall vision and goals.

Making the Best Decisions

Developing the core components of the visitor experience takes time. Building new collections areas is a multiyear, ongoing process. Advance time to organize new exhibitions and educational programs or even to book traveling exhibitions can be substantial. Thus the program development phase might take many years to evolve. Museum leaders need to facilitate the development through internal dialogue and engagement. This phase follows on the development of mission and vision in the strategic plan and is in fact the realization of long-term goals and objectives. This work is iterative and may evolve in tandem with the physical building plan.

Final plans for the exhibitions, educational programs, collections development, visitor amenities, and behind the scenes support will need to be approved by the museum's senior management and the board. Decision criteria will need to be considered in this effort, including

- Legal and ethical concerns for collections, exhibition themes, donor relations, and audience expectations
- Internal capacity for creating and managing projects, including following a process that is widely inclusive of museum staff
- Costs to acquire collections, mount changing exhibitions, and programs

Scope Creep

If there is any red flag to be worried about at this stage, it is scope creep. There is never a shortage of good ideas. Once a plan has been decided on, someone will want to make changes. Often the changes are legitimate and a vast improvement on the original plan. For example, there may be a desire to add a new space for retail or staff offices or any number of valuable ideas. It is here that the museum needs to take a hard look at the need to make major changes. Changes may be legitimate, but they may also add significantly to the cost or the time involved. Every effort needs to be made to assure adherence to the original plans for the sake of staying on schedule or avoiding cost overruns. Given the long time frame for building projects, there is frequently an opportunity for changes to be considered. This book will continue to emphasize the need to be vigilant about this.

IN SUMMARY

Do's and Don'ts

- Be sure to create working groups that are composed of the key functional areas of the museum.
- Allow sufficient time for planning the programmatic needs of the museums before launching the building planning.
- Consider the vision and mission of the museums in setting priorities for program development.

Red Flags

- Board does not agree with the program goals or understand the cost implications.
- Projects are initiated without stakeholder involvement.
- Collections management and scholarly research are under-resourced.
- Audiences do not respond positively to themes.
- Scope creep!
- Hard data are not used in setting priorities.

NOTES

1. Information about the numbers and types of museums can be found at the website of the American Association of Museums: www.aam-us.org (accessed April 5, 2008).

2. National Museum of American History, *"Our Vision": National Museum of American History Strategic Plan* (Washington, D.C., 2005), 2.

3. John Falk and Beverly Sheppard, *Thriving in the Knowledge Age* (Lanham, MD: AltaMira, 2006), 90–95.

4. Richard West, "A Song Made Visible," *Museum News* 83, no. 5 (September-October 2004): 34–40.

5. James B. Gardner and Elizabeth E. Merritt, *The AAM Guide to Collections Planning* (Washington, D.C. American Association of Museums, 2004). This book provides a good overview of the process and helpful examples.

5

Hiring Your Design and Construction Teams

You will need to hire many consultants over the course of your project to work with you, but it is doubtful you will work with any consultants longer than the design and construction teams. Hiring them, unlike hiring audience evaluators or historians, will probably involve your board, local political leaders, and other stakeholders. The process of hiring can take months, so care should be taken to form a selection committee and develop objective and subjective criteria in advance and establish a process that assures consensus so you can select the right firms for your project.

This chapter focuses on finding the design team (the architect and subconsultants), the exhibit design team, the construction team, and other specialty consultants not typically hired under the design or construction team's contracts.

THE DESIGN TEAMS FOR THE BUILDING AND EXHIBITS

Hiring building design and exhibit design teams are important steps, since these teams have a significant impact on translating the museum's vision and needs into reality. In selecting these teams, the steering committee should carefully consider their expertise and fit with your leadership team. Museum leadership must ask, "Do they understand who we are and what we are looking for? Can we work with this team day in and day out, trusting their advice, their ability to stay cool under fire, and work problems out when things go wrong—because they will?" This section focuses on the most common process and time frame used in hiring building design and exhibit design teams.

When Should I Hire the Architect and Exhibit Designers?

This section assumes that the museum will be undertaking exhibit design and building design construction concurrently. It is difficult to specify the best time to hire the design teams: some are expansive programmatic thinkers, planners, and designers, while others are siloed, focused only on the exhibits or building. You must decide what works best for your project. Your planning process may be driven by a wide range of needs, from analysis of your current building to the need to develop "beautiful pictures" of the new building for the development officer. A good rule of thumb is to hire the teams as early in the process as the museum can define what it needs them to do. This will allow the team to gel and add its expertise to advance early project conceptualization. Even if the teams' total participation at that point is a monthly meeting and bimonthly conference call for the first six months, the worst that can happen is that the museum learns it did (or did not) make the right choice. Remember, an early wrong choice can still be changed.

Museums should use the building design team's (usually an architectural firm) and exhibit team's (usually an exhibit design firm) contracts as prime contracts or vehicles to hire all the other specialty consultants (subprime or subconsultants) needed. This makes the prime firms legally responsible for negotiating scope of services, scheduling, directing, and coordinating their work, as well as paying their invoices, relieving the museum of a considerable amount of management time. While the museum will not have direct oversight of specialists, such as the lighting designer, it can work through the prime, who is accountable, to get the desired results and simplify the process.

Among the building design team consultants and subconsultants who may be needed are a museum planner, an architect, an interior designer, a landscape architect, HVAC engineer, plumbing engineer, electrical engineer, lighting designer, fire protection engineer, IT/registered communications designer, security consultant, audiovisual designer, media integrator, acoustician, vertical transportation engineer, food and retail consultants, kitchen designers, traffic consultant, and civil engineers. Sustainability, historic preservation architects, way finding/signage, cost management, and other consultants may or may not be required depending on core competency of the prime team. The museum may need to hire some consultants directly since most companies that insure design firms preclude hiring hazardous materials consultants, site surveyors, and geotechnical engineers. You will also need to hire a commissioning agent and a materials testing firm for third party verification of certain work.

For exhibit design, the team may include researchers, historians, story writers, curators, educators, lighting designers, and media and production consultants.

Should I Hire a Star, Expert, or Generalist (Local) Architect?

There are many excellent planners and architects who can work on museum projects. They can be found through museum peers, American Association of Museums (AAM) publications, and the American Institute of Architects among other sources. The hiring process is lengthy, but prior to issuance of the request for qualifications (RFQ), the steering committee must first do its homework and make sure it is in agreement about the type of lead design firm committee members want to hire. There are many qualified firms in each category which will be discussed, so selection is as much about your values and chemistry as anything else. Issuing the request for qualifications (RFQ) to a range of different types of firms will signal the board's division and make the project less attractive to any firm. Be assured, any divisions ignored now will surface when it is time to make the selection. The steering committee must do its homework and come to consensus to avoid a showdown, which could fracture the board and hurt the project's momentum.

- A star architect can add visibility, draw donors, and create a landmark that reflects the high aspirations of the community. Only a few museums can afford a star architect and there is no use in considering one unless the project type, size, budget, and visibility are appealing to that architect as well. The museum must have the money for a more expensive building, higher design fees, and an operating model that can support potentially higher maintenance costs. Most important, the steering committee must make sure the architect will respect the programmatic goals and priorities of your building vision statement so that the project can meet all the other goals of the strategic plan. Some star architects may not have the capacity to produce the design within the museum's time frame, so star firms often work with local firms to provide horsepower and local market expertise to the team.

- Museum expert architects are specialists in the design of museum buildings who have built their practice of architecture on working with museums. They bring a significant level of understanding of the way museums work and the challenges they face in navigating change. Many of these firms have excellent design credentials but lack the signature of a star firm while charging a lower fee. Depending on a museum's needs, often an expertise-driven firm will partner with a local firm to work on the project and provide local knowledge and support. Since most of these partnerships start as shotgun marriages, they can be challenging during the request for qualifications (RFQ) process and may be tension filled as the project progresses. One variation is to hire the expertise-driven firm first, and then have it interview and partner with a local firm so that there is a better chance of finding the right fit.
- Local firms may not have the programmatic expertise the project needs but are members of the community and can do a good job. Museum leadership may need extra time to educate the design team on the programmatic issues and may have to take a greater role in the process to ensure the museum gets what it wants. A local firm may work well for a small project, but a complex project may overwhelm your museum project manager and the local firm as they learn together how to plan and design a museum capital project. This can still be an effective approach, but holds risks in that leveraging the knowledge of trends and opportunities may depend completely on the museum to ensure the best possible outcome.

The only way to judge whether the firm and its lead staff will share the museum's design vision is to have them explain their work on other projects and how they came to their design solutions. This is a process of coming to understand their thinking and aesthetic response, which will provide a sense of how they will work with you and your committee.

Request for Qualifications (RFQ) and Request for Proposal (RFP) Processes

Hiring the prime building design team involves seven steps and can take from two to eight months, depending on the size of the project, the experience of the museum project manager, and the alignment of the steering committee. The process of hiring the exhibit design team is similar but is not likely to take as long, particularly since most museums are familiar with exhibit design teams and staff has experience in working with them. If the museum is working through a facilities department of a college or university, or through a city, state, or federal agency, the process and proposal format may be prescribed. If so, the steering committee should not shy away from the process since it will have a significant role in developing the content of the search and in prioritizing the key decision points in the selection process.

Step 1: Museum prepares and board subcommittee approves a request for qualifications (RFQ) (1–2 months). If the museum does not have a prescribed process, the steering committee should look for templates for a request for qualifications format used by peers or by agencies working with peer museums. If there is not a required public process, the steering committee can save time and prequalify a select list of firms by doing its own research: talking with peers, visiting websites or projects, calling references, and skipping the request for qualifications process altogether. Otherwise, all the steps apply.

The steering committee should do its homework in advance, since firms will expend a great deal of effort pursuing a project, and the museum's project manager will also spend a great deal of time answering questions, especially if the request for qualifications and request for proposals are not clear in stating the museum's expectations and project needs. If the steering committee is unprepared, it will spend even more time answering questions. The steering committee must keep the playing field level by requiring that all questions be submitted in writing and answered in writing. Do not do firms a favor by keeping the list long or feeling sorry to cut them early. Firms do not want to waste time and prefer to know early if they are not deemed qualified for the project. Your museum must be clear about what it is looking for in the process and state the criteria for selection at each phase. If it prefers that out of town firms partner with local firms, it should be explicit.

Design competitions provide a means of understanding the design skills and approach of the building design teams under consideration. While common in some countries, competitions in the United States are used significantly less frequently. Competitions are complex processes and should be held with a select list of firms after the request for qualifications process under rules such as those established by the American Institute of Architects (AIA). In the United States and most countries, invited competitions include a stipend for participation. Indeed, firms are likely to spend far more than the stipend to develop a convincing idea and graphic presentation. If a steering committee plans a competition, it should be prepared to supply a lot of information, be clear about its budget, and have the designs priced by an estimator so that the big idea is within the museum's fiscal capacity. The steering committee might want to add a dean of architecture or local design critic to the committee: his or her view will be important in seeing through the graphics to find a compelling design. The name of the winning design team should not be released until all key issues are reconciled with the building program and the estimate of the project's cost. A suggested table of contents for a request for qualifications appears in appendix B.

Step 2: Issue the request for qualifications (RFQ) to an open or select list of firms and receive responses (1 month). You may issue the RFQ to as many firms as you like. Some museums may issue an RFQ to fifteen, but be prepared to review many voluminous responses. Most of what you will get is boilerplate information, but some materials should be customized to the particulars of your project.

Step 3: Select a long list of firms to receive a request for proposal (RFP) (2 months). Often the museum project manager with the director or the head of the board steering committee will take responsibility to winnow down the list. Your museum project manager should start the review process by following up on references. Structure questions to ask of all references. Do not lead the reference. It is easy to be swayed by an applicant's strong qualifications and to invite reinforcement of one's favorable impressions during the reference check. That is why notes are important. Come as close to verbatim as possible in recording what the reference says, and read these remarks after initial excitement wears off. Select no less than three and no more than six firms for the next step. Any more and there will tend to be firms that are increasingly different on the list, giving way to skepticism by the design teams that the steering committee does not have a clear idea of what it wants. The steering committee should consider limiting the length of proposals to a specified number of pages with an established order. The more firms, the more proposals to read, so be selective and do the hard work now. This will help the steering committee evaluate what it receives and force the respondents to provide clear and concise information. At this point, be aware that fees are not reliable indicators of value, particularly when there is no fixed scope of work or clear requirements for number of meetings during design or construction. Most firms are competitive within a range, and if selected, will negotiate in good faith. If they will not, the steering committee should move to the second ranking firm. If the steering committee is required to ask for fees, firms should provide them in a separate sealed envelope, to be opened after the interviews and selection on all other criteria has been made. Then the cost proposal can be evaluated after a detailed discussion with the preferred firm of the scope of services needed. A steering committee should not be swayed by a low fee as the deciding factor. Building design teams sell their time, so less cost means less time spent on the museum's project. See appendix C for a suggested request for proposal table of contents.

Step 4: Issue a request for proposal to select list of firms (1 month).

Step 5: Short list of firms for interviews (1 month). Have the building design teams submit enough copies for everyone on your selection committee. Set a deadline for review and ask each member to rank each proposal using your previously established criteria. Ask for short narrative comments as a supplement to facilitate discussion. The ideal short list for interviews is three or a maximum of four firms; the longer the list, the more difficult it may be to get the steering committee to commit the time for interviews which will stretch over several days. Firms to be interviewed should be given at least three weeks advance notice—time to clear their schedules and be prepared. It is the steering committee's choice whether to assign the order or give firms the ability to select a timeslot. From the firm's perspective, the last interview is best, first is second best, and other positions are less desirable.

Rules of the interview process should be well understood by all the participants in advance. The steering committee should develop a list of topics and key issues to remind firms being interviewed of what should be covered. The museum project manager may also ask particular people to develop questions around particular topics in advance to ensure that everyone is not asking the same questions and all key topics are covered.

Interviews should be anywhere from one to two hours each with an hour between interviews to capture responses. Questions should be as specific as possible: open-ended questions may not yield enough information about the team. Questions should be designed to draw out the creative thinking of the team and test their ability to deal with difficult situations. Others should elicit a squirm: "What is the worst news you gave a client on your last museum project?"

Some steering committees may use standard scoring forms to level the playing field and to aid in deliberations. If the steering committee is using standard scoring criteria, the criteria should be clear to the firms prior to the interviews. This works if the steering committee is not a slave to the scoring system—selection is often as much gut as a point tally on criteria—some intangibles do not score well. You may elect in advance that if scoring is within a certain number of points, the decision should be based on a moderated discussion. Between interviews, members should write notes or fill out the scoring criteria.

Step 6: Selection. If the steering committee has done its homework and members are still in accord, the decision should be relatively easy. Often the top two firms are apparent as soon as the last firm leaves. The steering committee should be warned not to be overly swayed by a team that interviews well: it might not be the best firm for the job. The museum needs a firm whose key people have not only charisma, but also staying power and are not afraid to bring bad news. If scoring cards have been used and the scoring is very close, it is a good idea for the steering committee to throw out the cards and not make the decision based on a small point spread. Take a show of hands, continue discussion, and in particular, ask the museum's project manager to suggest who has the kind of personality best suited to the personalities of the working groups and stakeholders who will be involved in the project on a daily basis for the next few years.

Step 7: Contract negotiations and board approval (1–2 months). With your building design firm tentatively selected, the museum project manager should handle the contract negotiation process with support from legal counsel as needed. Assign or add additional consultants as needed to ensure you have the work scope and expertise you need under one contract. This will simplify your management time and provide a single point of responsibility. As the fee is negotiated, have your museum project manager and the design team project manager develop a detailed work plan and be explicit as to numbers of workshops and meetings and the project process. This is when the relationship between the scope of service you need and design fee becomes clear.

The museum is now ready to begin work with the design team. The process is described in chapter 6 and the work to complete design is described in chapter 7. The process to hire the exhibit design team is similar, though your criteria are different. Again talk with peer institutions and follow a vigorous process. One more major team remains to be selected—the team to construct your building.

HIRING THE CONSTRUCTION TEAM

Prior to selecting the construction team, the steering committee must decide on the method of contracting or construction that will be best for the project. Depending on the museum's needs, the steering committee may elect to hire a general contractor (GC) or a construction manager (CM); these and other approaches with the pros and cons of each are described in chapter 6. Once the decision on a general contractor or construction manager is reached, hiring follows the process described earlier in the chapter for the design team. If the museum is part of an institution of higher education or a government entity, the process may be prescribed and managed by others. The table of contents for preparation and approval of a request for qualifications (RFQ) is covered in appendix D.

The board steering committee and museum project manager should review the proposals carefully and ask for advice from the building design team or board members with experience in construction to review the technical aspects. When the construction teams have been selected for interviews, questions will be quite different from those asked during Design Team interviews. See appendix E for suggested interview questions.

As described in chapter 7, the general conditions of the specifications in the contract documents prepared by the design team set the requirements for the construction team on a range of issues. It is often a challenge to understand completely what is and is not included in the fee being presented. It is a good idea to ask for a breakdown of costs, or for a breakdown allocating all costs covered in general conditions and stating who is responsible for those costs. This is to ensure that shared items, such as cleaning the job site or removing construction waste, are included in one budget or another.

NOT ENOUGH STAFF FOR THE TASKS: PROCURING ADDITIONAL HELP

Over the course of your building project you may need temporary staff, particularly if you choose to assign permanent staff to key roles in the project, or the project involves other activities such as a major rehousing of your collections. One source is to use interns or temporary help from students in museum studies programs, or retired museum (or library) professionals who are comfortable in the museum milieu and bring professional demeanors.

Specialty consultants will be hired to support a large building program: consultants to conduct feasibility, marketing, and other specialized studies; to develop and lead capital campaigns; audience evaluators, conservators, and collections managers; public relations specialists; and caterers and events co-ordinators. Consultants connected to the design or building process but not hired directly by the design or construction teams such as hazardous materials consultant or a commissioning agent should be hired with the support of the design and construction teams. The museum should follow simplified but similar processes in hiring these consultants: issue a request for proposal for qualified individuals or firms stating clearly the goals and objectives of the project, qualifications required to be considered, and clear expectations for performance of the contract—deliverables, duration of the contract, quality of the service or product—and any other special requirements, selection criteria such as lists of clients, references, and successful projects of a similar nature. When a decision is made, make sure the scope of work is complete, stating consultant deliverables, performance expectations, and your schedule to complete performance of the task or tasks, with a payment schedule tied to deliverables. Include clauses for termination if performance targets are not met. Have all contracts reviewed by legal counsel before executing them.

IN SUMMARY

Hiring great people and firms is essential to your success. Spend the time to do it right, and you will be richly rewarded along the way with a team that works well with you and your museum staff.

Do's and Don'ts

- Do agree on criteria for hiring your design and construction teams prior to starting the process.
- Don't underestimate the value of team chemistry.
- When hiring services, don't overlook past performance and references of the individuals.
- Don't allow the donor to make the choice.

Red Flags

- Overstepping boundaries
- Going on the cheap when contracting for expertise
- Miscommunications among any working groups; conflicts of interest for board members in hiring any consultants

Project Management

Predesign, Design, Construction, and Closeout

This chapter provides an overview of the process of managing predesign, design, construction, and closeout of your building and exhibits. This process begins with the completion and approval of your strategic plan and ends the day you open your new building. This could range anywhere from two years for a project of modest scope to ten or more for a large multiphase effort. Since the useful life of some major building components, such as roofing or major mechanical systems, is around twenty-five years, the fact that some projects last that time frame reflects the fact that many very large museums are always in a planning and construction mode.

This chapter is organized to describe the

- Terminology used in the design and construction industry
- Phases of a project
- Communication tools and processes between the museum and the building design and construction teams
- Best management tools for controlling scope, building budgets, and schedules through predesign, design, construction, and closeout
- Options for bidding and construction of the building: general contractor, construction manager, or design build

This chapter covers the process (how to do it), while chapter 7 covers the work products (what you will know) in each phase. The goal of this chapter is not to make you the expert, but to demystify the process and help you become a more informed advocate for your museum. After reading this chapter, you can learn about standard procedures of design and construction from sources in the bibliography.

Consider the purchase of your home as an analogy for the planning, design, and construction process: Why do you need a new house, how big, is a yard important or do you need more bedrooms? What style of house appeals to you? What neighborhood do you want to live in, how much can you afford? You may not be able to find the perfect house, some criteria may give way, and some decisions may become more subjective (emotional) than objective (rational). Building a home for your museum is much more complicated and many more decisions need to be made. Along the way, you and your planning and design team will be making tens of thousands of decisions which will define in extraordinary detail your building as a reality on paper prior to becoming a reality during construction.

What is the design process and what is your role? Think of the design process as a decision-making and resource-allocation process. This is the time to define what you will and will not build to support your museum exhibits, programs, and staff activities as identified in your strategic plan.

- *Decision making.* A blank sheet of paper is full of opportunity; everything at that moment is a variable representing opportunity and a decision to be made. Each space, its location in your building down to the detail of how each light switch is located in relation to the door should be a conscious decision on the part of your staff and design team to support your activity in your building. There is an underlying logic to the sequence of the planning and design process as it progresses from broad general decisions (site, total size, functions) to the details (colors, types of light fixtures, etc.). Each decision is connected to dozens of past and future issues you will address. If you abdicate responsibility, the design team will have to make decisions on your behalf. If things are wrong, you share blame with the design team, so make sure your staff has the time and commitment to remain engaged and attentive to the detail that must be developed.
- *Resource allocation.* Every design decision, whether for materials selection (limestone or brick), building systems, or the building aesthetic, is a process of allocating your financial resources according to the values of your mu-

seum at every step along the way. Each decision you make sets a direction and encumbers funding that could be used in other ways. Your board and museum leadership must develop shared priorities and criteria well ahead of design to ensure that you are on the same page.

While the design phase is one continuous process, your design team views it as a sequence of phases which advance the level of detail. At the beginning, the number of decisions and pace will be all consuming. As design proceeds to the final details, the process relies increasingly on the design team to provide the technical solutions to the program problem. You do not need to know how the electricity gets to the lighting in the gallery, but you do need to remain involved to ensure your technical criteria are technically correct (does the fixture have the correct beam spread with enough lumens and a UV filter). The process and procedures used will determine your comfort level in making *informed* decisions and your ability to control what is going on.

TERMINOLOGY

Design and construction, like any industry, has generally accepted terminology and acronyms which will continue to appear throughout the process. It is the responsibility of the design and construction teams you hire to demystify the process and guide you through design and construction. If you hire someone with expertise in museums, you are several steps ahead: experience can be your guide. But if you do not hire someone who has expertise, expect to spend more time educating the design team and guiding the process yourself.

In this book, terms for the consultants you hire are meant to be inclusive and are used as follows:

- Design team includes planners, architects, engineers, and specialists such as lighting designers and acousticians who are subcontracted to the architects you contract with for services.
- Exhibit design team includes exhibit designers and their subcontractors, who may include a range of curators, historians, writers, and graphic designers.
- Construction team refers to the general contractor or construction manager and any of their subcontractors.
- Exhibit construction team may fabricate and install, and may be independent or part of an exhibit design/build firm.

- Owner's consultants are other consultants directly contracted to the museum for information technology, media integration, graphic design, retail and food and beverage planning, hazardous materials consulting, and so on.

See the glossary for further terminology definitions.

PHASES AND DELIVERABLES OF A PROJECT

This chapter approaches the deliverables (work products) of predesign and conceptual design in detail since the quality and depth of these planning and design documents will determine your ability to successfully complete the building your community expected at the cost and on the schedule your board mandated.

Predesign Phase

The predesign phase encompasses all planning and programming activities prior to development of a specific design solution. In a sense, predesign is the process of defining your *problem* and coming to a shared understanding of what you will build, at what cost, over what time frame.[1] Predesign should occur concurrently with, and be informed by, your financial and operational planning, so your project's scope remains within the fund-raising capacity of your institution and the project will be sustainable operationally and fiscally over the long term. Over the course of predesign, it is more than likely that there will be more scope identified than financial resources, requiring stakeholders to prioritize according to your strategic plan and potentially cut scope. The goal of predesign is to confirm alignment of your strategic plan's goals with your building project scope and budget, accompanied by a strategy for execution. Predesign management activities are covered in this chapter and deliverables will be covered in detail in chapter 7.

Design Phases

Design begins by turning the information developed in predesign into form, and ends with final deliverables, which are the contract documents that will be used to bid and build your site and building. There are four phases in design, each reflecting the development of a level of information as your site and building are increasingly defined:

- Conceptual design is where about 5 percent of your total project design is complete: the layout of your building, the building sections and elevations and selection of your basic building systems. Deliverables include drawings and narratives of site, building, building systems, and an estimate of costs that advance the information developed during predesign into the concepts of a built form. This phase is critical to your outcome since the criteria developed during predesign must be reflected in the concept of your building, its organization, and its image.

- Schematic design (SD) advances the understanding of your building to about 20 percent complete documentation where major elements are now shown in the drawings enabling you and the design team to understand the site and these spaces and their programmatic fit and visual appearance. Additional deliverables include outline specifications and an updated estimate of probable costs. Since the process of this phase is similar for all building types, this book will not go into greater detail and other books are referenced in the bibliography.

- Design development (DD) completes the design definition to 60 or 65 percent, showing all building elements and materials on all surfaces as well as building systems serving those areas in sufficient detail to reflect how your site and building will appear and how the systems serve them. Deliverables in this phase are similar to schematic design phase, but in greater detail in both drawings and specifications.

- Construction documentation (CD) completes the building definition to 100 percent, allowing the process of procurement of contracts with a construction team to commence. These are very detailed documents running into hundreds of sheets of drawings and thousands of pages for specifications for large complex projects.

Procurement Phase

Procurement is the process of obtaining bids or pricing and executing a firm contract to construct your site and building. Exhibit procurement is on an independent track but with a similar process. The different methodologies to procure the project are covered in detail later in this chapter.

Construction Phase

The construction phase begins with your construction team (construction manager or general contractor) mobilizing by assigning construction staff, ordering materials, obtaining necessary permits, placing trailers on the site, and preparing to begin construction. More detail on this phase is provided later in this chapter.

Postconstruction or Occupancy

   Your occupancy of your building may overlap with some on-site construction activity. It may start with essential staff for building operations, exhibit installation or testing, and increase as the construction team completes work.

- Beneficial occupancy is the date when a space is turned over to you. It may overlap with on-site construction work elsewhere and has legal ramifications in terms of safety of staff and warranty of systems.
- Substantial completion is a legal term for the date when work is 99 percent complete and turned over to you and your staff for move-in. You now cover insurance and building operations, while the contractor is still on site completing minor touchup or punch list items.
- Occupancy and operations.

MANAGING DECISIONS

What's the Importance of Early Decision Making?

   The cost of making a decision in predesign is comparatively small; all you have invested is your staff and the design team's time. Each decision becomes the basis for future decisions and project direction, so as soon as each decision is made new questions arise, and they form layers which become the bedrock for your building. Gradually they build up as the project proceeds, so that changing your mind later can involve throwing out the work of the working groups and design team potentially delaying the project and adding work and cost as you double back.

   The outcome of any capital project is determined by your diligence in managing a comprehensive predesign process. The quality and diligence of your predesign phase provides the greatest impact on outcome at the lowest cost to you. As shown on the diagram figure 2.1 (based on one prepared by the Construction Industry Institute [CII]), your influence is highest while at the lowest cost and declines rapidly in subsequent phases.

How Should I Manage Interaction, Communications, and Decision-Making Processes?

   Your museum project manager who has been tasked with coordinating the building project will work closely with the design team project manager throughout the design and construction process. You should expect collaboration in using a range of tools to expedite the flow of information. Project man-

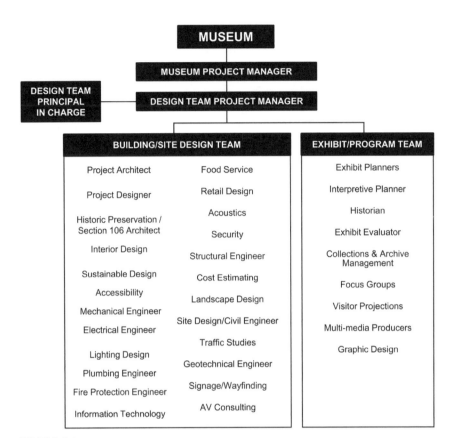

FIGURE 6.1
Sample Design Team Organization Chart

agement tools and procedures should not inhibit the free flow of information, but are needed to help to keep decisions on track and avoid possible misdirection of the work of the team.

Who's in charge? Communication flow between the museum and design or construction teams should always go through your museum project manager (PM) to the design or construction team project managers (figure 6.1). The reverse is true of subconsultants and subcontractors through their respective project managers to yours. Each of those individuals should be the point person for their team or organization to disseminate and expedite the flow of information to stakeholders and avoid any end run and costly ill-informed decisions.

What's the plan? A project work plan is a narrative of the sequence of activities of the predesign and design activities developed by the design team. A preliminary project work plan is often developed and submitted as part of the request for proposal by the design team to you in order to describe their services and activities. (A similar work plan is prepared by the exhibit design and construction teams.) It is, in effect, a work scope description which outlines each task, the numbers of meetings, major decision points, review periods, and deliverables so there is a mutual understanding of services, working process, and milestone schedule dates. The work plan is also the basis for fees: you are paying for the time for each task in the work plan. After you have hired your design team, this work plan will be detailed more thoroughly and will help your museum project manager organize the activities of the stakeholder working groups and become the basis for the design schedule.

Who knows what? A project directory should include a list of everyone associated with the project, internal and external. You should identify the museum department and working group affiliations of each person to ensure stakeholders are included in invitations to meetings, as well as subsequent distribution of meeting minutes. You should remember that most subconsultants are contracted directly to the design team who negotiated their scope of work, so this list should not be viewed as an invitation for you to call them directly and direct their work.

How will we stay on track? Meetings will be most successful if they are run with agendas created in advance by the museum project manager or design team project manager in consultation with each other. An agenda, distributed in advance, will allow participants to arrive prepared, focused and better able to make decisions in a timely way.

How do we interact with the design team and communicate our needs? Communication with your design team should use a variety of tools to engage stakeholders and bring them to consensus. The best way to understand the process of who needs to be in the various meetings is to look at your project organization chart responsibilities framework diagram (figure 3.1), where reporting relationships and stakeholder working groups are identified.

- Begin each phase of design with a plenary meeting, so that all stakeholders hear the same thing at the same time. The first meeting should focus on stakeholder understanding of the project process, their roles, the numbers of meetings or workshops, the schedule, and the lines of communication. Since schedule coordination is often a challenge, all major meetings with stakeholders should be scheduled two months in advance to ensure participation.

- Questionnaires are most useful for highly technical spaces and can be viewed as impersonal by stakeholders. A meeting agenda could be viewed as an interactive questionnaire and used as a to-do list after a meeting when an agenda is not completed.
- Benchmarking, as described in chapter 2, can be supplemented by visits shared by stakeholder working groups and the design team to peer institutions that have recently completed similar projects. Visits after the project kickoff provide a common point of reference for later discussions and breaks down the barriers between the stakeholders and design team.
- A significant amount of information will be collected from each stakeholder working group. A card show led by a museum planner uses index cards on a large wall as a visual outline of your workshop agenda. By following the cards, the discussion follows the flow of information which must be discussed. Posting the information as decisions are made provides a visual record which can be referred to as the workshop advances.
- Charrettes (from French for cart, reflecting a beaux arts tradition of the design process), or intensive interactive workshops, provide a two-way forum for engaging stakeholder working groups. Similar to those used in exhibit planning, these workshops which may occur over a series of days are generally interactive hands-on sessions where stakeholder input must be guided to stay on focus with an agenda. Dialogue structured by an agenda, use of sketches, and many other tools make these workshops very productive and enjoyable for everyone, and foster crossing formal barriers which may lead to the best ideas coming from your youngest staff or external stakeholders. The facilitator is often the leader of the design team, but should depend upon the subject at hand.
- Programming interviews with stakeholders will capture detailed information from departmental or individual stakeholders. Depending upon the complexity of the programmatic need, this can take two or three sessions, as issues more difficult to resolve are uncovered and addressed.
- Work shadowing allows your design team to spend a typical day to observe and question what your staff does and how they do it. Work shadowing should be an adjunct to the programming interviews to ensure the design team fully understands your staff needs.
- Depending on the phase of the project, regular meetings should be held at intervals which allow the predesign team and stakeholder working groups to

develop information and reach decisions. Pressure to move too quickly can result in failure to develop consensus or have the time to properly consider the implications of the issues at hand. Consensus may not always happen, so make sure your project leadership is prepared to step in where necessary.

- Weekly or biweekly updates outside of scheduled face-to-face meetings will allow your museum project manager to coordinate with your design team project manager and make adjustments in direction. It ensures that you relate new information in a timely manner and gives you the opportunity to understand the progress of the design team as they advance. There are a variety of conferencing, web, or video-enabled technologies which can be used. The most important element here is that you are communicating regularly.

- Email has emerged as the most frequent form of contact. Overreliance on email versus picking up the phone or any of the other means of communication has led to many misunderstandings undermining project process and teamwork. Email is an excellent tool to transmit information and confirm discussion, but it should not be used as a chat room by stakeholders who are seeking resolution of a complex issue or to avoid direct discussion of challenging project issues.

- Drawings, models, and digital animations all provide you with visualizations to communicate design intent. Diagrams will appear first during predesign, showing building functional adjacencies, collections movement, and visitor flow. Rough sketch drawings will begin during design offering alternative ideas, until a scheme is selected. Digital modeling software enables the design team to diagram the building, and as detail is developed, three-dimensional animations can be developed providing significant detail which will also be an important tool for fund-raising. It is unlikely there will be sufficient information for a complete realistic animation until the design is 50 percent complete (early design development phase) which will be a challenge to what the development department may need to approach donors.

How do we document our decisions? Documenting decisions made is a critical activity of the design process and each decision enables the design team to progress toward milestones of the project and completion of design. Changes and revisiting decisions, while your prerogative, can delay your ability to meet your schedule and give cause for the design team to ask for additional services.

Along the way, meeting minutes are the primary tool to document the process, and they are often an underused tool to track issues and ongoing discussions. Meeting minutes will serve as the institutional memory over the three to ten year life of your project. Since many of the participants in your project will not be present when the project is completed, this record is vital in tracking issues and later understanding the "what, when, who, how much" impact of the decisions made: minutes should be broken into four parts:

- Masthead
  a. Identify the working group name and purpose of the meeting.
  b. Identify who is present, as well as who was invited and absent.
- Discussion
  a. Each issue, numbered in sequence, such as meeting 2, item 3, first discussion, should be 2.3.1.
  b. Action by: Assign responsibility to someone present with date for providing resolution.
  c. At the next meeting, the items that are not closed are brought forward; discussed and new information should be noted as item 2.3.2.
  d. How much? Once there is agreement, note the decision, but keep the item open pending identifying cost or schedule implications of that decision.
  e. Decision to implement: After cost and schedule are known and the museum elects to approve the decision, keep the item open for one additional meeting. Then drop the issue from the minutes.
- Next steps
  a. Next meeting date.
  b. Action by (for open issues under discussion).
  c. Interim information covering telephone conversations prior to issuance of minutes.
- Issuance information
  a. Author, distribution list, and approval process.

If stakeholders miss meetings or workshops, make sure they review decisions and understand the implications as minutes are reviewed so that the next meeting does not backtrack.

Is it my job to know what's on the drawings? While you have had numerous meetings along the way, the design team is working daily refining the documents which have implications for how your building will function, so as your intent is translated onto the drawings, certain information may have been misunderstood or lost along the way. As part of the completion of each phase, you should undergo a rigorous document review process to ensure that reports and the design documents have captured your decisions and reflect what you expected.

How do we review the design team's documents and know what they say? Review of the design team's work is one of the most important museum activities during the design and documentation phase. A design review is a time to confirm the design is proceeding in accordance with your direction and the intent of the predesign planning documents. All key stakeholder working groups should be involved, but avoid using a review as an opportunity to reopen discussions or to make changes by stakeholders who did not buy into earlier decisions: this will undermine the process, add design cost, and may have schedule implications as well. You should schedule design reviews to last for two weeks, with design team response to your comments one or two weeks later. The museum's project manager should coordinate all stakeholder review comments onto one set of drawings and approve all changes.

Design reviews should occur at the end of predesign and each phase of each design phase. There are several suggested methodologies for the review process depending upon your preference of involving your staff, your staff's time, and their ability to understand documents that are becoming increasingly more complex to read and understand. Over the course of the project, you may want to change methodologies of review.

Method 1: Formal presentation by the design team. Have your design team, architects, and engineers formally present and walk you through the drawings in detail: from entering the site to the details of your conservation lab (where is the light switch, and is there an interlock between security alarm panel and the lock on the door to the collections storage space?). While this will be a lengthy process, working through drawings in detail ensures that you know what is intended by all the detail in the documents. Don't forget to use your basis of design report (described in chapter 7) as a checklist. Make sure individuals who are identified in the room definition sheets review the specific spaces they originally signed off on. You should bring in staff for the overview and specific staff for review of spaces appropriate to their area of responsibility.

Method 2: Formal review with written comments. This process can occur without a formal presentation or after a formal presentation. The same participants should be involved. Options are simply to have stakeholders mark-up sets of drawings, but the museum project manager should collate the markups to reconcile contradicting comments or scope change comments prior to returning the documents to the design team. The design team should review these comments and mark up the same set with any comments or questions which should be jointly reviewed with the museum project manager. A second option uses an online system for posting stakeholder comments and design team responses. Your stakeholders should review these responses to ensure the intent of your comments have been understood and incorporated.

Whichever method for review you use, your signoff is a formal acceptance of everything on the documents to date. Subsequent changes will be the basis for additional work and services for the design team with the potential for time delay to make changes retroactively. At the completion of your review, issue a formal notice to proceed letter to the design team to signal that this work has been accepted.

If the above processes of communication and teamwork are followed, your predesign and design processes should move forward with no more than the usual bumps and detours. If you communicate well, continuously manage the process to fit your budget and schedule, you will find success. The next two sections provide specific recommendations for overlaying communication with cost and schedule management to meet those expectations.

MANAGING COSTS

In a museum design project, there is never a shortage of ideas, only a shortage of money to build and support programs. In this environment, predesign planning to define scope is money well spent, but without a "culture" of ongoing management of project cost as part of your design process, you will find it impossible to make the predesign budget hold through the design process.

Reconciling the museum's capacity to raise money and the cost to build determines the final scope of what you build. If your predesign planning has more scope than you can afford, don't be optimistic, be realistic and develop an alternative plan by either cutting scope or phasing your project. Once your board hears a budget number, they will expect the project will be managed to meet that number. Resist the push for a quick study: if the feasibility is based on poor understanding of your project scope or the number is either too low or too high, it will be difficult to recover. Chapter 2 addresses development of an early feasibility study.

When should I develop estimates and what formats are most useful? Complete written estimates should be delivered at the end of each milestone during design:

- Predesign phase: During predesign, it is recommended that you develop a cost model for your first estimate. A cost model is a design tool as well as a method which looks at the building as a series of assemblies; for example, the exterior wall assembly (a sandwich of granite tied back to masonry, insulation, vapor barrier, plywood, drywall, and paint) has a cost associated with it. Once you know the area of the exterior wall, the cost can be determined based on a cost per square foot. If your building grows or shrinks, it is easy to understand the cost implications. If you need to cut project costs, by changing the cost of granite to brick you can immediately understand the cost implications of that decision. Even better, the format of a cost model allows you to quickly understand that adding a 2,000-square-foot gallery can be offset by substituting brick for the granite on your building's exterior. Your ability to understand the cost implications of design and materials makes it a useful tool as you decide to add or delete scope.
- Conceptual design through contract document phases: Your estimate may evolve from a cost model to one based on a format based on specifications sections following the Construction Specifications Institute (CSI) format. This is generally done to allow you to better understand the cost breakouts in the format used by the construction team and subcontractors, which includes the materials and the labor to accomplish work, with factors added to reflect the general conditions of the specifications. It is arguable whether the estimate is needed at the end of contract documents, since the documents have been completed and your bid information will be available in four to six weeks.

If you only use your cost estimator at milestones, you have a greater chance of going in the wrong direction or making decisions with unintended cost consequences. It is recommended that your estimator be available to the design team in a cost dialogue, or at the minimum provide feedback in a monthly cost meeting. Use your meeting minutes as described earlier in this chapter to track cost implications of your decisions and make sure the cost estimates are updated with the implications of these changes.

Who develops the estimate? Your process of managing costs during the predesign and design phases has a lot to do with your early criteria for hiring a construction team, which is covered later in this chapter. If you plan to use a general contractor, you will need to hire an independent cost estimator (some architects have this service in-house) as part of your design team. If you plan to hire a construction manager (CM) you will obtain these services from the construction manager directly. The greatest challenge for a construction manager or estimator in predesign phase is to estimate a project with unusual requirements from very few documents: having an estimator who understands the museum as a building type will help, but your design team must communicate the unique aspects of your project. While most estimators get the obvious bricks and mortar part of the estimate, the particular qualities of the systems, finishes, and equipment are more difficult to define.

For this reason, particularly if working with a construction manager, consider a process of using two estimators in parallel, so you can develop more cost dialogue around the project scope. In this method, one estimator will develop the format and spreadsheet for the estimate; then each estimator working from the same spreadsheet will independently estimate or review the first estimate, and subsequently reconcile their estimates. This dialogue will improve the accuracy of your estimate, and should be repeated at the end of each phase of design with the original estimate as the basis to manage scope.

How soon can I get a realistic first estimate? It's a chicken and egg problem, since the first estimate is always needed before you have sufficient information to create an estimate without a long list of exclusions and huge contingencies for unknowns: how much is enough, what's too small? Will the huge number scare the board or will a low number be the basis for a decision that will be a disaster later? This is where an experienced design team and estimator are invaluable. Using numbers from peers in other cities (whose true scope or market conditions differ more than they appear on the surface) or from a local builder (who knows strip malls but not museums) can be a very dangerous strategy as the basis for such a significant decision.

What is value engineering (VE) and how is it used? It's often said that value engineering isn't. Value engineering is a misused term in the design and construction industry often to the detriment of building quality and scope. As originally intended, value engineering was an activity to obtain the best value by finding the most cost-effective solution to a design question. Value engineering used in this way should not be confused with cutting the quality of the materials and systems or scope as a way of saving money which is how the term has been misapplied when projects are running over budget. When a project gets into trouble, cutting quality is never the best option since quality is the key to an institutional building you will use and maintain for generations.

What about the exclusions and notes at the bottom of the estimate? When you give your board an estimate, make sure you and your board understand the small type which includes qualifiers and assumptions in the estimate, including:

- Assumption of bid date or midpoint of construction. Since this date may change, you will need to track the overall cost changes. Update your board quarterly so that as costs increase over time, they understand the increase in project costs.
- Any allowances or lump sum numbers. These often indicate a scope of work not yet defined which indicates an assumption on the part of the estimator on the scope and cost of this work.
- Any exclusions, which may or may not include hazardous materials remediation, design fees, legal costs, furniture, collections furniture, computer network or servers, exhibit lighting track heads, or any other unknowns. Whatever you do make sure they are covered in a budget somewhere.

Project Phase	Scope Known	Design Contingency	+	Construction Contingency	=	Total Cost
Strategic Plan	0%	30%		5%		35%
Pre-Design	10%	25%		5%		30%
Project Design						
• Conceptual Design	10%	20%				25%
• Schematics	30%	20%				25%
• Design Development	60%	10%				15%
• Construction Documents	100%	0%				5%
Bid/Construction						
• Bid	0%	5% →		5%		5%
• Construction Complete	25%			5%		
• Construction Complete	50%			5%		
• Construction Complete	75%			2%		
• Construction Complete	100%			0%		0%

FIGURE 6.2
Contingency Over the Life of a Project

Contingency covers changes, but how much is enough and when should I use it? Your estimate should include an owner, design, bid, and construction contingency (figure 6.2), all of which are controlled by the chief financial officer of your museum with the recommendation of the museum project manager in consultation with the design and construction teams.

- Owner's contingency is generally held outside the construction estimate as a reserve based on critical scope changes or meeting needs as directed by a board or donor. This should be 10 percent of the overall budget for site, building, FF&E (fixtures, furnishings, and equipment), exhibits, and project soft costs (fees).
- Design contingency is used as scope becomes more defined to fill shortfalls. This contingency should be 20 percent at the start of design for a new building, 25–30 percent for a historic preservation project (due to the complexity of this type of work), and used or decline as the design moves forward.
- Construction contingency should be between 5 percent (new construction) and 15 percent (historic preservation) of the construction costs and used to cover unforeseen conditions (rock underground, pipes in a wall) and to cover scope gaps which may include omissions by the design team for work not completely covered in the construction documents.

While it is difficult to start with a bottom line and add an additional 20–30 percent for contingency since it may jeopardize project feasibility, your fiduciary responsibility demands a high level of care to ensure a successful outcome. At the completion of each phase, if there is contingency left, you may elect to roll the money into the contingency for a subsequent phase, use it for buying add-alternate scope, or for adding money to your endowment for future operations.

Do I have all the building and equipment costs included? Costs for various parts of your capital project may reside in many different budgets across the museum: hard construction costs, exhibit fabrication, equipment budgets in various departments, track lighting accessories, donor recognition signage, furniture, and so on. Assumptions on "which budget has it covered" could result in misunderstanding of scope coverage and subsequent gaps in budgets which may only become apparent late in the project construction. The museum project manager and the design exhibit and construction teams should

THE MUSEUM
Design and Budget Responsibility Matrix
Architecture / Exhibit Design / Museum

Area	Design Responsibility			Budget Responsibility			Notes
	Architect	Exhibit Designer	Museum	Architect	Exhibit Designer	Museum	
Exterior Building Signage							
• Exterior Building Mounted	X			X			
• Wayfinding Exterior	X			X			
• Wayfinding Interior	X					X	
Lobby							
• Architectural Lighting	X			X			
• Demising Walls	X			X			
• Donor Wall	X					X	
• Exhibit Lighting		X			X		
• Exhibit Entry		X			X		
Information / Admissions Desk							
• Desk (Info and Ticketing)	X			X			
• Signage	X					X	
• Events Announcement Board	X					X	
• Public Address System (Lobby)	X					X	
• POS/Ticket Equipment and software			X			X	
Retail							
• Fixtures/Furniture	X			X			
• Signage	X					X	
• Lighting	X			X			
• POS Equipment and software			X			X	

FIGURE 6.3
Cost Responsibility Matrix

prepare a cost responsibility matrix in each area of potential scope overlap: *what* is in each budget, *who* is designing it, whether cost responsibility is for supply only, supply and delivery only, supply and install, receive, store, install, hookup, test and warranty, and any combination of the above. As you can see, each item has many associated costs that must clearly understand and be accounted for.

How can I buy additional scope if the bids come in low? If you have more scope than you can afford, one option is to design the base building with add-alternates: work shown on the drawings and called out in the specifications as work which the museum may elect to build if budget permits. This can be done to improve the quality of finishes or increase the project scope if additional funding appears or bids are less than expected. An add-alternate must be exercised according to a schedule as determined by the construction team in order to allow them to build it in sequence with the rest of construction. In some cases, this is when the contract is executed (for a larger building footprint, for instance), or five months later when the light fixtures are ordered. Never use the deduct-alternate method (a scope reduction method), which means the costs are included in base bid, since you are less likely to get the full value back if you elect not to build the work. You should expect to pay extra to your design team to document an add-alternate since they are doing more work, and the decision to execute the design is in your control, not theirs.

Should I accept in-kind donation? Your development staff may encounter donors who want to provide an in-kind donation of building materials or services; be skeptical. Remember that 20 percent of all construction in North America is for worthy institutions like yours, so don't expect major manufacturers or suppliers to think you are special or are prepared to give you a "special deal."[2] It is best to establish a policy upfront with your development director to ensure they don't waste time chasing in-kind donations. If an in-kind donation is offered, have the offer fully appraised. Check with your design and construction professionals: designing with carpet of inferior quality that does not achieve LEED points, or designing around an elevator may save little or no money and may mean that schedules, warranties, and coordination become issues which involve significant problems.

What happens if the construction bids come in too high? Even with all the cost management processes in place, a bid bust can occur. Sometimes it occurs because of changes in the marketplace: increases in material prices or shortages of labor are common causes. Scope mistakes can be made as well, which is why parallel estimating is recommended. In the end, a bid bust will have significant impacts. It will

- Destroy confidence of your board in the project or within the team.
- Delay project start and finish.
- Disappoint the community if the project is not built as advertised.
- Disappoint donors' image of what they were getting.
- Discourage bidders from further participation when there are other potential projects.

Whatever you do, never cut quality and don't engage in finger-pointing. You may hear that the construction manager or estimator didn't understand what the design team meant, or the design team added scope in the final phase. Whatever the circumstances, don't allow the project to drift, or place blame (blame can come later). Call a meeting, set a tone of cooperation, create an action plan, and assign responsibility to team members to come up with solutions. Tasks should include:

- Comparison of each bid with the estimate
- Scope review and meetings with bidder
- Discussion of the requirements of the general conditions in the specifications, phasing, and other potential soft nonscope change solutions
- Scope change solutions, including phasing the work, changing material selection, or constructing the building shell without fitting out the interiors (an empty space shown to a donor is a better sell than empty ground)

In this atmosphere you will find a solution which may not please every stakeholder, but unless the cost discrepancy is significant, you will develop a solution.

MANAGING SCHEDULES
Schedules are used to organize the activities of the museum stakeholders and the predesign, design, and construction teams. Over the course of the project, you will develop several schedules which move from milestone schedules to very detailed schedules that describe activities and coordinate efforts of project stakeholders and the design and construction teams.

Presdesign schedule. The predesign schedule is prepared around major milestone dates which are timed to obtain approvals by the steering committee and coincide with scheduled board meetings. The museum project manager with the predesign team should be responsible for filling in the intermediate dates. The fundamentals underlying the development of a schedule recognize that project stakeholders (working groups) must make decisions which allow the predesign and design teams to proceed through a series of timely decision points to the next steps. These critical decision dates and document review periods need to be clearly defined as part of the schedule. Failure to provide adequate time to develop information and reach consensus will cause the schedule to fail.

There are different formats for schedules: the most common (figure 6.4), are created using software that allows increasing detail to be added over time. They consist of overlapping and linked working periods and are often called critical path schedules where failure to reach a decision or supply information to key decision makers in time will graphically show how this delay will jeopardize subsequent scheduled tasks.

Design phase schedule. This schedule is generally developed by the design team project manager to outline all major design phase deliverables, reviews, and sign-offs by the steering committee. Recommendations for effective schedule development include:

- Know the museum decision-making process. Track the time frame from submittal from the design team to museum working group recommendation to steering committee to museum board subcommittee to museum board. This should include time for board mailing package preparation and dissemination.
- Bury float time within a schedule in case consensus is not reached in a meeting, weather prevents a meeting from occurring, or your design team cannot complete a cost estimate in time. Not everything goes according to plan.
- If you have multiple working groups, develop a schedule which shows the path of information development and decision-making dates for each working group and interdependency of decision making among groups as their recommendations are sent to the steering committee. The schedule should show the interdependence of the tasks and decision points for each working group over the course of design.

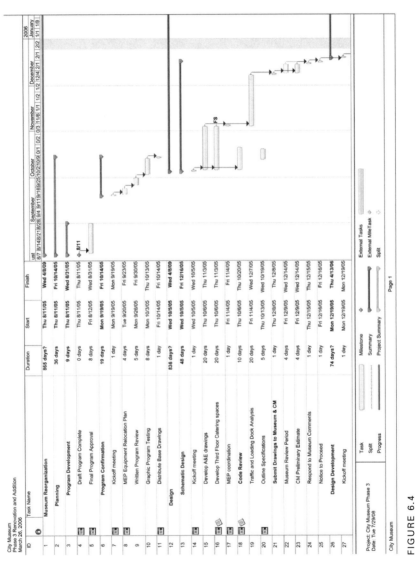

FIGURE 6.4
Project Design Schedule

Make sure your schedule shows milestone reviews and approvals by local code officials having jurisdiction over your site and building at the appropriate phase of work. These agencies include local and regional building departments, fire departments, and (for large museums) in-house safety officers; all of these groups will become design partners and can shape aspects of your project. Note that if you want to wait for certain approvals before proceeding with design work, you can add months to the overall schedule which may not be possible. This means your design team will need to proceed and you may be at risk if approvals are denied.

Update your schedule regularly and keep a master copy posted on a wall in the middle of your work space. Scheduling software can be cumbersome, so as you contemplate the implication of a change, use paper notes, sticky notes, and printed copies of email, color pencils and markers, whatever is at hand and whatever seems right to test the implications.

Construction phase schedule. As part of the specifications, there should be a time frame, generally noted in calendar days, for completion of construction with a requirement that the successful construction team will be submitting a more detailed schedule at kickoff for review and approval. Key things to review include:

- The schedule of completion of work will become the basis for the construction team's application for payment (done by percentage complete of various aspects of work). You should coordinate this information with your cash flow for construction payments during this phase.
- Coordination of your move-in activities with this schedule. Depending on your local building inspection rules and union work rules, you may or may not be able to take possession of spaces that are substantially complete (a certificate of substantial completion is a legal document) to install exhibits or furniture using your own labor or labor of exhibit installers. Check on the labor rules and your insurance regulations and adjust your schedule accordingly.
- Ask about the float time in the schedule in case of work stoppages, shortage of materials and labor, or other realities of construction which may slow down your progress.
- Identify dates when construction must cease. Special events, collections moves, exhibition installations, or public programs at museums often require several days of intense preparation, and these activities are usually incompatible with the noise and risk of a construction site.

Museum working schedule. Throughout design and construction, keep your own schedule for all of your activities which must be coordinated with design and construction teams. These include activities of consultants hired directly by the museum (food and retail vendors, ticketing systems, IT integration and software, exhibit fabrication, conservators, collections movers). During construction, as you gain occupancy of the spaces, the work of these same vendors and any other services you have contracted for directly must be coordinated with your construction team to ensure access, safety, security of installed work as well as potential union jurisdiction or work rules. Exhibit installation is usually one of the most challenging elements to coordinate, since interactive exhibits tend to have hard wire connections which must be made by licensed electricians and warranty application is of concern to the exhibit fabricator and electrician.

If any schedule seems to be sliding, ask questions early and challenge the reassurances of your construction project manager and design team. Develop a schedule recovery plan: you are better off addressing schedule problems early than disappointing your board and community closer to published opening dates when expectations are higher and you have spent money publicizing your opening.

SELECTING A CONSTRUCTION PHASE METHODOLOGY

Selecting the Best Process for Building Your Museum

As construction professionals and board members who are in real estate will tell you, you must select a methodology for how you build your project in the predesign phase. The construction methodology you select is related to your museum's approach and management of costs, risk and time, so it is a fundamental decision which has impact on the planning and design process.

While some government and higher education institutions have a fixed process, you must still understand the implications of the methodology in order to put other support in place to mitigate what you feel are the cost, risk, and time challenges of your project. This has as much to do with risk during design as with construction phase activities.

In brief, each methodology has numerous hybrid variations which reflect regulations and regional differences in practice. As an overview, your options are:

- Design-bid-build (DBB)
- Construction manager (CM)
  a. Construction manager as agent (CMA)
  b. Construction manager at risk (CMAR)
- Design-build (DB)

In order to better explain, a brief overview of each option includes a pros and cons description which is subject to debate depending upon your project needs.

Design-bid-build (DBB) is the traditional building methodology which reflects the approach of the sequence of design as independent from bid and build (construction). In this approach, when the contract documents are complete, the work is bid either to a select list (which could include general contractors or construction managers who have been identified through your request for qualification process) or in an open bid process to any general contractor or construction manager. Unlike most construction managers, most general contractors self-perform some trade work (such as concrete or carpentry) with their own labor forces and subcontract all other trade work to other companies. Implications of the design-bid-build approach are:

- *Schedule.* Design-bid-build is a sequential process, so there are no time efficiencies as in some methodologies. Documents must be complete for bid and construction.
- *Cost.* All preconstruction cost support will be provided through an independent cost estimator. Construction costs may be lowest with design-bid-build since market competition will provide competitive prices of all aspects of your project.
- *Risk.* The entire project scope is defined prior to pricing, so there are fewer gaps in scope than in other contracting methodologies. However, there is no market testing of your estimate until bids are submitted and reviewed so the assumptions by the estimator carry some risk of miscalculation. You do not have control over the general contractor's selection of subcontractors who may be selected for cost rather than best value, but the general contractor accepts the risk and owns all the work scope on the drawings. Scope creep problems at this point in time are more difficult to address since drawings are complete and the clock is ticking.

The basis for selection of a general contractor can be best value or low price. Best value is a preferred scenario which takes into account the reputation, experience, and team proposed. With best value, you are most likely to have a general contractor who is working with his reputation at stake. A purely low-cost basis for selection typically will result in more change orders and less cooperation from the general contractor and subcontractors.

Depending on your perspective, an additional advantage to design-bid-build is the traditional three-legged stool of owner, design team, and construction team keeps just the right amount of tension among the relationships so that all parties are clear in their roles and accountability.

Construction management (CM) is an approach that begins in predesign to develop costs, schedules, advice on constructability and market conditions, and in later phases manage the procurement and construction phases. If condensing your construction schedule is a requirement, then a construction manager using fast track is your best option. Fast track construction will bid the project in phases determined by the critical path or typical sequence of construction—site development, then foundations, structure, and major equipment, and so on, all of which will be designed and bid with construction starting prior to completion of the final documents for the building's shell and interior. This permits an early start saving time and sometimes money (due to inflation of costs or beating winter to place foundations during warmer weather) while increasing design team fees slightly. A significant problem for some boards is that the final bottom line is not known until the final bids are received when the building is under construction and partially built, well past a point of no return.

There are two variations of construction management methodology work worth considering:

- Construction manager as agent (CMA). Using this methodology, the museum will hire a fee-based construction management firm who is the owner's agent, and generally does not self-perform any work. The construction manager as agent will bid the work to subcontractors, provide recommendations on hiring, and oversee the scheduling of the on-site work. Implications of the construction manager as agent approach are:
  a. *Schedule.* The construction manager agent approach will permit fast track construction with no advantage over construction manager at risk. It is arguable whether the construction manager as agent has or will accept any control over the schedule and coordination responsibilities as

defined in your specifications of subcontractors, since the CM does not have any contractual relationship.

b. *Cost.* Predesign and design phase estimating are the responsibility of the construction manager as agent. By statute and industry standards they hold limited liability for the accuracy of the construction estimate based on the terms of their contract. You should verify whether trade subcontractors or the construction manager as agent is providing this information and how it is being tested with the market.

c. *Risk.* The museum, not the construction manager as agent, holds all trade contracts and their liability directly, so gaps in work scope, on-site damage for any cause, or out-of-sequence work are the cost liability of the museum.

- Construction manager at risk (CMAR). Using this methodology the museum will hire the construction manager at risk for a fee during predesign and design phases, converting the contract to a fixed-cost or guaranteed maximum price (GMP) contract at some point during design. The point of fixing the price can range from 65 percent completion to 100 percent completion of contract documents. The construction manager at risk may or may not self-perform work, and holds all liability for subcontractors and their work. Implications of the construction manager at risk approach are:

a. *Schedule.* Same as construction manager as agent, but the guaranteed maximum price is provided earlier with this approach.

b. *Cost.* Predesign and design phase estimating services are similar to construction manager as agent. However, the construction manager at risk has no incentive to develop a low estimate, particularly in a construction manager at risk variation which has a shared savings clause, where the construction manager at risk shares the cost savings of bids which come in below estimate.

c. *Risk.* The risk of cost is transferred to the construction manager at risk at the point of the GMP being set. This off-loading of risk can occur earlier in this methodology than in construction manager agent or design-bid-build. The guaranteed maximum price allows a board the comfort to lock in a price early based on drawings that are around 60 to 75 percent complete. Since the drawings are incomplete, the CMAR makes assumptions about the work scope not yet on documents at the time of pricing. This leads to the assumptions of what the design team believes is implied, and the construction manager at risk believes is implied in the incomplete documents. Gaps are inevitable, so a guaranteed maximum price cost can rise (team relationships play a major role in the process of working with a guaranteed maximum price form of contract.)

The challenge of this methodology is lack of incentive for a construction manager at risk to estimate the real market value rather than an inflated number: estimate high and add profit to the bottom line. This is not a recommended process unless you have strong ability to leverage strong relationships at a board level. Obtaining a parallel estimate can help keep the construction manager at risk numbers honest, but your ability to challenge the estimate remains very limited.

As another variation, once the contract documents are complete, you can convert from a guaranteed maximum price to a lump sum or fixed number as if the project was bid by your construction manager at risk.

Design build (DB) is a methodology where the design team and construction team form a legal entity which then contracts jointly for design and construction services with the museum. Design build is most often used where the project is simple from a programmatic and finish perspective. Conceptually, the design build entity provides a price based on scope definition provided by the museum to the design build team that interprets this scope in its proposal and develops a conceptual design and fixed price. Since the bid is based on incomplete documents, this may create gaps in scope of understanding and lead to cost and scope changes later in design and construction. Trust is one of the biggest factors in the design build scenario, and the complexity of a museum project mean you need to carefully assess the quality of the design team and construction team and the value of their bid.

No matter whether you elect to use a general contractor, construction manager or design-build, your goal remains to achieve a team approach to design and construction. Since you have successfully communicated your needs to the design team, managed costs and budgets, and have along the way, developed the physical framework deliverables at each milestone according to recommendations of chapter 7, it is now time to go to the marketplace and find out who will build your project and the costs for that work.

BID AND CONSTRUCTION PHASE MANAGEMENT

Bid Phase Management

No matter which construction procurement process is used, expect your time involvement, which may have slowed during later parts of contract documentation phase, to accelerate. During bidding, depending on the methodology, your museum project manager or your construction manager working with the design team will:

- Prepare bid packages for bidders.
- Send out contract documents and respond in writing or with additional drawings to any questions to all bidders on scope or intent. These formal responses become part of the contract documents and are officially called bulletins.
- Receive, open, and review bids for exclusions, compliance with specification division 1 requirements and glaring discrepancies in costs.
- Analyze bids, call in bidders that meet your criteria, and discuss any open issues or suggestions on potential cost or schedule savings.
- Select a construction team and complete negotiations for a final contract (chapter 5).

Once you have a signed contract, construction team mobilization begins where their staff is assigned, the project schedule is developed and materials are ordered. From this point on, the process follows standard procedures commonly found in other books and manuals listed in the bibliography.

Construction Phase Management
Prior to starting construction, you should make sure you understand the specifications stipulating certain activities and communication protocols that have been included to protect your interests during the construction phase. Sometimes the construction team may try to change the terms of the specifications directly with you, but you should avoid unilaterally giving permission without consulting your design team or attorney. More information on the general conditions of your specifications is covered in chapter 7. Specified processes and information which will require your project manager and design team's attention include a large number of submittals of information:

- Schedule of values, which is the breakdown of the costs for the building component by specification division or building trade. This is used for evaluating the costs of each portion of the building, valuing changes in scope, and reviewing applications for payment against work completed.
- A payment schedule enables you to anticipate the rate of payouts to the construction team (who submit on a form called an application for payment)

and plan for your cash flow. It should be in sufficient detail to allow museum and design team project managers to analyze the costs of work completed during construction. Along the way, you will hold back a percentage of each payment as retainage to ensure the construction team and subcontractors have incentives to finish the project close out activities and punch list. Retainage is set in the specifications, begins around 10 percent and is reduced to 5 percent at substantial completion of the project.

- Material substitutions may occur for a variety of reasons:
  a. With the bid, when the bidder identifies a product change in his/her bid based on superior quality of another product or based on offering cost savings to you. In either circumstance, substitutions should be reviewed by the design team to ensure the product is superior or that adequate savings accrue to the museum by using this material.
  b. Anytime during construction, when the contractor or subcontractor has difficulty obtaining a specified product and must suggest an alternate to maintain schedule.

  If a substitution is requested for any other reason, the contractor should be informed that the review by the design team will be at the contractor's expense and written approval is required. This requirement prevents specious requests.

- Submittals are product selections sent by the construction team by various subcontractors which include physical samples, printed materials on a wide range of building materials (such as hardware, gravel, or paint), material data safety sheets (identifying safety and toxicity), and shop fabrication drawings (such as ductwork) to show compliance with the project specifications. On a larger project, there will be anywhere from three hundred to eight hundred submittals, some with one to two hundred drawings each.

- The submittal schedule is prepared by the construction team to coordinate the arrival of all the submittals by all the subcontractors. Since review is a lot of work, this schedule facilitates three activities:
  a. Establishes that there is sufficient time for review and (if necessary) resubmission prior to fabrication and installation of equipment as shown on the project schedule.
  b. Allows the design team to understand how much staff time to set aside over the course of each month for the review of submittals and shop drawings.

c. Enables your project manager, facilities staff, conservator (for off-gassing and environmental concerns), and select staff whose space is affected (exhibit lighting, furnishings for a conservation lab, etc.) to review and approve certain submittals. You should work with the design team to understand what you should review.

- A safety plan for the job site identifies the person responsible for safety of construction staff and emergency procedures. In an existing building, the approach to protect ongoing activities of the public and your staff are identified.

- A project milestone schedule shows the work of each construction activity *and* where it is occurring. This helps establish the flow of work and if work is occurring in an occupied building, understand the implication of these activities on your visitors and staff. This also becomes the tracking mechanism to see if the project is on time.

- Coordination drawings are often required to ensure the final fabricated assemblies for your building systems (ductwork, plumbing waste and water, electrical power, IT trays, lighting, and sprinklers) fit between your finished ceiling and the structure of your building. Failure to require coordination drawings may mean conflicts between building components which must be resolved in the field and can prove costly or delay construction. With the increased use of building information management (BIM) documentation, the need for coordination drawings may be built into the contract documents. Remember, it is cheaper to solve these issues on paper than it is when pipe and ductwork have been fabricated and taken to the site.

Construction Phase: Ground Breaking, Finally

You've planned carefully, reviewed documents carefully, worked with a great design team, and have a great construction team on board. What can go wrong? Murphy's Law: forget perfection and don't imply you expect it, since any architect, engineer, consultant, or contractor will laugh at the suggestion that everything must be perfect. The planning, design, and construction process are human endeavors, so in spite of everyone's best efforts and following every suggestion in this book, things will go wrong. You too will initiate changes for a variety of reasons.

Most "oops" or changes will be modest and the process to review and approve them ongoing and at times burdensome. But that's the responsibility of your construction and design teams who will work with your museum project manager to come to a resolution. You will pay for changes with your construction contingency. The most important suggestion is to look for solutions, not blame. Establish an atmosphere of teamwork for resolving all issues quickly to avoid delaying the construction activity on-site. There is a well understood concept of a standard and reasonable level of professional care which acknowledges that a certain level of mistakes are inevitable in a process involving thousands of decisions, hundreds of pages of documents, and work by many people. Be realistic. Some legal counsel may bristle at this, but if you spend all of your time establishing blame with the intent to back-charge the architect or contractor, you will find them more likely to spend time finger-pointing and worrying about covering their liability than responding to problem solving. Expect to spend that contingency; don't treat it as extra money that you will have at the end of construction.

Sometimes bigger problems can come out during construction or after construction is complete: 80 percent of all building problems involve design or construction issues around roofing or HVAC systems. Whatever you do, maintain the solutions approach and worry about placing blame later. This is crucial, because when things do go wrong, the tendency for parties to run for cover may delay finding a solution and put the parties who are in the best position to find a resolution in a defensive (or offensive) role rather than a problem-solving role. In addition, delay is only going to make things more expensive. Throughout construction, demand teamwork, expect conflicting opinions and recommendations, and never tolerate design professionals and contractors bad-mouthing rather than making constructive suggestions.

Since there is a great deal of expertise on the construction process resident in your project manager and your design and construction teams, as well in many publications, standard procedures will not be covered further in this chapter.

COMPLETING CONSTRUCTION AND CLOSING OUT YOUR PROJECT

As construction moves toward completion, there is a great deal of excitement as well as activity which must be coordinated by your museum project manager in order to bring construction to a close and your new facility online. Depending on the size of your project, your museum project manager may need additional assistants who can take primary responsibility for coordinating other activities such as exhibit installation, IT/AV/media installation and integration, FF&E (fixtures, furnishing, and equipment) fit-out, and so on.

This section provides an overview of project closeout procedures and the beginning of your obtaining beneficial occupancy of your space. For the most part, activities that are governed by terms of the specifications on final payments, release of liens, reducing retainage, and other financial obligations will not be covered here as these are standard procedures which are covered in other books and understood as a matter of good practice by most design and construction teams.

What kind of schedule should I create to manage move in activities and how do I know when I can start? Depending on your local building inspector, fire marshal, insurance requirements, work rule jurisdictions (if you are in a union contracting environment), and your agreement with your construction team, you may or may not be able to take possession of parts of the building as each area is completed. It is important to understand these parameters well in advance in order to coordinate with the construction team project manager and schedule a host of activities that you now have to manage that are outside the work scope of the general contract for construction. These include the work you contracted for directly (exhibits, furnishings, server room, etc.) as well as turnover activities including hiring and staff training for building operations and taking over insurance and security in those areas. You will need to coordinate reserving space at the loading dock with clear paths through the corridors to move material. There are many details (who pays to haul the Dumpsters with your construction waste?), so meet weekly over the last few months with the construction team project manager knowing full well that those turnover dates may slip for any one of a number of reasons which will require you to reschedule work for your subcontractors. You may want to request that the contractor prepare a detailed schedule fragment for closeout and turnover of spaces.

Who prepares the punch list (list of things to be corrected)? As is logical, according to most specifications, the first punch list is developed and work is completed by the construction team (simply finishing the work they are responsible for) prior to the design team or museum punch list being developed. Don't punch list a space that is not complete: listing obviously incomplete unfinished scope is not your job. When the construction team has completed the work on your punch list, the design team and museum project managers should walk through again and verify the work has been completed satisfactorily.

When should I formally accept a space? Turning over spaces is a legal and contractual milestone. It means you accept the space as complete, you are prepared to operate the systems and insure it, and hold all liability for the space in case of any occurrence. It is also usually the date which begins the warranty period.

What is owner supplied fit-out? Just as with exhibits, sometimes you may decide to have work installed outside of the construction teams work (the data center, loose furniture, or collections furniture), particularly when a product or fabrication is independent from the building or the manufacturer must install a piece of equipment, or you may want to save money and avoid the contractor mark general conditions or markup. In taking responsibility, you must recognize that there may be union work rule jurisdictions, considerations about responsibility for installed items (did that sofa walk off by itself?), concerns about the safety of your staff or your subcontractors on an active construction site (what does your insurance say?), access issues due to ongoing work, and concern about responsibility for damage to the building or collections by a worker. Whatever you do, make sure you include all activities on your work schedule and coordinate your loading, receiving, and security needs. Careful consideration must be given to the true cost of your handling these types of things yourself, the money "saved" by not having the construction team manage this may be less that your direct cost to execute.

When do I start installing my exhibits? Your exhibit space may not be totally complete by the time you start installing your exhibits, particularly if some work is set into the walls being built by the construction team. Coordinating this work is the responsibility of your museum project manager working with the construction team project manager to ensure access from the loading dock to the exhibit space for movement of collections or exhibits. You must also make sure that any exhibits or equipment you install in space still controlled by the construction team is secured and insured to ensure it does not "walk off the job site." You must make sure all required rough in (framing, power, IT, etc.) is or will be 100 percent complete prior to commencing exhibit installation.

How does my staff get trained to operate the building? As part of your specifications, there will be a stipulated amount of training prescribed for particular building systems, and an operations and maintenance manual (O&M) will be given to you which will have the instructions and maintenance procedures for your building systems and components. It is best to prepare your staff for operating and maintaining systems well ahead of turnover. In the case of complicated systems, you may want to consider having additional staff training for building mechanical systems and their controls, electronic keying systems, security systems and your server rooms, among others. One session is not enough. Only when the system is operational and things begin to happen will your staff really know whether the training has prepared them, so make sure you buy additional support for your staff for an extended period; it will be a good investment. There are many stories of poorly trained facilities staff reacting when the system malfunctions, making things worse. Besides the usual operating and maintenance manuals, it is a good idea to have the training for complicated systems videotaped so your staff has this for future reference.

What is commissioning? Commissioning, further defined in chapter 7, is a process which a commissioning agent, generally hired directly by the museum, undertakes third-party verification that the building components or systems are operating to their design expectations. Commissioning can be for particular building systems or for many components of the building including roofing and skylight systems. With the advent of LEED, commissioning is a prerequisite activity to achieve certification. The commissioning process begins in design, as the commissioning agent establishes an understanding of design intent, and includes attendance at meetings with the design team (generally monthly), reviews drawings at milestone completion dates and at closeout, and finishes with a process of system performance checks. With the concurrence of the design team, the commissioning agent directs the construction team to make modifications to improve system performance to the criteria of the specifications and the intent of the design.

Who installs the exhibit track heads? Unless you have been through the process before, this may seem like an odd question. In short, your electrician expects to put up lights, and in the bid will make an assumption of the time it will take to complete the activity. Hanging heads, but not aiming or installing and changing the accessories, is in your bid unless contract language in the specifications is clear on the time required for this work. In fact, it is best to make sure you buy the hanging, accessorizing, and aiming of the lighting from either your lighting or exhibit designer. If this is not possible, buy a number of hours from the electrician, but do not expect that the electrician is going to have the same level of concern about the aesthetic effect.

Who prepares the record or as-built drawings? Record drawings are the final set of modified contract documents which contain the changes that took place over the course of construction to the original design drawings. The construction team project manager will keep a set throughout the construction process, marking up the changes and taping any sketches which were made by the construction team, design team, or the museum onto the set. If compensated under their contract, the design team will pick up these changes and prepare a final set for you to keep. These drawings, along with photographs taken prior to and during construction, will provide you with invaluable information of what was built when you maintain or plan to alter the building in the future.

How long are my warranties and when do they begin? Warranties generally begin when you take possession of the building and the length of your warranty is communicated in the specifications. It is possible to obtain longer warranties, but it is best to obtain them during project procurement to get the best value. For certain systems, particularly building controls, lighting controls, and security you should consider including a service contract for the first year in the base bid contract with an option for a second. You must remember that a warranty covers only defects. After project closeout, the contractor and/or subcontractors do not owe you any service work unless there is a specific requirement in the contract.

IN SUMMARY

Management of the process requires teamwork, trust, and a management process which is clear and rigorous while allowing the creative process to flourish. This is easier said than done, but the trust and understanding that tether you as a team will enable you to weather the bumps along the way.

NOTES

1. HOK Group, William A. Pena, and Stephen A. Parshall, *Problem Seeking: An Architectural Programming Prime*, 4th ed. (New York: Wiley, 2001).

2. Over the past five years (2003–2008), institutional building comprised 20 percent of total building in dollar terms, according to the construction start statistics compiled by McGraw-Hill Construction.

Physical Framework

Defining What You Will Build

The physical framework will guide the design of spaces you will build, how they are organized in relation to one another, and the criteria defining what goes into each space to support your museum's activities. This information is scoped during the predesign phase, documented during the design phase, and built during the construction phase. Developing this framework is challenging, since it moves between being an objective and subjective activity: the quality as well as the function of the spaces are both critical parts of meeting your strategic plan's goals. To develop this framework, your planning team must know in detail how the public and museum staff will use each space on a day-to-day basis to translate your needs into an effective solution.

It begins with organizing stakeholders (chapter 3) and building the right team (chapter 5) while employing a process in a creative yet rigorous structure (chapter 6).

The planning of the physical framework requires museum stakeholders to begin with a shared understanding of your priorities and how they relate to your strategic plan. The understanding of the planning process particular to museums among interested parties is diverse: some may have building industry experience, but not with museums; others have not been involved in a building project but understand how a museum works and what it needs. There will be a process to develop information which seems obvious to some stakeholders but is new to others. This chapter will focus on a predesign process to guide stakeholders to capture and analyze information as early as possible, in order to make decisions and define the requirements of your project in detail.

The process and tasks are different if you have an existing building or site, but it is recommended that you read all sections of this chapter regardless of whether you are starting on a new (green) site, working on an existing site, or working with an existing building.

CHAPTER ORGANIZATION

The physical framework starts in your strategic plan with narratives of needed space, and by the end of the design phase includes a huge number of drawings and books of specifications of materials that have been selected. The fundamental goal of this framework is to ensure you have developed an appropriate level of documentation at each phase of the project along the way.

This chapter is organized as follows:

- Building project vision statement (your building goals)
- Setting criteria (adopting standards)
  a. Museum policies and procedures
  b. Site
  c. Building architectural criteria
  d. Building engineered systems
- Sustainability
- Codes and stipulated regulations (impact of external standards)
- Existing (or new) site and facility assessment (impact of what you have)
- Site and building space programs (sizing your spaces)
  a. Site space program
  b. Building space program
- Site and room definition sheets (applying criteria to each space)
- Functional relationships (how you organize your spaces)
- Phasing or closing down (sequence of implementation)
- Estimate of probable costs (financial resources needed); covered in chapter 6, page 86
- Schedule (time to implement); covered in chapter 6, page 81

These headings are also intended as a suggested table of contents for your final predesign phase report.

Predesign phase. An explanation of predesign is found in chapter 6. In brief, it is the phase where you define your *problem* prior to design of a specific site or building *solution.*[1] You may develop it with a museum consultant or an architect who has expertise in museum planning. While terminology for the final predesign report may differ, a basis of design (BOD) report developed by the design team defines the characteristics of a future design, and the best basis of design report will include technical information which may require architectural and engineering expertise to properly scope and develop a first cost estimate for your project.

While few museums will undertake a complete basis of design report in predesign due to upfront costs, those that do find the outcomes more clearly match the ideas, scope, and budgets promised to the board and community with fewer bumps along the way. Since you will need to develop this information by the end of conceptual design phase, completing this work in predesign offers the museum distinct advantages. The basis of design will be:

- The *definitive* reference guide throughout the entire project design process and the most effective tool you have in maintaining scope control and collective memory of the project team.
- A documented basis of understanding between the board, museum leadership, and stakeholders of scope, cost, and budget.
- The most efficient manner to capture of your stakeholder needs while enthusiasm for the process is high and collective memory is fresh. Remember, the design process will go on for another year or longer and a successful basis of design can capture 80–90 percent of stakeholder technical input.

Since design is an iterative process where new layers will be added in subsequent phases, your design team will develop the details based on the information the basis of design report captures.

Let's see what information goes into your predesign basis of design report by following the recommended table of contents.

BUILDING PROJECT VISION STATEMENT: YOUR BUILDING GOALS

It is assumed that your strategic plan is complete and all your stakeholders share common goals with an identified facility need. Strategic plan goals left unresolved at the outset will return, often presenting significant issues later in the process. As covered in chapter 2, board and staff preparation is critical in achieving a common understanding and vision and a commitment to work together to accomplish these goals. It is recommended that you start with a building project vision statement which should include:

- *Shared values.* What values developed during the strategic plan will guide decision making and keep stakeholders on the same page?
- *Priorities.* What are the most important strategic plan initiatives which must be met in order to make the building project successful?
- *Performance evaluation narratives.* Define in words your case statement and outcome expectations for the program of public and support spaces you need. This should be written from two perspectives: external (visitor experience) and internal (museum operations), and include input from each stakeholder working group. More on performance measures is included in chapter 12.
- *Stakeholder working groups:* Develop working groups as covered in chapter 3 with clear roles and establish clear reporting and decision-making authority. (See figure 3.1 as an example.)

SETTING CRITERIA: ADOPTING YOUR INTERNAL STANDARDS

Criteria are the measurable standards or attributes you set for each part of your building and site that determine their performance based on your strategic plan and building project vision statement. Criteria must be set during predesign, so that their cost implications are understood and budgeted. Sources of information and advice for your institution will come from knowledge of best practice, benchmarking your peers, attending conferences, asking Listserv communities, consulting with experts, determining your risk tolerance and financial capacity through your lens of shared values. Criteria for museums are not strictly objective standards. They evolve and require compromise by some stakeholders.

Museum Policies and Procedures

A building will change not only your capacity as an institution, but also your internal working processes. Winston Churchill once said, "We shape our buildings; therefore they shape us."[2] All of us adapt to the conditions we work in, so the planning process for your physical space is a chance to improve your internal work processes and adopt new procedures across the museum as defined in your strategic plan. As part of predesign planning, you must reexamine all your official procedures and policies to improve them and fight the tendency of some staff who believe things work fine as they are.

Your operations plan must identify your staffing needs to implement major initiatives, exhibits, and programs. It is helpful to develop a staffing matrix by museum department, showing current and projected staff and space. The projection can be based on benchmarking, consulting peer museums, or working with consultants.

Major contributing factors, most of which will be covered in your strategic plan are:

- An established time horizon for the facility. Develop a clear statement as part of your project vision statement such as "This project will enable us to collect, process, preserve, and access artifacts for twenty years while decompressing our current collections."
- Philosophy of using permanent or contract staff for key functions such as exhibit design, security, retail/food and beverage operations, technology hosting service, communications, fund-raising. Permanent staff will need more space than sourced work. Decisions mandated by hiring freezes should be examined, since a change in this status will affect your allocation of space.
- Decision to consider or develop an off-site museum support facility as a lower-cost option which permits more public functions on-site, particularly if your site is limited in size.
- Building system redundancy in case of system shutdown or due to a loss of power.
- Protocols of handling collections including staff safety such as standards for use of hazardous materials in conservation labs or the ergonomics of collections storage.
- Incoming collections processing, conditions assessment, pest management, crating and uncrating procedures all have impact on space needs and the sequence of spaces. Set your standards and make sure you understand the protocols of lending institutions.
- Museum work protocols will be covered under individual function space descriptions. A key challenge is for staff to change how they work rather than working "to" their space.

- Food policies establishing where food may be present, the paths of how food and waste may be taken through the building.
- Approach to building-wide security and safety, specifically collections, visitors, and staff. This will include developing an approach to use of security staff, monitoring systems, and hardware.

Site

If you are an urban museum, your site may indirectly include the streets and sidewalks that surround your museum. If so, your need for identity and working with your local government to create signage and a sense of arrival will be different from a museum on a site where the building itself may occupy 10 percent, the roads and parking 30 percent, and landscape 60 percent. Do not underestimate the potential of your site for supporting a rich array of programs which can provide a great experience, but can be built and operated at significantly lower cost than inside your building.

The experience of your site is the first impression by visitors, so organizing your site for the types of visitors and addressing the challenge of supporting peak visitation will have an impact on visitor experience. Key site issues for museums during predesign phase planning are:

- Identification and preservation of significant features, such as trees, landscape elements, or historic features.
- Site utility capacity in the street or on-site including availability of water, sewer capacity, and electrical power from a reliable substation.
- Design of specific site elements programmatically includes sculpture gardens, concert spaces, outdoor classrooms, school picnic areas, and paved space for an event tent (with appropriate utilities to support lighting, the needs of a caterer, and restrooms nearby).
- Segregated and safe on-site roads for buses and cars, with pathways for visitors with minimal crossing of roads. Parking for seventy buses may be a requirement that is not determined by local codes.
- Develop signage from regional roads to the site synchronized with directions from your website and third-party directions such as MapQuest.

Building Architectural Systems

This section addresses setting criteria for overall building design, individual spaces and building systems. These criteria use your building project vision statement and financial capacity as filters which will determine which criteria you will adopt to guide design.

Architectural design goals are difficult to define as a narrative. In the early 1900s, there were fewer aesthetic options, and the beaux arts neoclassical vocabulary dominated the development of large and small museums reflecting a community view of the importance of the museum as a democratic institution. Today, the range of aesthetic expressions is much greater, and coming to consensus around a shared design aesthetic will have an impact on the content of your basis of design report. The aesthetics of your building (and site) have a lot to do with the influence of major donors and board members, so development of a shared aesthetic may be a challenge depending on the role of your museum's senior leadership. Apart from the objective functional aspects of what makes a great building, defining beauty in the eyes of each (stake)holder is a challenge until everyone sees renderings of your future building and come to consensus.

Find ways to develop a shared vision in advance: a PowerPoint presentation of museum projects of peer institutions by faculty from a local architecture program is a good way of establishing a common point of reference without ever referring to the specifics of your building program and site. You may find it is easier to learn the vocabulary of expression, and include those in your basis of design report using other projects as reference points for your museum: massing, context, materials, light, the experience of space, and so on. If your museum is on a college campus with written design guidelines or requirements to work only within a traditional building style, a firm with a contemporary aesthetic may not be a good fit. Design can be the point where a building committee can come apart: the mind's eye and expectations are different. It is critical to have substantive discussions within the architect selection committee prior to any solicitation of qualifications or proposals to ensure that all members of the committee are on the same page. Regardless, your aspirations as a museum should be reflected in the design of your building, and finding the right fit is a challenge that should not be underestimated.

Building Engineered Systems

Building systems include heating, ventilation, and air-conditioning (HVAC) systems, electrical (power and lighting), plumbing, risk reduction (security and fire protection), information technology/audiovisual systems, and structural systems. Engineered systems are significantly more complex and demanding in museums than in most building types. An overview of each follows.

Mechanical, or heating, ventilation, and air-conditioning systems (HVAC).
Criteria setting will have huge impact on first cost and operating costs, quality of systems (due to the ability to meet strict criteria), and long-term serviceability. Make sure the engineering team is prepared to help you understand the implications of your system selection based on the criteria you establish. The more strict your criteria, the higher the first cost, operating costs, and maintenance costs, no matter how high the quality of the system.

Temperature and humidity have been the two criteria of environmental systems most widely discussed in the museum world in terms of collections conservation, and yet the proof of these commonly held criteria is still an open discussion. The 70°F (± 2 degrees) and 50 percent relative humidity (RH) (± 5 percent RH) standard is just that, a standard, but by no means is it universally accepted for all types of collections. It represents a compromise that is suitable for the widest range of artifacts. Taking a position in this book does not advance the discussion, since there are many other factors which will impact your choice of criteria.

Over the past decade the dew point and the rate of change of temperature and relative humidity have been recognized as equally important criteria. Since a change in temperature results in a change in relative humidity, temperature stability is very important. Establishing a standard, 70 degrees (± 2 degrees) over twenty-four hours, with humidity at 50 percent(± 5 percent) should be considered for its efficacy against more liberal criteria with a measured gradual rate of change. Where some collections lending agreements are set, you may need to consider options, such as more stringent conditions only in special exhibition galleries. Some museums are varying their conditions criteria by season, slowly reaching 70°F / 30 percent RH in winter due to the difficulty of maintaining high relative humidity in very cold climates, particularly in historic structures. The key to this strategy is to change RH over a period of weeks, not days. Excellent research on this issue is available from a variety of research institutes focused on collections conservation.

In the end, good judgment is the primary tool to make the best decision, since other factors have a significant or greater impact in terms of risk to collections: frequency and length of display, fire, direct sunlight, UV exposure, theft or vandalism, vibration, off-gassing of contaminants by other collections or building materials, location of collections in the discharge air stream of a duct or a window, and storage of collections on open shelves rather than inside cabinets.

Regardless of the ideal standards, unless your collections are very large and you can afford multiple environments, the size of each collection relative to your total space may force you to set a single criterion which is "ideal in the middle." Many conservators, collections managers, and researchers continue to discuss this ideal, and you will join in the debate as you set the performance goals for your HVAC systems. Whether you are preserving paint on canvas, wood, metal, or plastic or any one of dozens of combinations, the ideal will suit some of your collections perfectly, but not all.

As you consider the selection of building systems, these additional issues will impact your decision:

- First cost discussions need to separate quality from complexity. As an institution with fiduciary responsibility, and with significant challenges raising money to renew or repair HVAC equipment, you should direct your design team to specify the highest-quality systems. Designing more complex systems may not improve the conservation goals, particularly if you cannot afford to maintain the system or obtain exotic parts.

- Maintenance costs due to numbers of devices and sensors in the system.

- Energy use and ability to use energy recovery equipment (which is quite large) to lower operating costs.

- Reliability of system performance, since all systems break down. Redundancy of systems (particularly crucial in collections areas) can be accomplished by tying two systems together with crossover ducts rather than buying redundant or oversize systems.

- For the HVAC engineer, a narrow range for temperature and humidity criteria will drive the complexity and expense of the building system needed to comply with your request. For some engineers, the complexity makes the project more interesting, but what you don't want is interesting, you want simplicity to ensure performance and maintainability. Spend the time and ask your facilities staff (or if you don't have one, borrow someone else's) to discuss the system operational attributes.

- Existing and historic buildings have additional challenges, including:
  a. The lack of a moisture vapor barrier and appropriate insulation preventing moisture migration within the exterior wall system. In some historic structures in colder climates, preventing moisture from condensing or freezing within the walls may be impossible to achieve without destroying

historic building interiors. Beware of easy fixes: you may end up with systems that are too complex or rely on untested wall systems.
  b. Size of major equipment.
  c. Ability to thread ductwork through building in ceiling cavities.
  d. Zoning the building systems by area and function.
  e. Sustainability goals may be impossible to achieve with historic windows and uninsulated walls.

  Building controls are the digital or electronic sensors which allow you to monitor and operate all the elements (chillers, boilers, cooling towers, pumps, valves, dampers, humidification equipment, reheat coils, sensors, humidistats, thermostats, etc.). With all these points to monitor the controls system may become very complicated, but as the brain of your HVAC system, it is a crucial. A well-designed and programmed controls system can reduce operating costs, provide historical records of temperature and humidity fluctuations, assist in system troubleshooting, and provide early warnings of potential problems before they become catastrophic failures. While there are open systems that can be modified by anyone, in general you will be married to the controls system manufacturer and one of their approved installation contractors. It is not your job to know, just to challenge.

  The single largest cause of HVAC systems failure is that they were never properly installed and tuned up to meet the design engineers' intent for performance. Commissioning is the process of third-party verification that all systems components are properly installed and operating. Since the control system is the brain of the system and the last component to be installed, proper operation is frequently unchecked unless third-party commissioning occurs. An experienced commissioning agent should be hired directly by the museum early in the design process to ensure understanding of system performance goals, to conduct early design reviews, and to have more insight into the project design and its goals. In any case, make sure that you find an independent firm, and that you, with assistance from your mechanical engineer, are involved in qualifications review and commissioning agent selection.

  In design of HVAC systems, consider:

- Laying out building systems serving any space requiring special security such as collections storage or conservation labs, where maintenance of equipment serving those spaces can occur without entering the space.

- Developing an understanding of the hours of operation of each program area in order co-locate functions which have similar operational criteria (24/7 operations, similar temperature and humidity criteria, need for system redundancy, etc.) for building systems efficiency during operations.
- Programming uses of collections storage space to exclude occupancy by staff for any activity except for the retrieval and cataloging of collections. If your occupancy of the space is incidental (all other collections management functions occur in other spaces), your system can be designed with less outside air resulting in significant energy savings.
- If possible, provide doors between areas with different uses and climate requirements such as gallery spaces and atriums/lobbies to minimize their impact on one another.
- Provide an area for collection acclimatization. Make sure that collections are allowed to slowly change temperature and humidity when they are moved from areas with different temperature and humidity.
- Even though it is hard to give up space in a building, provide sufficient area for easy maintenance and adjacent storage of maintenance supplies (filters and equipment). The easier preventative maintenance is, the more likely it will occur and the better your systems will perform.
- Energy-saving technologies will be covered in the sustainability section in this chapter. Always start with the simple systems with short paybacks such as CO^2 sensors, which bring in outside air only when the room is occupied.

Electrical systems. The electrical systems in your building consist of incoming utility service and switchgear (the backbone), convenience power, lighting, and emergency power for life safety.

Incoming service is not always reliable. Power outages happen for a variety of reasons, and your electric utility has data indicating the historical outages of the substation serving your site. This is important information, since frequent outages (and you may be surprised at the frequency in some areas) will impact your ability to operate. Power redundancy, which is very expensive, will require a second incoming service from another utility substation.

Convenience power consists of the plug load in your building. For the most part, the codes will dictate the minimum quantity for specific locations such as offices. Discretionary convenience power is another story. In setting criteria, particularly in lobbies, exhibit galleries, and classroom workshops, consider the cascade effect of requesting outlets everywhere and the currently held standard of a grid of power on ten-foot centers in the floor in gallery spaces. More on flexibility of power is covered later in this chapter.

Clean power is power which comes from dedicated electrical panels to supply audiovisual equipment, and exhibit interactives free of distortion caused by vacuum cleaners, personal fans, task lighting, or other equipment which can cause power distortion. Discuss these criteria with your electrical engineers, exhibit designers, and exhibit media integrators to ensure that interactives work properly.

Lighting. The criteria for lighting vary across the museum. For spaces without collections, consider lighting options for energy efficiently, but remember the best savings occur by managing how you organize and operate your building by providing:

- Housekeeping lights in gallery spaces for use during exhibit installation and cleaning
- Occupancy sensor to turn on lighting only when spaces are occupied
- Task lighting in office areas or conservation labs where intensive light levels are needed only in certain areas
- Light sensing dimming technology allowing dimming of light when daylight is available or the space is unoccupied
- Sensor-controlled lighting or shelf-mounted local lighting in collections storage

Lighting in gallery spaces has different criteria, but there are operational opportunities in how you light your spaces to save energy and still accomplish the exhibit design goals: Prior to consideration of lighting your curators, conservators, and your lighting consultants should review the collections to be displayed. Lighting needs are very different for paintings, drawings, three-dimensional objects, objects in vitrines, film, video art, and interactive displays. Understanding the medium will allow you to further set criteria for brightness (illuminance), light exposure (with a concern of exposure which is measured in terms of lux over time), and Color Rendition Index (CRI).

Architecturally, the volume of the building and height of the gallery play a significant role in the ability to properly use daylight or select a fixture to properly place light on the wall or floor where collections are displayed. During design, computer lighting simulations are easily developed once the room cavity is known to visualize how and where to place lighting of different types and to understand the impact of various lighting sources.

There is nothing more beautiful or orienting within a museum than using natural light for your galleries. It goes without saying, that in spite of UV filters, heat blocking coatings on glass and scrims to block daylight, too much light can be very damaging to many types of collections. Skylights are expensive to build, allow significant heat gains or losses, and provide a surface for condensation which can drip on collections below during dry winter conditions in cold climates. If you are considering day-lighting, discuss your goals and make sure you have a computer model for day-lighting developed to understand the lighting and energy implications.

Artificial lighting and lighting technology are changing more rapidly than any other building system. Collection conservation concerns (lighting levels and UV exposure) and curatorial concerns (controllability and proper color rendition) have been extensively discussed and written about, so they will not be covered here. In North America, incandescent remains the lighting of choice for exhibit spaces for its color rendition, controllability of beam, dimability, and low first cost. Current incandescent lighting technologies consume in excess of 40 percent of the power load and air-conditioning load of exhibit spaces, so from an energy use and lamp life perspective, incandescent is problematic. With the energy bill of 2007, incandescent lighting will be phased out over time starting in 2012. With the technology ready to change, at this moment, there is no equal, but options include other technologies that may be appropriate for some types of exhibits and collections:

- Halogen is a more efficient type of incandescent lighting, and is the current state of the art option for gallery lighting.
- Ceramic metal halide PAR lamps are an excellent solution where dimming is not required, due to their efficiency and long life. (As of 2009 dimming technologies have been introduced but are not widely tested.)
- Fluorescent systems have been utilized successfully for laylight and indirect lighting applications, and general house lighting. Fluorescent is dimmable and energy efficient, has long life, but has poor color rendition and is not a point source. While fluorescent fixtures have been accepted by many museums in Europe, resistance remains in most American museums.

- LED technology is advancing every day. But as of 2009, first costs are very high. Along with extremely long life and efficiency, there are options for color temperature adjustability and dimming. Investigate this worthwhile technology for your project.

The code mandates that emergency power be provided by an on-site power source, typically an emergency generator to power egress lights, exit signs, fire alarms and pumps, the elevator for firemen, and the operation of equipment which is used in emergencies. You must develop criteria for your engineer to size the emergency generator to provide the additional power for mission museum functions such as security systems, critical computer systems, and equipment (such as ultracold freezers if you have tissue collections or freezers with film or other special collections).

The cost of providing an on-site generator is quite high, so look first to passive and operational strategies to minimize the need to add optional non-code-mandated power load to your emergency power system. Since most power outages are relatively brief, most museums will get people out, shut down areas where collections are kept, and keep them as locked boxes which will minimize any change in temperature over the course of twenty-four hours.

Plumbing. Plumbing issues are straightforward in the museum environment. Key issues specific to museums for consideration are:

- Keep water supply and drainage piping away from areas where collections are present. Leaks are infrequent, but most often occur at valves. If piping is present, consider placing drip pans under piping with a drain that is piped to drip into a janitor's sink where it will be noticed.
- Treat roof drains in a similar manner. Make sure they are insulated to prevent condensation during colder weather. Again, the drip pans apply.

Risk reduction systems: Fire protection and security systems. Fire protection and security (theft and damage to collections, personal safety for visitors and staff) are key design criteria which use a combination of passive and active systems to deter any threats to the museum visitors, staff, building, and collections with an identified goal. Suggested fire protection objectives include:

- *Life safety.* Design and maintain an egress system to protect occupants for the time needed to evacuate the building.

- *Building protection.* Locate the devices to be unobtrusive and off surfaces which may detract from exhibit experiences.
- *Collection preservation.* Fire safety and fire protection features must be designed, approved, implemented, and maintained to preserve the original qualities of the collection (a zero net loss goal).
- *Continuity of operations.* Fire safety and fire protection features should be designed, approved, implemented, and maintained to minimize disruption of operations consistent with the organization's fire safety goals.

While building codes address life safety for people, they typically do not recognize the value of your collections. It is recommended that you undertake a risk assessment analysis for both fire and security. Each assessment will establish clear goals and objectives, describe threat scenarios, and establish mitigation strategies of those threats. The goal is to identify the risks, develop response plans, and design the building and systems which enable a cost-effective (initial and lifetime) risk mitigation effort utilizing a combination of daily prevention measures using passive and active systems. Keep in mind that lowering risk of loss due to fire or fire-related perils will involve reducing both frequency of a fire event (i.e., limiting potential ignition sources) and lowering the impact of an event (i.e., evacuating smoke via a building system).

You should develop a risk assessment working group which should include your curator, conservator, collections manager, security director, facilities manager, insurance carrier, local first responders, fire protection engineer, and security consultant. It goes without saying, the best protection is a prevention strategy based on risk reduction. The starting place is to identify passive strategies, supplemented by active building systems. Passive strategies do's and don'ts include:

- Security
    a. Design for sight lines and visibility in exterior and interior spaces.
    b. Prepare procedures and standards for accessing, exhibiting, and storing collections. There are all too many examples of theft by outside researchers who were trusted and not watched or searched.
    c. Train all staff and maintain plans for disaster response and mitigation.
    d. Locate museum operations that pose an inherent risk to security (retail, restaurant, coat check, and mail) outside the security perimeter.

e. Locate departments visited by unknown persons such as shipping and receiving, and human resources just inside the perimeter at an entrance.

f. Isolate curatorial activities to a curatorial suite.

g. Provide a single after-hour employee entrance with a twenty-four-hour security control room.

h. Develop a program that conforms with "Recommended Guidelines for Museum Security," a document prepared jointly by insurers, the ASIS cultural property committee, and the AAM security committee.

i. Create a comprehensive security policy (access control, sign-in, and screening) with a manual for guard training and building operations.

j. Train all staff and maintain plans for disaster response and mitigation.

- Fire Protection

a. Cross-train security staff to be an active part of monitoring for fire and to respond during accidental sprinkler discharge.

b. Locate building systems (motors, valves, etc.) and dimmer panels for lighting outside areas where collections are present to remove potential sources of ignition or water, and maintenance activities.

c. Compartmentalize your building where possible. A large collections space may be efficient, but subcompartments and smoke drops can contain a fire or smoke damage.

d. Remove combustible materials and materials that may be toxic when burned including plastic boxes for collections and wood pallets for sculpture storage.

e. Implement policy changes:

   i. Minimize work in collections storage areas.

   ii. Remove trash and refuse as frequently as possible.

   iii. Administratively control on-site construction. Do not permit welding or other activities with sparks or open flames unless strict procedures are in place. Sample policies are available in various National Fire Prevention Association (NFPA) and Occupational Safety and Health Administration (OSHA) codes.[3]

The second strategy, using active systems, is more expensive to implement and maintain. Inherent in reliance on any active system is a chance of failure, particularly if the system is too complex, requires extensive maintenance and testing, or is prone to malfunction due to human or hardware overreliance on "foolproof" design solutions. In general as a system's complexity increases, human error increases and its reliability decreases.

- Security systems
  a. Understand the cost of security personnel as a supplement to monitored systems.
  b. 24/7 on-site versus off-site monitoring.
  c. Look at risk and cost of outsourced versus in-house security staff.
  d. Card key access hardware systems are recommended as a strategy across the museum. The building lock system should use a proprietary keyway so keys can't be made without your authorization.
  e. CCTV is the best expenditure of your security dollar for daytime protection; if a system is too expensive now, prep spaces for future installation.
  f. Object protection systems are effective, but expensive, so prep for future installation if budgets are tight.
  g. Modern burglar alarm, access control, CCTV, and object protection systems are computers operating on a network. Resist the temptation to converge these onto a common building-wide network.
  h. The guard radio system must extend to all parts of the building, and repeaters should be included if necessary.
- Fire protection systems
  a. Smoke detection includes devices with a range of sensitivity for activation that respond to temperature rise or presence of particulate matter (smoke) in varying degrees of sophistication.
  b. Provide a rapid entry key for fire departments for emergency responses.
  c. Active fire suppression systems include the five following options:
     i. Wet pipe sprinklers
        a. Pros: Lowest first and maintenance costs; effective in response; extremely reliable and recommended by NFPA's Cultural Property Committee.
        b. Cons: Potential for damage to collections if accidental discharge occurs, but documented instances are extremely rare.
     ii. Preaction sprinklers are similar to wet pipe sprinklers except water is held back from system piping. Two actions must occur for water to discharge: an integral smoke detection system must sense smoke and a sprinkler head must operate due to heat (or mechanical damage).

   a. Pros: Has failsafe check prior to discharge.

   b. Cons: Higher first and maintenance cost; modifications are difficult; potential decreased reliability due to the additional complexity; regular maintenance is essential to ensure reliability.

iii. Gaseous and dry chemical

   a. Pros: Potentially less harmful to collections when discharged.

   b. Cons: Higher installation and maintenance costs; health hazards are uncertain; relies on room containment (doors being closed) to be effective; difficult to modify.

iv. Water mist

   a. Pros: Effective with less water damage; may be used in facilities with a limited site water supply.

   b. Cons: Significantly higher installation and maintenance costs; relies on room containment (doors being closed) to be effective.

v. Reduced oxygen

   a. Pros: Significantly higher installation and maintenance costs; no collections damage.

   b. Cons: May be unhealthful for persons with respiratory problems.

With the possible exception of environmental conditions criteria for collections, the controversy over fire protection systems is the subject of the most intense debate. While wet pipe systems seemed to be increasingly criticized for accidents and potential damage to collections, the actual data show very few accidental discharges occur. In your discussions with your risk assessment working group, raise questions and address a variety of approaches, always keeping in mind that passive risk reduction and simple systems can be the best choice.

Information technology (IT) systems. Since 1990, IT systems have evolved from independent systems of voice, data, and media to converging systems on a single network. The pace of change has also created a perpetual process of obsolescence, making design of systems difficult. Voice Over Internet Protocols (VOIP), new data cable types to handle capacity and speed demands have driven up first costs of these systems substantially. Wireless systems while useful (as of 2009) are limited in size of file transfer, and are a supplement rather than a backbone in terms of systems for museums.

Provide dedicated space for incoming utilities for telephone and data. The central location of the information technology system is the data center (or computer server room) which will house servers, routers, switches, and storage systems and be the origin of distribution of the data, media, and voice services throughout the museum. Distribution from the data center is accomplished via multipair copper trunk, fiber optic, coaxial, and unshielded twisted pair (UTP) cabling. Each cable terminates in a properly sized data closet on each floor back to the entry point.

When considering IT design:

- Develop a clear plan for use of media in your building. Overdesign of capacity can be very costly; however, keep flexibility in mind as technology continually changes and you want the ability to modify the IT systems easily to accommodate change.
- Consider the cost of the active components necessary to support the data, media, and voice systems of the building and establish a budget for these systems. Include the costs for telephones, computers, monitors, printers, and similar office equipment as these costs are typically not included in the construction budget.
- Maintain separate cable tray pathways and tag cable for IT systems, security systems, low voltage wiring for HVAC systems, and power distribution.
- Centrally locate the data center within the building to minimize backbone riser cable and utility cable runs reducing costs and locate data closets in order to minimize cable lengths and reduce costs. Locate the data center, demarcation room, and data closets clear from potential building hazards such as flooding caused by broken pipes.
- Engage media consultants early in the design process to assist with planning and design.
- Overhead distribution should always be through dedicated cable trays, with care to distance the cable from electrical interference from "dirty power" and to minimize the potential of damage from maintenance activity.
- Expect change, since IT technology is constantly changing.

Flexibility of power and data systems. Creating a flexible electrical and IT system in public spaces is a challenge for museums; no matter how many points of connection, placing them in exactly the right places is impossible. For the most part, the ten-by-ten-foot grid on the floor is the gold standard, but regardless your exhibit designers must design to the grid. A benchmarking study by this author in 2006 revealed that no science center (which are heavy users of interactives) out of a sample of twenty centers used more than 24 percent of their floor grid plug capacity.[4] This translates into having four times the capacity (and initial installation cost) needed in these spaces, whether used or not. This design load translates into larger electrical panel boards, a bigger switch in the basement, a bigger transformer, and bigger incoming service. Compounding this is the requirement to cool the space, since all that power being burned translates into heat. While the code and good practice recognize every point of connection will not be used, the percentage reduction in total capacity allowed (called a diversity factor) is still low. Therefore the large grid of power and data, designed to provide flexibility, whether utilized at 50 percent or 24 percent, increases the size of the HVAC ductwork, air handlers, central plant, and costs. Whatever your need, carefully consider the criteria you develop and understand the construction cost implications fully.

Structural systems. Structural systems include everything from the footings to the top of the building. Design of these systems for most museum buildings does not require your input except to set criteria in certain circumstances.

Ordinary floor loading assumptions by a structural engineer will include the people and collections or displays you might expect and are driven by codes. Extraordinary loads to consider for your structural engineer include compacted collections (now or later), heavy sculpture or artifacts (think twisted columns of the World Trade Center), and ceiling loads for sculpture, banners, and other objects. In some museums, a ten-by-ten-foot overhead grid of unistrut—threaded rods supporting small structural sections—are installed to enable easy connection of minor loads.

SUSTAINABILITY

The twenty-first century has brought new emphasis and consideration for the usage of sustainable design principles. Sustainable design is most commonly used to refer to "designing building systems and programs that meet the needs of today's building occupants while being respectful of the needs of future generations." The terms "sustainable design" and "greening" are used and often abused when the talk turns to changing the way in which buildings are designed and operated. Sustainable design practices in some countries are far ahead of North America. Since 2000, the movement to adopt more sustainable building design and operational practices has significantly accelerated and is altering the design, construction, and operation of buildings. Even experienced design teams must constantly revise their processes and procedures to incorporate innovative thinking that effectively integrates sustainable practices into your museum building. This integration process is a work in progress, with the team working to improve your building's performance and ultimately achieving significant and measurable outcomes that will simultaneously reduce utility costs and minimize the environmental impact of new, renovation, and construction projects.

Sustainability is arguably a return to tradition, not in form but in practice. Our earliest buildings used local materials, had no mechanical systems to move air, were oriented to maximize use of the sun and wind, mass, and vegetation to bring in light and air and temper the interior environment. With the advent of long-distance transportation and cheaper energy, buildings quickly evolved to the sealed systems which require enormous energy inputs to maintain comfort levels and conditions. The biggest challenge to today's success stories evolves from the creative blend of lessons learned from traditional practices with technology and building practice innovations that create the most sophisticated and exciting building strategies.

For most museums, sustainable practices are directly or indirectly a part of their mission as public institutions that see stewardship and conservation as core to their values. Museums are also realizing that the donor community is increasingly motivated by sustainable design which creates the opportunity to attract new community support (suddenly HVAC systems are of interest). Not surprisingly, many state and local codes are starting to mandate levels of building performance. There are some local, state, and federal incentives and some funding sources available to help fund green building technologies and renewable energy practices. Foundations are increasingly making grants toward sustainability initiatives for operations and building projects.

In the United States, as sustainable design becomes more mainstream, the systems for assessing and certifying environmental performance have increased dramatically. Product manufacturers, service industries, and professional organizations have created countless environmental performance systems. The large number of alphabet soup benchmark systems, tools, and products has caused an enormous amount of confusion in the industry. Two benchmark systems have emerged as the most commonly used set of standards for sustainable design and construction:

- *LEED.* Leadership in Energy and Environmental Design (LEED) administered through the U.S. Green Building Council (USGBC).[5] This program has had the largest impact to improve environmental performance of buildings in North America. As of February 2009, four programs of LEED are likely to be used in a museum:
  a. LEED for new construction: LEED NC is the first rating system developed and is the most familiar rating system to the museum building industry. It can be used on any project of a minimum size or in a renovation with an addition.
  b. LEED for commercial interiors: LEED CI rating system was developed to serve tenants in multitenant buildings. In the museum world, this could include smaller renovations within a museum or where a separate 501(c)3 operates the museum while a government entity is responsible for core and shell building services.
  c. LEED for existing buildings: LEED EB has the greatest possibility of actually saving a museum on operational costs when working within an existing building.
  d. LEED for core and shell buildings: LEED CS is designed for building projects that have critical building envelope systems, engineering systems, and shared circulation and core systems. In a museum application, LEED CS would be appropriate where critical systems were put into place previously.

The U.S. Green Building Council is constantly upgrading and improving the rating system based on feedback and recommendations of its membership. The historic preservation community has influenced changes in the LEED rating system, stressing the value of embedded energy in reuse of existing buildings. Phased projects which occur frequently in museums are not easily accommodated within the current system, but these challenges should not prevent you from applying LEED principles or trying for certification.

EnergyStar is administered through the U.S. Environmental Protection Agency and is best known for certification of electronics and appliances.[6] However, the program also applies to energy efficiency for buildings, focusing on energy usage in the building. It requires much less paperwork documentation than the LEED program, and a building can receive and EnergyStar designation if it performs better than 75 percent of the buildings being recorded in a specific building type. Unfortunately as of 2009, a museum as a building type cannot receive an EnergyStar designation; however, an off-site facility such as administration, lab/research, and other building types which may be part of a large museum can receive certification.

Both programs emphasize a range of metrics to benchmark performance either during construction or during operation of a building. Depending on your project's aesthetic needs, programmatic needs, and funding, different benchmarking tools may be appropriate.

Who Should Be Involved in Our Sustainability Effort?

You should set up a sustainability working group and include a variety of project stakeholders. Cast a wide net and make sure you include your conservator, building operations, and food facility operator. Before adopting a level of certification, recognize that certain benchmarks are at odds with programmatic or conservation needs of collections. However, most of the core values of the sustainable building practice are in direct alignment with the goals of conservators and curators: highly filtered clean air, elimination of off-gassing from building materials, lower lighting levels, and so on. Other core values pose some challenging opposition to museum design strategies: use of energy efficient lighting (poor color), extensive day-lighting, and temperature levels.

While you are planning your new facility, there are things you can do now that are simple and effective and can test your organization so that there becomes a culture of sustainability in your museum. Below are some of the "low hanging fruit" strategies:

- Maximize recycling: Create measurable goals for reducing the amount of waste in your facility and increasing the amount of recycled content you buy. What can you reuse, such as furniture or crates, that might be disposed of currently rather than refinished or repurposed?
- Occupancy sensors everywhere possible: Install sensors, which are very affordable, to turn off lights when rooms are not occupied.
- Water-efficient plumbing fixtures: Install energy efficient toilets and faucets and eliminate paper towels by using hand dryers.

- Encourage alternative transportation modes: Offer discounts to visitors and provide incentives for staff who use public transportation in conjunction with your local transit authority. Remember, it costs over $8,000 to build a parking space (2008 dollars) and money each year to maintain it.
- Use low-emitting products: There is no additional cost for low volatile organic compound (voc) paints, sealants, and adhesives in today's marketplace.
- Durable and reliable products: Buy for the long term.
- Green housekeeping strategies: Identify cleaning products and procedures which use fewer chemical and greener cleaners.
- Measure your energy performance: Develop specific practices which can allow you to turn off lights, change the temperature (in noncollections spaces) or otherwise decrease your energy use.
- Purchase power from renewable resources: Your museum can make this shift with no operational changes.
- Green your food operations: Eliminate the use of disposable products. Consider serving food according to the "100 mile diet" using local and/or organic food, while eliminating bottled water and composting food waste.

What Are the Benefits to My Museum?

Adopting high standards is good for not only the environment but future operational budgets. Just as having a hybrid vehicle with higher mileage performance has lower operating costs, a high-performance building will lower energy costs. Investments in sustainable performance in the private sector are often performed strictly on a five-year payback analysis, while for museums, the metrics are completely different: lower operating costs translate into less endowment needed for operations.

Do I Need to Register and Certify My Building?

Remember, you are really doing this for the quality of outcome: you can do it all and not register. With certification you will have proof of your commitment and the bragging rights that go with it. If you are in a location where government funding agencies will not pay for project registration with the USGBC and LEED certification, consider finding a donor with a particular interest in sustainability to bear the costs.

What Does It Cost to Obtain Certification at Each Level?

Again, this is changing rapidly as the design and construction markets move sustainability into the mainstream. The answer is almost nothing for basic certification to much higher if you decide to generate your own energy on-site and head toward a zero net energy goal. There is a design cost in having your design team work with you to develop project documentation and submit certification information, but overall it is modest in terms of project cost impact.

CODES AND STIPULATED REGULATIONS

Codes and regulations establish *minimum* standards for your site and building performance. They are generally enforced by state or local code officials known as authorities having jurisdiction (AHJ). Codes can have a significant impact on your ability to function, expand, or even add a few parking spaces on-site, so early code review is essential.

Some codes provide two means to achieve compliance:

- Prescriptive codes prescribe the means for achieving an accepted outcome.
- Performance codes describe an accepted outcome and leave the means to a number of design solutions.

The following section will provide an overview of six types of codes or stipulated regulations that may apply to your project:

- Zoning and land use
- Impact codes
- Historic preservation
- Building
- Accessibility
- Additional stipulations

Zoning and Land Use Codes

Zoning codes were developed in the early twentieth century to put compatible uses on adjacent land and over time has become an important force to allow communities to have a voice on how land is used. Under zoning codes, land may be used "as of right" without community input if your use is zoned for institutional use. In older communities, house and history museums find themselves "nonconforming users" in residential areas which may require that a variance must be applied for any time land or building change is needed. A variance opens the project up to public comment and a ruling by a board of adjustment. There are cases such as the Woodmere Art Museum's expansion on its site in Philadelphia, which has been delayed for more than three years due to the opposition of one or two nearby residents.

Specific requirements of zoning in your district may govern:

- Lot coverage, limiting how much of your site is impervious surface: the sum of building footprint and paved surfaces (the walks and parking areas that are surfaces that do not allow water to return to the water table)
- Setbacks, or the distances of your building from front, side, and rear property lines
- Height restrictions, which are usually determined by some aesthetic issue or the capacity of local fire department to reach upper levels safely
- Site attributes including lighting, materials, and aesthetic concerns

A site master plan may be required by local authority and it is in your best interest in order to ensure your long-term ability to continue to grow on-site and limit your need to return for approval of future projects. Exceptions to zoning, such as grandfather clauses, are generally noted in the code or run with property title. The process to obtain a variance can be lengthy and should entail legal counsel with documents prepared by the design team.

Impact Codes

Typically required only for larger projects, impact codes may be stipulated in local, regional, or federal regulations and govern a wide range of issues.

- Traffic studies are concerned with the number of car trips and truck traffic the museum generates daily and their impact on local roads.
- Environmental impact statements (EIS).
- Carbon impact statements are new and emerging regulations appearing in some municipalities as they work to comply with voluntary caps on carbon emissions.

Historic Preservation Codes

Since the destruction of Pennsylvania Station in New York City in 1963, historic preservation codes have been implemented locally and nationally with varying degrees of success and enforcement. Historic preservation should be seen large: you may be part of a historic district, part of a historic landscape, or in a historic structure. For many museums, an existing site and building may be considered a part of your identity; a de facto nonaccessioned part of your collection, or the key to your interpretive mission. Changes will be closely watched, whether or not your building is on a local or national listing (such as the National Register of Historic Places administered by the Department of Interior).

Engaging community input early and consulting with historic preservation experts, including your state historic preservation officer (SHPO) or local historical commission, will enable you to understand the key areas' significance which must be respected. Various studies such as historic structures reports will become baseline documents to form the basis of setting criteria to enable you to then plan how you may use and modify your structure to meet your programmatic needs. See the bibliography for more information.

Building Codes

Building codes are legal requirements imposed or administered on the state or local level. Code compliance is legal responsibility of design team, enforced by local authorities having jurisdiction who have the right to interpret the code's intent. Codes are written to define criteria for safety in this order of importance:

- Building occupants and first responders
- Protection of your building
- Protection of your building contents

Since protecting collections is equally important, and any collections loss is unacceptable, the criteria you adopt for protection of your collection (and by extension people and your building) will most likely be even more stringent. Performing a fire risk assessment or elevating your protection in excess of the code is covered earlier in this chapter.

Several additional issues may impact your project are:

- Code interpretation by the local authority can be different from interpretation by your design team. In some cases, local authorities will accept written interpretation by a national board, accept a fire risk assessment, require a local board hearing and determination, or reject any outside interpretation. The time and cost implications of these interpretations should not be underestimated.

- In historic structures, certain requirements may be waived in formal hearings or with written notice by local authorities based on alternative strategies for compliance. These nonprescriptive approaches will take time to develop and should also be reviewed by your insurance carrier.

Accessibility Code

Accessibility standards under the Americans with Disabilities Act (ADA) is another prescriptive code for providing equal access to all public areas and most support spaces for staff. The ADA addresses the mobility, visual, and auditory challenges of visitors and staff and the minimum standards for design compliance to allow equal access. State or local amendments may also apply. Compliance is the responsibility of your design team, so your concerns should be limited to supplementing the requirements to address the special considerations of your visitors and staff:

- Elevator size. If your visitors include large groups, consider enlarging your elevator to accommodate a full school or group of older visitors (consider being the person in a wheelchair separated from your class). This may require little more than having your freight elevator located near your lobby.
- Access inside collections spaces can be considered a staff facilitated process and outside the requirements of the ADA. However, depending on your policy, staff or visiting researchers may be allowed unaccompanied access to collections storage areas and may affect design.

Additional Stipulations

Other requirements impacting setting your building criteria may be imposed by:

- The accreditation process by the AAM and other accrediting agencies such as higher education institutions
- Insurance requirements
- Lending agreements

- Donor stipulations, including environmental, security, and segregation of materials
- Cultural sensitivity, including co-location of materials

It is your responsibility to inform your design team of these issues and to carefully develop a plan for compliance where these stipulations may exceed code requirements.

Remember the following about codes:

- Identify all applicable codes early and integrate the time for approvals into your planning and design schedule.
- Recognize that interpretation of codes can be subjective and result in delays.
- Exhibit design firms or fabricators are not licensed design professionals, and may not know local codes or carry insurance for errors made in their design in regard to code compliance. In many jurisdictions, authorities will require an architect to take responsibility for this work and seal the exhibit design drawings. Talk with your code official during design and work with the exhibit and design teams to develop a strategy for compliance. If the design team is to take responsibility for review and liability, budget for additional costs.
- Sleepovers or camp-ins are popular in some museums, but in some jurisdictions, code officials will require museums meet the requirements of a hotel in terms of parking, bathroom fixtures, and fire safety or smoke detection systems.
- Even the best efforts of the design team may result in changes. Most frequently during construction, local building officials will walk through installed exhibits and ask for additional exit signs based on obstructed sight lines due to exhibits within the space.

EXISTING SITE AND FACILITY ASSESSMENT: IMPACT OF WHAT YOU HAVE

Presumably your strategic plan identified site and facility needs, or you would not be planning for a building project. Do not proceed on the basis of the strategic plan alone since stakeholders or staff who did not participate may be aware of other programmatic space needs as well as needs for site or building infrastructure upgrades for building systems at the end of their useful life. Values based goals will influence your decisions: a building needing programmatic improvements whose envelope and systems are problematic from a sustainability perspective may still be worth renovating since renovation is a more sustainable approach than new construction.

As part of your basis of design report undertake a complete assessment during predesign to proof your needs by starting with staff. Consult peers, attend conferences, and then hire a design team to assess, with a dispassionate view, the site and building physical conditions and programmatic fit, its serviceability over the long run, and key impediments to implementation. Among issues to study are your:

- Site's external conditions such as neighborhood support, site use permits, historic preservation or district designation, traffic, or other impacts
- Site's internal conditions such as aesthetic appearance, programmatic opportunities, access (public transportation, cars, bus), and pedestrian movement
- Building's existing conditions, including envelope, thermal performance, and vapor barrier location, interior fit out, and building systems' remaining useful life
- Organization and flow, from visitor, collections, and support perspective, and the programmatic appropriateness of each space (size, ceiling heights, adjacencies, ability to expand)
- Implementation challenges, including phasing, schedule, and costs to implement

Consideration of Off-site Facilities

Embedded in the analysis of your existing facilities is consideration to develop an off-site facility. While this will functionally break up the museum family, the reasons which drive it generally relate to the cost of building on-site versus off-site, the location of swing space, time frame for implementation of a multiphase project, and the lack of space on-site to accommodate the program due to zoning. Programmatically, off-site facilities typically include noncollection functions such as offices for finance or other administrative functions, "dirty" workshops including exhibit/carpentry shops, and storage for institutional archives, crates, or exhibition furniture. If you elect to move collections off-site, don't forget things go with collections, like collections management and research areas. Make sure you operationally budget for collections transportation, extra security, and maintenance of additional equipment.

If your conclusion is a phased renewal or an addition, there are special advantages and challenges to this approach:

- Garnering donor support if the project is perceived as less significant
- Visual linkages of stylistically different architecture
- Impact of construction on daily life and perception of visitors
- Limited chance to provide ideal spaces for activities and improved visitor flow due to working with existing constraints
- Time to complete a phased renewal
- Work outside the building envelope has less impact on daily visitor/staff

Your existing facilities study will provide objective information which will increasingly become more subjective as your stakeholders and institutional silos come into play. Often the discussion evolves into questions of legacy of the board and other intangibles which will influence your decision to proceed using your existing building or to develop a new building.

Assessing a New Site

A new site, called a *green* site (if never before developed) or a *brownfield* site (if developed previously) should be approached with legal and design team support. Most of the requirements are similar to issues previously covered.

Do not expect, however, that public use and your mission will automatically mean you will be welcomed everywhere and that opposition will not develop over your hours of operation, water runoff into local streams, or the traffic you will generate. Work with a real estate adviser, examine sites dispassionately and rigorously. Develop a matrix of issues, including visibility, access, public transportation, neighbors, demographic opportunities, and political climate for funding and support. The visual quality is equally important, such as the quality of context, mature trees, ability to minimize the visual impact of parking, and so on. As part of your study of a new site, the reliability and capacity of infrastructure such as power, water, or gas may impact your initial and ongoing operating costs to develop your site. Whatever your needs, develop a site master plan and project forward in time to fully understand the potential for the site to accommodate your needs in the long term. Commission a geotechnical report of subsurface conditions: finding rock or a high water table will impact your plans and costs significantly.

SITE AND BUILDING SPACE PROGRAMS: SIZING YOUR SPACES

A space program is a quantification of all functional areas of your site and building to ensure proper accommodation of all staff and functions. Useful tools include benchmarking space needs for some functions (parking spaces per square feet of gallery, seats in your lunchroom per square foot of exhibit space; square feet per office by staff position). It should be formatted as a spreadsheet allowing you to document current and proposed space and staff, program options (1, 2, 3, etc.), and final space size as designed.

One of the greatest challenges is to understand how much space is needed that could be viewed as nonprogrammatic but is essential to the operation of the museum: circulation, bathrooms, shafts for ductwork, fire stairs, rooms for building systems (HVAC, electrical, fire pumps, IT closets, etc.). There is no rule of thumb: a ten-foot-wide corridor between your loading area and primary support areas may be required for movement of collections or access for replacing large HVAC equipment. If you are working without planning or design professionals in preparing your first space program and budgeting by the square foot, do not leave these areas out or you will be significantly underestimating what you need to build by a factor of 30 to 60 percent.

Prior to starting, adopt a standard for sizing your building spaces. Although there are different methods for calculating size, the definitions used here are based on standards developed by the Building Owner and Managers Association (BOMA).[7] Since your goal is not for leasing purposes, the definitions here are simplified and geared toward developing an accurate space program for your museum:

- Gross square feet (GSF) refers to measured space from the exterior surface of your building and includes all enclosed and covered spaces (loading area, porte cochere, etc.).
- Net square feet (NSF) refers to space that excludes shafts, elevators, stairs, exterior walls, and rooms for building systems.
- Net assignable square feet (NASF) refers to the net of all other factors and assigned to a department within your museum solely for its use.
- Net to gross ratio describes a building's efficiency of net assignable to gross square footage. This can range from 1.3 to 1.6 depending on whether corridors are considered usable, and building layout efficiency.

ART MUSEUM

Division of Conservation

DESCRIPTION	Cat.	W/S No.	Room No.	Qty × Area	NSF	Cat. Total	Work Area	Swing Room	Swing Staff	Swing Qty × Area	Swing NSF	Swing Total	Decomp Room	Decomp Staff	Decomp Qty × Area	Decomp NSF	Decomp Total	Post Ren Room	Post Ren Staff	Post Ren Qty × Area	Post Ren NSF	Post Ren Total	Notes
SCULPTURE CONSERVATION																							
Lab/Workroom																							
Object Lab	ANP	4	B201	1 × 808	808	912	6	B149		1 × 419	419	419			1 × 1,200	1,200	1,304			1 × 1,600	1,600	1,704	Explore integration into Lab 5
Object Lab / Shower	ANP	4	B201B	1 × 104	104					0 × 0	0				1 × 104	104				1 × 104	104		
Inergen Tanks	ANP	4		0 × 0	0					0 × 0	0				0 × 0	0				0 × 0	0	0	
Equipment																							
X-Ray Room w/Wet Developer	ANP	4	B233	1 × 306	306	357	2			1 × 306	306	364			1 × 306	306	357			0 × 0	0		Locate in X-Ray Suite.
Spray Booth	ANP	4	B253	1 × 49	49		2			1 × 58	58				1 × 49	49				0 × 0	0	0	
Office/Common Area																							
Office w/Equipment & Storage	O	1	B221A	1 × 169	169	484				1 × 150	150	511		1	1 × 150	150	547			1 × 175	175	824	Swing assumes most staff to be elsewhere @ other institutions.
Office (Dept. Head)	O	1	B21C	1 × 130	130		5			1 × 25	25			0	1 × 25	25			0	1 × 25	25		
Workstation in Lab	O	1	B202	1 × 25	25		5			1 × 48	48			7	7 × 48	336			9	9 × 64	576		
Workstation (currently in corridor)	O	5	B206B	4 × 30	120		6			7 × 48	336			7	1 × 36	36			1	1 × 48	48		
Scanner Station (currently in corridor)	O	0	B102	1 × 40	40																		
Files/Storage																							
Storage (Chiller Room)	O	4	B202E	1 × 12	12	27				0 × 0	0	15			1 × 100	100	205			1 × 120	120	225	
Files	O	4	B206B	1 × 5	5		2			1 × 5	5				1 × 5	5				1 × 5	5		
Sculpture Garden Storage	ANP	4	B233	1 × 10	10		2			1 × 10	10				1 × 100	100				1 × 100	100		
Total Object Conservation		8				1,780			8			1,309		10			2,413					2,753	
PAPER CONSERVATION																							
Lab/Workroom																							
Paper Lab	ANP	4	B102C	1 × 816	816	816	6			1 × 451	451	451			1 × 1,100	1,100	1,100			1 × 1,240	1,240	1,240	50% increase.
Inergen Tanks	O			0 × 0	0	0				0 × 0	0	0			0 × 0	0	0			0 × 0	0	150	
Equipment																							
Light Bleaching	ANP	4		0 × 0	0	327									1 × 150	150	150			1 × 150	150	648	
Office/Common Area																							
Office (Dept. Head)	O	1	B302A	1 × 252	252		2			1 × 150	150	367		1	1 × 150	150	367			1 × 175	175		
Workstation (in Lab)	O	2	B102	1 × 25	25		2			1 × 25	25			0	1 × 25	25				1 × 25	25		
Workstation (currently in corridor)	O	2	B106A	2 × 25	50		2			4 × 48	192			4	4 × 48	192			7	7 × 64	448		
Files/Storage																							
Storage - Paper Sample Archives	O	1	B69H	1 × 140	140	140	4	G150A/B		0 × 0	0	0		4	0 × 0	0	0			0 × 0	0	0	Will move back to G2 after swing.
Total Paper Conservation		5				1,283			5			818		5			1,617		8			2,038	
PHOTOGRAPH CONSERVATION																							
Lab/Workroom																							
Lab	ANP	4	G102B	1 × 149	149	149	2	G150A/B		1 × 166	166	166			1 × 400	400	400			1 × 900	900	900	Provide independent space.
Inergen Tanks	O			0 × 0	0	0				0 × 0	0	0			0 × 0	0	0			0 × 0	0	0	Currently share w/ Paper Conservation.
Equipment																							
Office/Common Area																							
Office (Dept. Head)/located in photo cons. lab	O	2	G102B	1 × 0	0	246	6	G156	2	1 × 100	100	100			1 × 150	150	246		1	1 × 175	175	367	Currently share w/ Paper Conserv.
Workstations	O														2 × 48	96			3	3 × 64	192		
Files/Storage																							
Storage	O					0						0			1 × 50	50	50		1	1 × 120	120	120	Currently share w/ Paper Conserv.
Total Photographic Conservation		2				149			2			266		3			696		4			1,387	

FIGURE 7.1

Database Space Program

Site Space Program

The site program should quantify:

- Site's natural and historic features, aesthetic and view sheds issues, and site civil engineering concerns regarding storm water management and availability of utility infrastructure
- Signage and way finding
- Vehicular movement, including entrance from surrounding streets, drop off and parking areas for group and family visitors
- Visitor/pedestrian circulation, including sidewalks and paths and their materials
- Programmatic areas, including gardens, memorial spaces, sculpture gardens, outdoor learning spaces, and event spaces such as terraces or event tent pads
- Service zones

Building Space Program

The building space program is a document to quantify internal space and should be organized by the presence (or absence) of collections and the public, which will allow you to categorize types of systems, level of fire protection, security needs, and other criteria differences enabling you to zone and operate your building more efficiently.

This results in a space program as a four-part matrix.[8]

- Public, with collections present
- Public, without collections present
- Support, with collections present
- Support, without collections present

Appendix F contains a list of spaces you will need to consider in your program which should inform your thinking, but not be considered exhaustive or directive of your planning effort. The bibliography also has references to other books on museum planning.

There are highly specific criteria to consider when programming and sizing for every museum space. This chapter cannot cover every space, but consider the following functional aspects of your front entrance, lobby, and loading dock areas:

- The entrance vestibule is one of the most important tools you have to maintain environmental conditions in your lobby (and by extension, nearby galleries). The vestibule should be deep and the doors oriented away from prevailing winds. Doors let four times as much energy escape as revolving doors.[9] Security is increasing at the door in many museums, so provide adequate queuing space indoors to prevent doors from being held open in inclement weather.

- Your lobby should speak to who you are. If it is devoid of collections, check your reasons: security concerns, the cost to provide proper environmental systems at the front door, or the concern of using a lobby for events where collections are present are often offered as reasons to keep collections out. Is this the best first impression?

- Consider ticketing a hospitality function. A long row of ticket booths on a slow or busy day is not welcoming. Consider handheld ticketing devices and using technology to avoid dedicated ticketing real estate to visually make your lobby more of an event rather than a transaction location.

- Coatrooms should include space for wheelchairs, lockers, strollers, and additional security screening equipment. Locate oversize restrooms near your entrance so visitors can use them when they arrive and leave.

- Your education center should be accessible for buses and include adequate storage, coat carts, and offices. Take care that it does not look like what children left at school. The size of your school lunchroom space will dictate how many groups can visit. Provide vending or a staffed cart for snack or drink purchases if you are not near the café or don't want younger visitors in your café.

- Consider separating school group retail from other retail functions. Your income from a well-placed cart for school groups may exceed the return on investment from the fit-out and operational costs of a larger store.

- Make sure events can be set up without disrupting visitor or ongoing operations.

- Separate collections receiving and delivery from food or other supplies to prevent contamination. While trash seems like a straightforward subject, loading areas for trash are becoming larger due to the need to separate types of trash to enable recycling. This may require compactors or Dumpsters for paper, plastic, glass, and metal as well as trash in two additional categories: wet or food based which may require refrigeration or daily removal, and mixed trash, which is trash that cannot be recycled. Count them up: there could be six containers behind your museum.

- Back corridors leading off a loading dock should be ten feet wide to be used for temporary holding of deliveries or items like forklifts, pallet jacks, or rolling ladders. Check with your local fire marshal regarding tolerance for the use of this type of space in terms of clear paths to exits and combustibility of what may be sitting in a corridor.
- Near your loading area, provide secure dirty holding areas and decontamination equipment (treatment tents or freezers) to manage infested collections as well as a clean holding area for collections which have been treated.
- Provide a space for collections processing and inspection near the loading area. This area must include a place to open crates, locked storage for tools and photography equipment, and task lighting for conditions assessments. Make sure this room is environmentally conditioned for collections and adjacent to a secure collections holding area. Crate storage is always undersize, no matter how large.
- Location of your fire/emergency command center should be coordinated with first responders as well as a security consultant to ensure the location itself is secure.

SITE AND ROOM DEFINITION SHEETS (RDS): APPLYING CRITERIA TO EACH SPACE

Many experienced museum design teams use room definition sheets as a way of developing a more in-depth project scope well in advance of design. Room definition sheets are developed for each site feature and every room as a way of capturing all the criteria of those spaces.

There are numerous reasons to develop room definition sheets:

- Scope definition. If properly developed, the room definition sheet captures every attribute of every space.
- As a basis for pricing, the room definition sheets permit your estimator to perform a quantity takeoff of everything in a space. This forms the basis for the engineers and cost estimator to size and price your project with a high degree of accuracy well ahead of design.
- Room definition sheets form the basis of understanding between the design team and the museum for the project scope. It will truncate the data collection process well before museum stakeholders reach fatigue.

EwingCole

Art Museum
Room Data Sheet

Date: _____
Revisions: _____

	Existing	BOD	Proposed	Notes

Room Data Sheet:
Room Name _____
Room Number/Floor _____

Department:
Primary Use _____
Event Use _____

Responsibility for Signoff:
VP _____ Tel: _____
Staff _____ Tel: _____

Room #
Net SF
Of Staff Occupants
Of Visitor Occupants
Of Event Occupants

Architectural/General:

Notes/Comments

Space
Dimensions:
Min Clear Ceiling Height:
Artifact Containing Space:
Dedicated Storage:
Other:

Finishes
Wall Finish:
Ceiling Finish:
Floor Finish:
Base Finish:
Window Treatment:

Doors
Clear Door Dimensions:
Special Entrance Doors:
Folding Partitions:
Locking Requirements:

Accoustical Requirements
Conferencing:
Sound Control/NC Rating

Built-In Millwork
Base & Wall Cabinet & Top: _____ LF _____ PLAM _____ WD _____ HT
Shelving: _____ LF _____ PLAM _____ WD
WD Paneling: _____ SF

Special Conditions
Special Loading - Floor:
Special Loading - Ceiling:
Special Wall Ratings:

Special Equipment Needs
Laboratory Needs:
Mobile Equipment Needs:
Special Event Equipment:
Note: See Attached Equipment List.

FIGURE 7.2
Room Definition Sheet

- As a reference book room definition sheets link needs, attributes and budgets so all stakeholders understand what is in the project scope during design for the museum leadership, staff, design team, and construction team.

It is highly recommended that preliminary room definition sheets should be developed in predesign, with final room definition sheets at the completion of the conceptual design phase. At a minimum include:

- Name and room number
- Programmatic uses including occupancy (your engineer needs to know a party for 250 may occur in a lobby typically serving 100)
- Staff responsible and place for signoff (critical for ownership and scope control)
- Spatial attributes such as area and height
- Finishes
- Doors, locks, window treatments
- HVAC system criteria, including redundancy
- Power and data connections
- Lighting and dimming systems
- IT and AV requirements
- Security systems
- Equipment and furniture needed, with cost responsibility matrix

FUNCTIONAL RELATIONSHIPS: HOW TO ORGANIZE YOUR SPACES

Adjacency diagrams, often called blocking and stacking diagrams, are abstracted plans showing adjacencies of your primary function spaces on each floor to help you understand the amount of space needed on each floor and how spaces work together from a functional and circulation perspective. The diagrams should use color blocks which relate to use and should be keyed to indicate the presence (or absence) of collections. These diagrams should also relate to the site itself and indicate points of access, parking, and program areas, as well as undeveloped zones. Anticipating the future, show where the building is likely to expand to ensure future galleries, venues, collections storage, or support spaces work diagrammatically.

Your blocking and stacking plan should have an overlay of circulation, each color coded based on three patterns of movement:

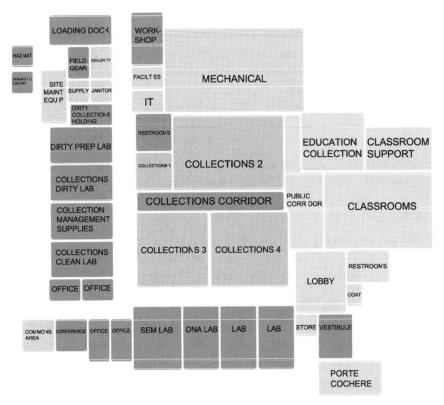

FIGURE 7.3
Blocking and Adjacency Diagram

- Visitor flow, from off-site to the front door, whether pedestrian, car, or bus. From that point, diagram movement of family and groups through the museum public spaces, looking for areas of decision to ensure their clarity.
- Collections flow, both clean and dirty, from loading dock through collections management and research suites, storage areas into exhibit areas.
- Food and catering supplies in and out of the facility, checking areas which cross paths of travel with collections and the public.

Develop two additional sets of overlays: zones of security with points of access and control, and zoning of building mechanical systems to ensure a cost-effective solution has been developed. This process has a tendency to "read like a building," but you should make sure that during the predesign phase you do not get engaged in giving form to a specific design.

PHASING OR CLOSING DOWN: SEQUENCE OF IMPLEMENTATION

Whether new, expansion, or renovation, your building project may require phasing if you are planning substantial renovations and do not plan to close your facility, or the availability of financial resources requires phased implementation.

As you see in figure 7.4, the Philadelphia Museum of Art started construction of the two wings to its neoclassical building without the central pavilion that connects them with the goal of "shaming" the local community into finishing the building. (This was, by the way, a successful strategy.) Phasing is easier said than done: implicit is a prolonged construction process which will impact the public perception of your being a desirable destination and your daily operations in many ways. Unless you are constructing a new building well away from your current facility or are creating an addition which can be

FIGURE 7.4
Philadelphia Museum of Art Construction Photograph. Used by Permission from PMA. PMA Construction photograph scrapbook 1, photograph 201. Photograph by William R. Hellerman.

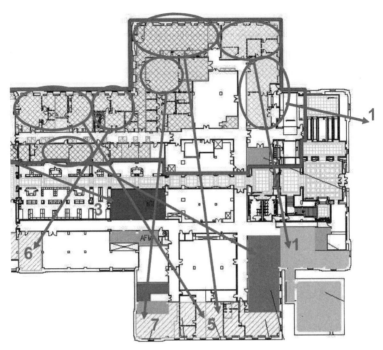

FIGURE 7.5
Phasing Diagram

safely constructed while you are open, phasing must be as carefully designed as the building itself. Even with an addition, you will be doing some work in your existing facility to tie them together.

Phasing diagrams consist of plans which show the sequence of construction and departmental moves needed to complete your building project. Unless you are adding new space, swing space will be needed off-site or in trailers to house functions displaced for construction. Make sure you coordinate your phasing plans with a detailed schedule for each move, and a cost management plan identifying the additional costs associated with swing space, moving, downtime, and the reinstallation of exhibits, furnishings, and staff workspaces.

Since you will, in effect, be finishing the same building as a series of projects over a longer time frame, cost inflation and additional general conditions (construction team operating costs) must be identified and budgeted. Recognize that phasing may not be based on your programmatic priorities, donor goals, or need to show the public that your renewal is under way:

- A new-building HVAC system central plant or fire protection system may force you to start with a central plant and infrastructure backbone as part of the first project. This is a tough donor sell and hardly going to generate excitement in your community.
- The area of the building covered by a particular air handler may determine the blocks of space which are renovated in each phase.
- If you are not planning to close, maintaining operations and keeping yourself in the public eye must be planned carefully and coordinated with your communication strategy and financial forecasting to allow for a drop in attendance and revenue. While there is no rule of thumb, don't close too much public space at a time or visitors will feel you are only partially open. More on closing or maintaining operations is included in chapter 11.
- Available cash may determine the size of each phase of work.
- The use of an addition as swing space may mean it is completed first but not occupied for its ultimate use until your project is completed.
- Access to your facility during construction may influence the location of the addition or sequence of construction.

If you need to rent swing space, you may find donated space in another institution, or empty space or in a building owned by a museum supporter. Functions that typically are prime candidates for moving into swing space do not involve moving collections: administrative support offices, library or research spaces, institutional storage, and collections furniture storage or exhibit workshops. Collections storage including collections management and conservation functions will of course be more difficult to house with their need for more exacting environmental conditions (see article by Martha Morris in the bibliography).

FINISHING YOUR BASIS OF DESIGN REPORT

The last two sections of the basis of design report include the estimate of probable cost and schedule which are covered in chapter 6. When you complete your predesign basis of design report, you may have several hundred pages of information. Even if some factors change, all of it will be usable through the design process. You will know a lot about your future building without having drawn an architectural plan or elevation. In fact, there is a use for the basis of design report which has not been discussed: a detailed cost estimate. When a cost estimator is "taking off" a building, he or she is performing what's called a quantity takeoff, tallying areas, finishes in those areas, quantities of outlets, and so on. Your room definition sheets and the information you have developed provide enough information to help develop a detailed estimate.

While there is much more to be done, consider this predesign effort a good investment of your time and money. You would need to know this information sooner or later, but now you have it ready to use moving into the design phases. This book will not go into depth describing the subsequent phases of design in detail. There are other excellent guides for the nuts and bolts of design and construction process in the bibliography. Your project manager and design and construction teams should be executing those tasks as a matter of professional practice.

DESIGN PHASES WORK PRODUCTS

Design moves from diagrams and narratives into giving form to a building. Using your basis of design report as a guide, you have a great deal of information developed, whether you are just hiring the architect or used an architect to develop the basis of design report and are continuing with the same team based on a good working relationship and the confidence that you have developed over the past few months. Pay the same attention and take the same level of care over the next few phases, in particular during conceptual design and schematic design phases, when your design teams will be taking the *basis of design* and turning it *into a design.*

Schematic design and design development phases. As previously discussed, these design phases represent the realization of 60 percent of the project documentation as you and your design team develop the details of your building in the documents. As details are developed, continue to be engaged, although the intensity of your input will lessen. Review the design team's work at the end of each phase as discussed in chapter 6.

Contract (or Construction) Documentation Phase

As you move into the final documentation phase, focus your design input toward final selection of materials and on the general conditions (which define your relationship with the construction team). Construction documents (drawings and specifications) are often called contract documents. They are the basis for a legal contract between the museum and a construction team for the scope of what will be built, under what terms, and at what cost. They are the final work product of the design team.

The final documents consist of two components: drawings and specifications. The drawings are organized by a numbering system coded by design discipline (A for architecture, C for Civil, etc.). Specifications are the second work product of the design team. Think of the specifications as the project manual that clarifies what is in the drawings, what materials go in your building, how they are to be installed, and the terms of engagement with the construction team to perform the work. Each specification division follows a standard three-part format edited to your project requirements by the design team. If you have not been through the construction process, the specification book(s), which can run to 1,500 pages or more for a moderate size project, may appear to be only the design professional's responsibility, with little need for input from you. But taking this approach is not a good idea. If you are familiar with the specifications from an exhibit design project, then you are familiar with specifications, but for major construction projects there are significant differences. For exhibit installations, there is limited scope and exhibit fabricators already understand the complexities of working within a museum. Your general contractor or his field superintendent may not have the same understanding. You are not expected to be the expert in specifications, but as with the drawings, you must expect to work with the design team to make your requirements known. The rest of this section is focused on listing the issues where your input is most critical.

There are two parts to the specifications:

- General conditions contained in Division 1, which sets the terms of your relationship with the construction team: project procedures, scope, schedule, cash flow, and other contractual requirements. As a rule of thumb, the costs for general conditions are approximately 15 percent of total project costs for a new building. These costs can increase to 25 percent if the contractor is working inside your building while you are open and you, of course, are placing restrictions on construction activity. Carefully balance these restrictions with the understanding that your goal is to balance your operational needs.

- Materials specifications contained in Divisions 2–49, which focus on the choice of materials, building assemblies, and equipment with information on quality and how they are installed in your building. While these are the bulk of the specifications and are highly technical, your input will be focused primarily to ensure continuity of systems you may already have (hardware or valves for instance) rather than technical oversight.

An excellent white paper has been produced by the Construction Specifications Institute.[10] It describes how standards have been adopted across the construction industry to help find common language to ensure these conditions are met. You should try to understand how a museum's specifications differ from those of an office building, which may be the last building your construction team completed prior to starting yours.

Up to 25 percent of your construction team costs are the costs of Division 1 requirements, so waiving these requirements is not in your best interest, but some construction teams will attempt to skip procedures to save money or time.

Division 1 Issues to Review

- The project construction schedule can be stipulated in terms of months and is provided in order to enable the museum to plan dates for installation of exhibits, hire and train staff, and meet the opening date you gave your community. Build float time in your project schedule to provide a cushion for unforeseen construction conditions, delivery delays, and labor shortages to ensure timely opening. Do not be tempted to compress your own schedule, since you will discover that exhibit fabricators delays and getting the bugs out of your IT system may take more time than expected. At worst, you will have additional time to train staff and have a longer soft opening so that your new building is really ready for the grand opening.
- There are options to incentivize the construction team with an early completion bonus or late penalty charge. However, a smart construction team (and most of them are) will be much better at justifying delays leading to late completion than an owner will be about holding the construction team's feet to the fire. Early recognition of schedule slippage and pressing the construction team for a recovery plan and schedule update is better than relying on any penalties or bonuses.
- Clarify who furnishes and installs a wide variety of museum equipment and exhibits. In most contracts, for a variety of reasons, not all work is supplied

by and installed by the construction team. For this reason, you should create a responsibility matrix which clearly defines design, procurement installation, and coordination responsibility. These items include:

a. The track for exhibit lighting but not track heads.

b. Donor recognition signage.

c. Furniture, including visitor, lobby, and office furniture.

d. Specialized environmentally conditioned exhibit casework.

e. Ticketing systems and point of sale systems software and hardware.

f. Collections storage cabinets or compactors. Compactor rails are sometimes supplied by owner, set by the construction team which often subcontracts this work back to the museum's preferred compactor manufacturer.

g. IT servers, racks, and final connections in the server room.

h. Terminal devices for interactives and final connection of interactives.

i. Exhibits and exhibit signage.

j. Security system installation.

- Terms of payment to contractor

a. The schedule of values for analysis of the application for payment.

b. Applications for payments are monthly requisitions for payment.

c. Retainage is the money held back by the museum (usually 5 to 10 percent to ensure the contractor completes the work).

d. Closeout terms for final payment.

- Contract modification procedures (there will be changes in the base contract due to any number of issues)

a. Owner-initiated changes, including your decision to increase project scope or eliminate certain work.

b. Unforeseen field conditions, which can include everything from finding rock underground to pipes inside the wall of your existing building.

c. Omissions in scope or errors in the technical aspects of the contract documents.

d. Construction team–initiated schedule changes, substitutions of materials, or scope gaps.

These changes sometimes begin as a request for information (RFI) which is initiated on a standard form by the construction team to the design team to clarify work scope or intent of drawings and specifications or a field report observation. The design team's response may identify a change in work scope, which may or may not have any impact on cost or schedule. The museum project manager will then be notified in writing by the construction team that there is a potential cost event (or potential change order or any one of a number of other names). These are tracked on a log which should be reviewed at the regularly scheduled project weekly job meeting. These changes are the reason for you to carry a construction contingency.

The procedure you follow is critical to maintaining control over the process. All changes, no matter how small, must have a paper trail with a description of the issue, a reply by the design team, a cost and time proposal by the construction team, an evaluation by the design team and museum project manager, with a final negotiation and written acceptance by your CFO or the museum project manager. Except in extraordinary cases, there is no reason to skip any of this process. Your construction team may claim this process is delaying the work but your weekly or biweekly construction meetings are the best forum to address and work toward resolution on issues like this. For the most part, only at certain points of construction or at the very end of the project will time be so critical that work cannot be shifted to another project area as the issue is being resolved. However, this approach may result in out of sequence work, so timely decisions and prompt paperwork form the best approach.

- Coordination drawings are specified to require that the construction team and all subcontractors produce a single drawing with layers showing the location of all building systems (mechanical, plumbing, roof drains, power, data, sprinklers, and lighting), to ensure they fit within the zone between structure and the finished ceiling. Remember, the fabrication of ductwork may deviate slightly from the design drawings, and that deviation may lead to problems in the field. Keep the requirement for coordination drawings. It will help ensure problems are identified before fabrication and long before installation when the cost or schedule impact will be greater. Simply by going through the process, the subcontractors interact and are more likely to work well together in the field. The advent of building information management (BIM) documentation methodology may help the contractor with this final field coordination, but not totally replace it.

- Site use by the construction team is critical if you occupy your site/building while construction is taking place within or adjacent to your current building.

a. Construction team behavior on-site is significantly less an issue now than when the ethos could be sexist and racist. However, strong, unequivocal language about respecting your visitors and staff with a zero tolerance policy makes your expectations clear to the construction team. Other behavior outlined should address appropriate clothing, eating inside the building, and smoking on-site.

b. Security procedures must be developed or reviewed by your security staff and/or insurance carriers if your project is on an occupied site. Among issues to be outlined are:

   i. Clearance requirements for construction workers, including advance notice for your security clearance process

   ii. Responsibility for the cost of overtime for your security staff for work initiated by the contractor

   iii. Screening and scheduling of incoming deliveries

   iv. Protection of on-site collections, including collections left in-place in galleries

c. Cleanup on a daily basis.

d. Protecting your existing building and site from damage during construction.

e. Early turnover dates and occupancy of specific spaces.

f. Noise and vibration.

g. Construction tours by dignitaries and donors.

h. Use of utilities on your meter.

i. Restrictions on access to portions site and building.

j. Hours of construction activity at particular times of day including special events (2 days around your gala, for instance).

k. Use of your loading dock where activity may impact access, screening, and elevator use.

l. Temporary use of restrooms or museum facilities.

m. Holidays observed by the museum not necessarily observed by the construction team.

n. Photo documentation and notation of your building and site of existing conditions (cracked sidewalks, stained marble floor in your lobby) prior to the construction team taking possession will ensure clear understanding at construction closeout of responsibility for repair of damage that occurs during construction. Ongoing photography of construction before walls are closed up will document where the plumbing or electrical wiring was routed and will allow future design and construction teams to know what is inside the walls they may want to remove or change.

o. Salvage of materials. If you have an existing building, particularly a historic structure, an alteration may produce salvageable materials which could be useful for future repairs, particularly stone or historic doors and hardware.

Divisions 2–49 to Review

Through the design process you have been involved in the selection and discussions about the quality of many finish materials. Since thousands of other less glamorous materials will be specified, review of these materials for toxicity and impact of off-gassing by an industrial hygienist or conservator will enable you to understand their potential effect on your visitors, staff, and collections. Material safety data sheets (MSDS) are manufacturer-supplied sheets for virtually all construction materials and the mastic or glue to install them. The advent of green design or sustainable design is improving manufacturers' awareness of these issues, but there is still a long way to go toward improving these issues with all materials.

IN SUMMARY

You are now ready to bid your project. Information covered in chapter 6 outlines what you need to know to go to the marketplace to procure construction contracts to get your building in the ground and built. In the next chapter, you will learn about managing your financial health throughout the process of planning, designing, constructing, and start-up operations of your new facility.

NOTES

1. HOK Group, William A. Pena, and Stephen A. Parshall, *Problem Seeking: An Architectural Programming Prime,* 4th ed. (New York: Wiley, 2001).

2. Winston Churchill, quoted in James C. Humes, *The Wit and Wisdom of Winston Churchill* (New York: HarperCollins, 1995).

3. NFPA 909, Code for the Protection of Cultural Resource Properties: Museums, Libraries, and Places of Worship.

4. Walter L. Crimm, "Trends in Design of the Best Temporary Exhibit Spaces: Results of a Benchmarking Study" (unpublished benchmarking study presented at Association of Science Technology Centers Annual Meeting, Los Angeles, California, October 2007).

5. "LEED Rating Systems," a third-party certification sustainability sponsored by the U.S. Green Building Council, 2008, www.usgbc.org/DisplayPage.aspx?CategoryID =19 (accessed May 5, 2008).

6. "Information on the EnergyStar program Sponsored by the U.S. Environmental Protection Agency," 2008, www.EnergyStar™.gov (accessed May 5, 2008).

7. "Building Owners and Managers Association," which has information on standards of how space is calculate for commercial buildings, 2008, /www.boma.org (accessed May 5, 2008).

8. Gail Dexter Lord and Barry Lord, eds., *The Manual of Museum Planning*, 2nd ed. (Walnut Creek, CA: AltaMira, 2000).

9. "Sustainability: How Does Using the Revolving Door Save Energy?" 2007, www.sustainability.mit.edu/Revolving_Door (accessed May 5, 2008).

10. Charles E. Gulledge III et al., *MasterFormat 2004 Edition: 2007 Implementation Assessment* (Canada: Construction Specifications Institute and Construction Specifications Canada, 2004).

Financial Planning and Cost Management

The purpose of this chapter is to identify the requirements for a financially successful building project and how to meet them. It will elaborate on the importance of a sound business plan and how to ensure its success; the role and responsibilities of the financial or business officer; the elements of total project costs; and the resources and tools needed to plan for, secure, and manage project financing, including developing and implementing budgets.

This book mentions many types of studies and plans. All are important, and none are discrete from one another. Each study or plan grows out of the museum's strategic plan—its mission, its vision and direction for the future, and a set of goals for attaining the vision. Each study or plan informs the museum about specific aspects of the tasks leading up to the project and each builds on information gathered in earlier or parallel studies and plans. The first section of this chapter focuses on the business plan, a tool flowing directly from the strategic plan that frames how the museum should think about and present its project to potential funders and partners.

IMPORTANCE OF A BUSINESS PLAN

Given the intense competition for the public's leisure time and for donor, government, and granting agency dollars, museums can no longer assume that visitors will come when they open their doors nor donors write checks when asked. In order to position themselves, museums have begun to adopt business practices once thought applicable only to the private sector, becoming more entrepreneurial in seeking new sources of income, new partnerships, new offerings, and a new way of thinking about their constituents as customers.[1] A business plan based on the museum's strategic plan is a key tool for entering the world of nonprofit enterprise.[2] While not every museum chooses to develop a business plan, in today's competitive environment more and more funders expect them; they are becoming not only commonplace but obligatory. Even if a museum does not have a current project requiring funding, it needs to demonstrate a readiness and capacity for action. Rather like having a current résumé at hand, the museum should be able to spring to action with its credentials when opportunities arise. Thus a museum should always have a good business plan, validated on a regular basis by looking back at targets set and milestones reached, and updated annually with new targets to maintain currency and vibrancy.

How Business Plans Add Value

A well-developed business plan provides value in a number of ways:[3]

- *Attracts investment.* Museums need to demonstrate to foundations, corporate sponsors, potential business partners, individual donors, and their own trustees that they have well thought out plans and the capacity to deliver with the resources they are requesting. A business plan bridges the language divide between the nonprofit and for-profit worlds and showcases the museum's team, its ideas, and its programs.
- *Identifies risks and checks the feasibility of the venture.* Few museum players in a building project are likely to have had experience in renovating or building a museum. The business planning process calls for thorough, research-based analysis similar to the SWOT (strengths, weaknesses, opportunities, and threats) analysis frequently used in a strategic planning process to uncover information about competition, expose vulnerabilities within the museum organization, and ferret out potential opportunities for collaborations, niche initiatives, and the like. It can also inform the project design process by assisting museums in weighing opportunity costs among design choices, such as building exhibit versus events space.
- *Measures outcomes.* The business plan focuses on the strategic goals of the project with clear targets and pathways for successful project implementa-

tion. Donors and other supporters can track the museum's performance on the project.

- *Builds alliances.* The business planning process can tease out the potential and build the case for benefits of strategic partnerships with other organizations.
- *Supports critical thinking.* With staff often caught up in the day-to-day activities, developing a business plan forces the museum to engage in self-reflection and objective analysis and to ask and answer key questions about its ability to accomplish strategic goals.

Museums should undertake business plans not only for the product but for the process itself, for the latter helps to clarify mission and vision, provides a reality check for the museum's aspirations, offers insights into the museum's competitive markets, motivates and becomes a rallying point for staff and other stakeholders. It may also serve as a vehicle for restructuring or even repositioning the organization. Similar to capital campaigns, a business plan can be modest or complex. If you are hesitant about a comprehensive business plan, start with a small initiative to test the business model, and get the practice and experience before undertaking a larger plan.

DEVELOPING YOUR BUSINESS PLAN

Where to begin? As noted earlier, a museum should have a business plan, based on its strategic plan, at the ready. If that is not the case and you are considering a building project, the leadership team must make the commitment to undertake the business plan. This is not the time for lengthy discussion of tactics. It is the time for strategic thinking and action, to demonstrate an entrepreneurial nature, to rise above the daily grind and work toward a vision that positions the museum to attract and engage its customers—visitors and supporters.

Think of all the procedures you use in a strategic planning process, starting with, "Do I need a consultant?" And you probably do need, if not a consultant, a small group of experienced stakeholders who can serve as advisers or mentors throughout the process. Board members or longtime supporters or even volunteers with experience in business planning may be able to serve in this role. Corporate board members may be willing to lend staff from their business planning and marketing divisions to get you started. Graduate students may assist in data collection and analysis or someone on the business school faculty of a local university may advise you. Make sure it is still your plan, however, and if you are adventurous, there are dozens of tools, starting with the Small Business Administration, which has a host of online tools, including tutorials and sample plans. There are also inexpensive software packages such as Bulletproof Bizplan and Biz Plan Pro that can guide you through the process.[4]

Review all of your other plans, particularly your strategic plan, for useful data. If you have been assessed recently in an American Association of Museums (AAM) accrediting process, materials developed for that activity will be useful. Unlike a strategic plan, the business plan is a plan of action to mobilize the resources of others. It must compel them to invest in you. Its focus is entrepreneurial rather than organizational, financial rather than programmatic, and it uses for-profit terminology such as "market" and "customers."[5] While it builds on your strategic plan, it is tightly focused, and the broad spectrum of stakeholders who are engaged in the business plan development must be able to rise above the particulars of daily and short-term operational thinking. The museum director must commit to being a change agent who cannot be limited by current resources. At the same time, the process must include regular communications with other stakeholders, keeping them abreast of what is happening and inviting them to contribute ideas and data. Once the plan is complete, it needs to be operationalized so that it becomes an integral part of doing business, that is, the museum applies organizational resources to enhance the museum's position vis-à-vis its competition and improves services by thinking of audiences as customers to be served.

Who Is the Audience for the Business Plan?

Think of the business plan as a loose-leaf document with chapters that can be deleted or moved around, depending on the audience. While the plan is comprehensive, the audience is broad: individual, corporate and foundation donors, investors, lenders, vendors, partners, the board, volunteers, local and state government officials, staff, and the community. Some will be more interested in your building, some in the programs inside the building, some in your financial position. Do research on their interests. You should be able to tailor a message quickly by pulling together only those sections relevant to your specific audience.

What Are the Components of a Business Plan?

The business plan begins with an executive summary, which you don't write until you have finished the business plan and can distill it to its essence. A standalone document, it should be in a capsule form that allows someone who needs to know to make a decision. It may be the only piece of the plan a potential supporter reads, so it must make clear the relationship between the museum's purpose and the project or venture as well as its capacity to deliver. In short, it must both capture the imagination and convince the hard-headed business side of a supporter. The executive summary answers a series of questions:

- What do you do?
- Who are your customers?
- What are your programs?
- Who is your team?
- Where are you located and how do you operate?
- How does the proposed plan support your mission?
- What are your projections?
- How much money do you need, for what, and how will you repay if you borrow?

While museums may differ in the focus and structure of their business plans, they must cover information summarized below. For convenience, suggested chapters of a business plan might include the following:

The enterprise. This section, chapter 1 in your business plan, provides the demographics: the museum's purpose, its history, its legal foundations, where it is located, its facilities, the nature of its collections, baseline data such as staff size and attendance, and a profile of its programs. It identifies where the museum ranks among its competitors, some indicators of success, what makes it unique, separating it from the pack. This section also includes a summary of the strategic plan and other pertinent plans, as well as the scope of the business plan.

Management team and organization. This section of the plan describes the functional organization; areas of expertise relevant to the project, including the expertise of the board of trustees; information systems; compensation packages; any liability issues. This is also the area in which the museum separates its business ventures from its nonprofit activities, including spelling

out any differences in compensation packages for staff in each area. This is
the section that showcases the management team—its strengths as a team,
its demonstrated accomplishments, its management skills, and its confidence in the future. If a donor or lender dips into the plan beyond the executive summary, this and the following section are the two he or she is most
likely to read.

Programs and services. In a for-profit business plan, this section would describe products and services. Here it describes the museum's range of programs and services and the major inputs—personnel, financial resources, and
processes—required for each to bring the programs to its constituents/
customers. It also defines how it measures the results of programs and services, comparing them with the programs and services of other organizations,
and its capacity to fulfill the requirements of the project, including how it uses
tools and technologies to accomplish its goals. This section must quantify the
amount, cost, and frequency of use of the resources and tie the descriptions to
the museum's financial reports. It also needs to demonstrate the power and effectiveness of the museum's programs and their delivery.

Market analysis. This section is likely to be unfamiliar territory to many
museums and must be supported with solid market research and analysis to
demonstrate that the decisions of the plan are based on facts. It examines the
competition and how well the museum is doing vis-à-vis its competitors; the
current and projected customers, what they want and need, and strategies to
attract and keep them; pricing and positioning of museum programs and services, including membership benefits offered and a marketing plan for its proposed new initiative, including a budget, an action plan, and how progress will
be monitored.

Strategic alliances. If the aim of the business plan is to attract partners, such
as retail vendors or food and beverage caterers, to participate in the construction project, a section on strategic alliances may be needed. This section
would focus on how the museum plans to create one or more long-lasting,
mutually beneficial relationships. It would address strategies and various scenarios involving product and service mix, costs and pricing, who is responsible for what, the operating plan for the new venture, and measures of success.
For example, where a partner might be a private operator of retail activities in
a new facility, it would address how the two parties in the alliance would share
costs for developing and operating the new space, manage inventory, assess

and respond to the competition, analyze and segment the market, develop and market product and service lines, set prices, control costs, manage cash flows, and share the risks.

Challenges and risks. This section provides a hard-headed, fact-based assessment of major risk areas in the project and strategies to minimize the risks. Real-life examples of risk include the death of a major donor without documented provision for the promised gift or a sharp increase in the cost of borrowing money just as design is nearing completion. The plan should include various scenarios that might occur, milestones, strategies to mitigate major risks—or to exit the project—and clear delineation of how decisions will be reached on overall project scope and cost, on whether to scale back, or whether to abandon the project.

Financial projections. If there is strong interest and support for the project among stakeholders, this section may not be required; do not present it unless asked. However, this section is the one that funding entities will pull out and hand to their accountants, who will not have benefit of any rosy scenarios in other sections of the plan and will look only at the data in front of them. This section must fully document the museum's financial structure and its current financial condition. It must include the following financial reports: the balance sheet (statement of financial position), the income statement, also called statement of profit and loss (P&L) or statement of financial activities, and cash flow statements. These reports are the same as those routinely provided in an annual audit. The section should also include three years of projections of income-generating activities along with their cost estimates. While not as detailed as an operating budget, this chapter should have enough data to give the reader a good idea of how the museum plans to cover start-up, cash flow during the project, and other working capital; equipment and furnishings that are not part of the construction contract; its current and anticipated debt; and its plans to retire debt. Despite the quantitative focus, this section must be both realistic and optimistic, covering aberrations in income and expenses. For example, a reduction in income this year compared to a prior year may be the result of a onetime spike in income created by a blockbuster exhibition, not a downturn this year in normal retail activities or attendance. If benchmarks are available, they can be helpful. Budgeted to actual performance may also demonstrate effective management and good financial controls. Even if this section is never requested or presented, the exercise itself is useful. It is important for the management team and the board to watch the financial situation over the years, tracking fixed and variable costs, following cash flow over time to see when cash comes in, where it comes from, how it is used, and when it is used.

To summarize, a winning business plan must demonstrate with data that the museum has a strong management team, that the constituent market wants its programs and services, and that it has a complete and realistic financial plan. While you can pick and choose among the parts of the plan to show to different audiences, the most important ingredient from among the three above is a strong management team. If a strong team is missing, no amount of positive data will give a lender or donor the confidence to invest in your enterprise.

PLANNING AND MANAGING PROJECT FINANCING

The chief financial officer or business manager is the management staff member responsible for the overall financial health of the museum before and during the construction and after the new space becomes operational. He or she is an integral part of the steering committee and works closely with the director, the museum project manager, and the development officer in the development and implementation of budgets for the construction project, the capital campaign and associated communications plan, and ongoing operations. The chief financial officer supports the steering committee in establishing policies for managing project expenditures, such as authorities for approval of payments or use of contingency funds.

The chief financial officer also plays a major role in developing the business plan and securing capital and operating funds. Ultimately, the chief financial officer has overall responsibility for covering the full cost of the project (the total cost to acquire property if needed, to plan, design, and construct the project, to borrow money, to cover operations during construction, and to open, start up, and operate the completed facility) as well as responsibility for the appropriate use of funds, such as restricted gifts, and in managing cash flow, particularly for the construction project, to ensure there are sufficient income streams to pay the bills on time. He or she must work closely with the development officer to recognize and receive gifts; with financial advisers, legal staff, and public officials to develop the prospectus if funds are borrowed for the project; and with the board of trustees throughout to ensure they understand and are mindful of their fiduciary responsibilities.

Developing Budgets

In addition to the financial statements, particularly cash flow statements, the primary tool for managing a building project and ongoing operations is a budget. The budget is a plan that grows out of the strategic plan and annual plans. It projects the museum's needs, where funds are coming from (sources), and how they will be used (uses). It is also a control mechanism by which the museum can monitor its expenditures against the projections. The chief financial officer works with the project manager in developing and executing the project budget, including use of the design or construction contingency funds and when to engage the steering committee in budget decisions.

For actual management of the budget, the chief financial officer develops two types of budget for the museum's project and for sustaining operations during the project:

- The capital budget covers everything related to the building project: cost of acquisition of land if needed, and the cost of design, construction, and fixed equipment (equipment installed by the construction contractor and considered a permanent part of the facility). While the chief financial officer has ultimate responsibility for overall cost management for the museum, the museum project manager has day-to-day responsibility for monitoring the project budget and making recommendations for changes.
- The operating budget includes the costs of ongoing operations as well as additional costs related to construction that are not part of the capital budget, such as campaign consultants, furniture and supplies for the new space, and contract employees to assist in moving collections.

For accounting purposes, capital and operating budgets are managed separately, but for reporting purposes to the steering committee, the museum will monitor total project costs, which combine capital and project-related aspects of the operating budget. Detailed in figure 8.1, they include

| Hard costs | Preparation of site and infrastructure, construction of the building, fixed equipment and furnishings installed by the construction contractor |
| Soft costs | Fees for consultants, permits, and costs to finance the project |

Program costs   Start-up of new space, such as collections moves, new
                       and reinstalled exhibits

Internal costs   Staff time and expenses to support the project,
                       including the development office and additional
                       consultants such as an outside project manager

Contingency costs   Amount set aside for unplanned events, such as change
                       in scope or program, unforeseen conditions, or code
                       changes that occur after the construction contract is
                       awarded

Endowment   Funds set aside by the board for maintenance and
                       renewal of the new space

OPERATING BUDGET REQUIREMENTS

When a museum undertakes a building project, funds are dedicated to the direct costs of design, construction, and equipping the facility. However, there are other substantial costs that must be funded from the operating budget.

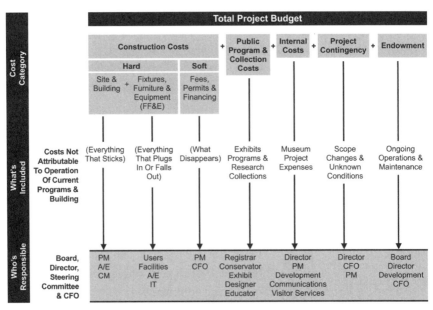

FIGURE 8.1
Total Project Cost Management

Some of these costs are onetime and some will have an impact on the operating budget well into the future, if not forever. All these additional costs over and above normal operating costs must be taken into account when the museum prepares an operating budget when undertaking a building project.

Depending on decisions to remain open or to close, whether the museum borrows to pay for the construction project, and the extent to which contract staff support is used, these additional costs can be extensive, as indicated below.[6]

Before and During Construction

- Cost of borrowing funds, including ongoing debt service on borrowed funds. When a museum opts to borrow funds, whether by issuing a bond, obtaining a bank loan, or turning to a third-party financing mechanism, there are costs for the process and for use of the funds. Just as purchase of a home has closing costs (cost for the process) and interest on the mortgage over and above the amount of the loan, so a museum has borrowing costs for the process (e.g., for financial advisers, bond underwriters, legal advice) as well as for interest to be paid on the loan. Costs to process can be budgeted in the operating budget on a onetime basis, but the interest costs must be included in the operating budget for years to come, depending on the loan period.
- Relocation of staff and/or collections to swing space during construction or protection of staff and collections on-site during construction
- Costs to conserve and move collections during the project
- Communications costs to keep visitors and the community engaged with the museum and its programs during construction
- Alternate program venues outside the museum and/or traveling exhibitions during construction
- Contract staff to assist in collections relocation and care
- Capital campaign start-up and implementation, including consultant assistance, temporary staff, communications tools, including publications and DVDs, and fund-raising events
- Reinstallation of exhibits, including additional contract staff for design and installation
- Opening exhibit installations, including additional contract staff for design and installation
- Costs for fit out of new space not covered in the construction contract, such as for office furniture and equipment

- "Test-driving" new systems and spaces with school and community groups before opening
- Special events for opening
- Staff and volunteer orientation to new space
- Staff training to use new equipment (IT and facility systems)
- Legal fees to review/prepare contract documents for consulting and contractor services
- Added security

After Construction

- Ongoing debt service on borrowed funds, plus repayment of the loan in predetermined increments over an agreed period of time
- New program staff to occupy and use the new space
- Additional maintenance and operations contractor or museum staff, supplies, equipment, and service contracts to care for the additional square footage, additional parking and grounds, and new systems equipment
- Service contracts and staff for delivery of enhanced IT capabilities
- Utility costs for the additional square footage
- Added support costs for additional staff

WHERE CAN WE GET THE MONEY?

Typical Funding Sources for Capital and Operating Budgets

Figures 8.2 and 8.3 display sources of funding for both construction costs (capital) and operations. The most common include:

- *Gifts.* May be restricted by the donor to specific purposes, for example, capital or operating budget purposes. If unrestricted, can be used for purposes determined by the museum management.
- *Appropriated funds.* May fund either operations or capital projects. The appropriated language will specify the purpose for which the funds are intended.
- *Grants.* Generally restricted to a specific purpose, either capital or operating uses.
- *Partnering.* Joint undertakings with other museums or nonprofits or with vendors on projects or endeavors of mutual benefit. Division and use of proceeds will depend on agreement with the partner.

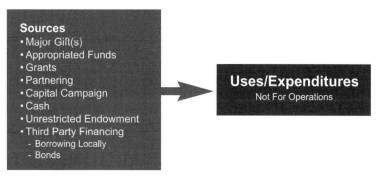

FIGURE 8.2
Project Financing

- *Capital campaign.* Discussed in chapter 9.
- *Borrowing.* Can be for a variety of purposes ranging from a bridge loan to maintain operations and pay the contractor while awaiting arrival of a major gift or grant to a line of credit to smooth out cash flows to direct borrowing or issuance of bonds through a government entity to cover costs of construction.

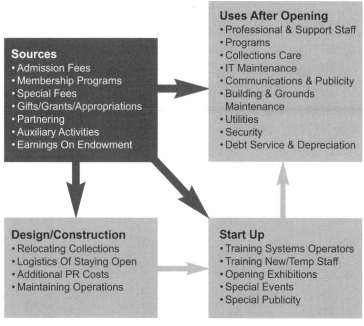

FIGURE 8.3
Sources and Uses of Funds

- *Cash or unrestricted endowment.* Funds with no restrictions on their use except by the board of trustees. In the case of endowment, the board may limit withdrawal to a percentage of earnings only, not of the principal.
- *Membership fees.* For general operating use unless otherwise specified.
- *Admission fees.* For general use unless otherwise specified.
- *Net auxiliary income (rental of space, net retail activities).* For general use unless otherwise specified.
- *Earnings on endowment.* Use depends on donor-specified restrictions.[7]
- *Restricted endowment.* Donor has restricted the use of these funds.
- *Special fees,* such as for use of copyrighted images for general operating use unless otherwise specified.

HOW WILL WE ENSURE GOOD MANAGEMENT OF THE MONEY?

Funds that are borrowed or raised specifically for the capital project—restricted gifts and grants—are to be used specifically for the project, not for operations.

Funds in the operating budget may be used as follows: personnel costs (salaries, wages, benefits), collections care (supplies and materials, rental of storage space), program support (supplies and materials, contractor services, travel), IT maintenance, buildings and grounds maintenance and operations, utilities, security, and depreciation.

Following a general rule of good budgeting, unless a museum has acquired a reserve of funds over and above its regular operating requirements, it should not dedicate income generated from its ongoing activities to a capital project. Typically, capital projects are funded by onetime-only sources dedicated to the construction project, such as from gifts, grants, or borrowing. As part of a borrowing agreement, however, projected new income from fees and memberships as a result of the new space could be pledged to retirement of the debt. Museums must ensure, however, that income generated from the new space should first cover the cost of activities and operations in that space before dedicating any of it to debt retirement. Either the capital or operating budget may be funded by gifts, grants, or appropriations as specified. Depending on the nature of the relationship and transactions, outside partners could be the source for either capital or operating funds.

Appropriate Uses of Funds

At all times, but especially during the period leading up to and immediately following a construction project, the chief financial officer must pay close attention to when funds are received and how they are recognized, or recorded, on the museum's books, as well as for what purposes they are spent.

The chief financial officer must pay particular attention to the following:

Gifts and grants, including donor intent and timing of the gift or grant, when or whether cash is actually received, and how pledges should be received—or written off. At all times the chief financial officer and the development officer must partner on gift recognition matters. From the donor's perspective, the development officer must secure a record of the donor's intent as to use of the gift or grant and keep donors informed of timing of gifts to meet their tax year requirements. Working with the development officer, the chief financial officer must determine when a pledge should be recorded as equivalent to funds in hand and when it should it be written off as uncollectible. The two can examine the history of yield on pledges to determine the best method of projecting an amount to record for gifts expected but not yet received. Together they can determine the likelihood of a gift's arriving in time to meet obligations or whether bridge financing may be required. In all cases the chief financial officer must ensure that funds equivalent to the amount of the gift or grant are spent for the purposes intended and properly accounted for.

Borrowed funds, in addition to requirements for repayment, may have restrictions, such as loan covenants requiring the museum to dedicate certain income streams to retirement of the debt. Funds from the sale of municipal bonds may also be governed by arbitrage rules. Requirements on accounting for and repaying borrowed funds are complex and vary from state to state. Museums should not enter into debt financing without sound legal and financial advice from outside experts, and without being aware of the risks, including restrictions the lender may place on the museum's future income and its management practices.[8]

Management of Cash Flow

Cash flow is the movement of funds into and out of the organization. Tracking the museum's cash flow is an important financial monitoring activity at any time and should be done regularly—annually, monthly, weekly, and in a large operation, daily. The monitoring process also includes reviewing cash flow patterns over time in order to be prepared for seasonal highs and lows or large onetime events. There is ample software available for tracking and for graphical displays, especially useful in tracking seasonal fluctuations. The need for good cash flow management is heightened during periods when large amounts of cash are moving rapidly into and out of the institution. A good record of cash flow history, tight budgetary controls, and regular monitoring will serve to cover current demands and predict and plan to meet future requirements on time.

Prior to the beginning of a building project, the chief financial officer should contractually require and obtain payment schedules from the design team (architects and consultants) and the construction team (CM or general contractor) in order to project cash flow the museum will need to meet obligations to the design and construction teams. Similar agreements and schedules may be necessary for exhibit design, campaign consultant support, and caterers. In addition, during a construction project sufficient cash must be on hand to

- Ensure the museum can meet its ongoing obligations (e.g., payroll, utilities, and contract services).
- Cover large payments in addition to the design and construction teams (e.g., consultants, musicians for opening events, new furnishings not in the construction contract).
- Cover future financing (e.g., long-term debt, short-term credit line, permanent working capital).

The latter two upfront mechanisms allow the museum to smooth out the lumps of in and out flow of cash.

IN SUMMARY
This chapter sets forth the requirements for a financially successful project. It offers a primer on preparing a business plan and the tools for sound financial management before, during, and after the project and suggests vehicles for project funding. Careful planning and execution of the financial management process is essential for project success, requiring oversight, courage, and engagement of museum leadership at all key decision points.

Do's and Don't's
- Include the chief financial officer in all major planning decisions throughout the project.
- Don't overwhelm potential partners, lenders, or funders with your business plan; make it succinct and compelling.

- Put strong financial management controls and accountabilities in place before the project begins.
- Have risk mitigation strategies in hand before the project begins, and revisit risk scenarios frequently.
- Don't allow the chief financial officer and the development officer to engage in turf battles.
- Seek expert advice when borrowing.

Red Flags
- Changes in scope during design
- Change orders during construction
- Loss of major donor(s) support or slowdown in arrival of pledges
- Major increase in cost to borrow money
- Sharp increase in materials or labor costs

NOTES

1. Douglas McLennan, "Culture Clash: Has the Business Model for Arts Institutions Outlived Its Usefulness?" *Wall Street Journal*, October 8, 2005, 11.

2. In recent years business schools focusing on nonprofit management identify nonprofit organizations that generate earned income as "nonprofit enterprises." See the Yale School of Management Program on Social Enterprise and the Duke University Fuqua School of Business Center for the Advancement of Social Entrepreneurship for extensive coverage of this topic. The Yale-Goldman Sachs Partnership on Nonprofit Ventures has sponsored an annual competition for the best nonprofit business plan since 2003. That activity is now under a new organization, Social Returns, led by the founder of the Yale-Goldman Sachs Partnership on Nonprofit Ventures. See www.socialreturns.org/businesscompetitions.asp (accessed November 24, 2008) for winning business plans.

3. This list draws on material prepared by Ann-Clayton Everett for a presentation by Tom Berger, Ann-Clayton Everett, and Dr. Wharton, "So You Need a Business Plan," at the AAM annual conference in Portland, Oregon, May 22, 2003.

4. See Small Business Administration, www.sba.gov/smallbusinessplanner/index.html (accessed November 24, 2008); *Bulletproof BizPlan* (Denver: DoubleDown Capital Partners), www.bulletproofbizplans.com (accessed April 5, 2008); and *Business Plan Pro* (Eugene, OR: Palo Alto Software), www.paloalto.com (accessed April 19, 2008).

5. Vicki Gillette and Susan Christian, *Planning to Succeed: Preparing a Business Plan for Your Nonprofit Organization* (National Trust for Historic Preservation, 2000).

6. Decisions made during the planning and design stages, such as whether to close or travel exhibits during construction, will determine many of these costs.

7. Distribution of earnings depends on restrictions placed on use by the donor of the endowment and by board endowment spending policy.

8. See Barton Groh, "Timeline on a Mount Vernon Tax-Exempt Bond Offering," presented at the Mid-Atlantic Association of Museums 2008 Building Museums Symposium, illustrates the labyrinth of steps, players, and institutions the museum negotiated and raises important questions that an organization should answer before entering the world of bond financing. Also see Robert Yetman, "Borrowing and Debt," in *Financing Nonprofits: Putting Theory into Practice*, ed. Dennis R. Young (Lanham, MD: AltaMira, 2007).

9

The Capital Campaign

This chapter will consider how to determine a museum's readiness to undertake a fund-raising campaign, primarily for a major building project and related activities, such as costs to reinstall or mount new exhibits for the building's opening, new program offerings and expanded operations, endowments to support ongoing programs, and a restricted endowment for future renovation of the new facility. It will also cover how to plan, organize, and staff the fund-raising effort and how to identify sources of funding other than borrowing, covered previously, and to cultivate and engage sources. Finally, this chapter will address ethical considerations with respect to donors and how to present naming opportunities.

Few museums can rely solely on a generous donor or state appropriations to fund a major construction project. Nor can many museums accumulate sufficient reserves for such an endeavor. Almost all of you will seek outside funding in the form of gifts, grants, appropriations, and borrowing. Pursuit of multiple funding sources requires careful planning and close coordination among key players. Almost all museums undertaking a major construction project will develop a capital campaign based on a carefully planned strategy to identify and cultivate partners, matching donors with project goals to maximize gathering funds from all available sources.

THE FEASIBILITY STUDY

When you are in the early stages of developing a major construction project, you should undertake a feasibility study to determine the museum's readiness and its capacity to undertake a capital campaign. The steering committee should hire a proven, impartial consultant, preferably one who knows and understands the museum, to undertake the feasibility study of its community, purpose, programs, audiences, and current supporters. Additionally, the consultant must understand the donor base in the museum's sphere of influence: who the major givers are, what other organizations they support, how much they give to other organizations, how much other organizations are raising from donors, and which donors can bring other donors to the table. The feasibility study is a delicate undertaking, and you should choose the consultant with great care.

The feasibility study employs techniques similar to the SWOT (strengths, weaknesses, opportunities, and threats) analysis used in strategic planning. The study looks externally and internally with a twofold purpose: to determine whether there is sufficient donor support in the community, and whether the museum has (or can build) the capacity to undertake a capital campaign.

The consultant will conduct research on philanthropic support in the community from annual reports of nonprofit organizations and corporations, interviews, and media announcements and accounts of major gifts. That research will be followed by confidential interviews with members of the museum's board of trustees, community members of influence, current major supporters, and potential individual and corporate donors. Interviews will focus on how well donors and potential donors understand the museum's mission and its programs, how they view the museum as a community asset, whether they think the museum can conduct a major campaign, and whether they would be willing to make a major contribution. Other questions may probe in depth: How often do you visit the museum? Is the director well thought of in the community? Is the museum making a difference? What is the most important part of the museum's collections? How could the museum improve its offerings? Does the museum have a strong board? Current contributors are queried about their willingness to increase their giving levels, and board members are asked to indicate their level of commitment to make major gifts and to solicit gifts from others. Much of the value of the study depends on the experience and judgment of the consultant in analyzing the body of subjective information from the interviews and the trust he or she can command in the interviews.

The consultant must also weigh another external factor: whether the giving community has temporarily "given out." A decade or two ago capital campaigns were rare; only in major metropolitan areas would more than one be launched at the same time. Publicly supported institutions seldom engaged in fund-raising; nonprofits typically relied on membership drives, annual giving, and gifts from their boards or a few major supporters. Today, museums face stiff competition for all donor dollars—gifts or grants. Hospitals, public and private universities, community-based organizations, and museums have become increasingly sophisticated fund-raisers: more and more of them are mounting major campaigns with heretofore undreamed of targets. And they are all casting their nets in the same donor pool. A new leader of today's large nonprofits knows that a campaign early in his or her tenure is a given expectation of the board. Thus the consultant for the museum's feasibility study must factor the timing of competing capital campaigns into the analysis of a museum's readiness to undertake a campaign.

The companion piece to the external analysis portion of the feasibility study is an examination of the museum's ability to develop, run, and sustain a campaign throughout the life of the project and perhaps beyond. Is there paid staff or a strong volunteer cohort, including trustees, who are prepared and committed to conduct the campaign and related activities? Experienced development staff members are in great demand, especially in urban areas where several organizations may be engaged in capital campaigns. Do the director, staff, or trustees have experience in asking for major gifts? Does the museum's membership program have a good track record? Is annual giving strong and steadily increasing? Has the museum been able to move members to successively higher giving levels in a significant way? How much care and follow-up is given to cultivating major donors? How successful has the museum been in attracting major gifts in the past few years? Does the museum have modern systems and support for donor research, record keeping, and follow-up? Does the museum know how much it spends on donor development and fund-raising? What is its true yield from special events? From direct mailings? Answers to all these and many more related questions will give the consultant the information needed to identify the museum's readiness to undertake a major campaign.

Using data gathered from interviews and other research and analysis, the consultant will weigh several factors and present an assessment to the board and the museum's senior leadership on whether the museum should proceed with campaign planning, recommending measures to mitigate negatives. Factors selected and means of "scoring" will vary, depending on instructions to the consultant at the outset and on an individual consultant's modus operandi.

A feasibility study is far from an exact science. The decision on whether or when to proceed must be made carefully. Together the board and senior leadership must weigh all the factors. If potential donors and persons of influence

Factors	+	-	Actions to Mitigate Negative Scoring
EXTERNAL			
1. Perception of value to community • mission or purpose congruent with community values • programs a credit to the community • programs serve the community • museum well known and respected			• Conduct assessment on reasons for negative perception • Undertake steps to change perception before proceeding
2. Confidence in leadership • Museum trustees and management team strong and creative • Board of trustees respected and viewed as good leaders			• Examine reasons for lack of confidence • Board may need serious self-examination or evaluation of museum's leadership or both
3. Willingness to support			• Further study to determine reasons • Delay or scale back campaign
4. Timing • Other campaigns underway or soon to be launched			• Delay campaign or break into phases
INTERNAL			
5. Staff experience and track record • Museum can identify a select group that could and would likely make significant gifts • Staff has made successful requests for large gifts • Museum has a strong membership program • Museum has successfully moved members to higher levels of giving over time • Staff experienced in managing special events			• Current staff could be trained and/or augmented with experienced contract staff • Special events staff can be augmented with contract staff
6. Supporting infrastructure • Automated systems in place for donor research, tracking of gifts • Past record keeping meets acceptable accounting standards			• Consultant can recommend systems, oversee their selection and installation, or assume responsibility • Consultant can recommend policies, procedures, and best practices for record keeping

FIGURE 9.1

Factors Influencing Whether the Museum Should Undertake a Capital Campaign

in the community support the museum's mission and believe its programs bring credit and make a major contribution to the community, there is a strong likelihood that they will support a campaign. However, if there is little or no community confidence in the board or museum leadership, a consultant would be foolish to recommend proceeding. Some factors can be mitigated by changing schedule or scope of the anticipated campaign. For example, if another major campaign in the community is under way or nearing launch and likely to be targeting the same donor pool as the museum, the museum leadership (the trustees and the senior leadership of the museum) would be well advised either to delay its campaign, perhaps continuing its planning and strengthening its internal support while lengthening the "quiet phase" of the campaign, scaling back the scope, or staging its phases to avoid overlapping with the other campaign in the same donor segment. If the museum is not as well known as its competitors but is otherwise well regarded and has a good record of retaining a small and loyal membership, a campaign can be delayed in favor of a program restructuring and/or a public relations campaign to become better known. There is no easy formula for making this decision. Museum leadership must approach the task with a combination of realism and optimism.

If the consultant has concluded that the museum can garner sufficient support from the community and has the capacity to undertake a campaign, he or she will likely recommend a next step: a plan outlining goals, board members or other strong supporters who could lead a campaign, donor targets by type, and estimates of how much the museum could expect to raise from each, as well as a time line, budget, staff, and support issues that need to be addressed. The plan is likely to be a proposal indicating the services the consultant recommends bringing: expertise—and perhaps staffing—to the effort throughout the life of the campaign. Should the leadership decide to move forward with a campaign, the relationship between the consultant and the museum thereafter will fall on a continuum ranging from ending the relationship after completion of the feasibility study to planning, training of staff and trustees, and oversight by the consultant, to contracting for all campaign activities. The extent of consultant assistance will depend on several factors, including the museum's resources to contract for outside assistance, the availability of staff and volunteers with campaign experience, and the museum's capacity to move forward on it own.

Once the board decides to proceed, many players will be engaged in fund-raising and related activities during the course of the campaign. With their connections to community leaders, public officials, and major donors, board members will assume a strong leadership role in this undertaking. The first critical task for the board is selection of a campaign chair who may be a board member or a well-known supporter of the museum. It is a great honor to be entrusted with such an undertaking, but it is also a great responsibility. Regardless of where the chair comes from, he or she should be well known and highly regarded in the community, a recognized supporter of the museum, experienced with fund-raising, comfortable in a highly visible position, and prepared to make the lead, or largest, gift. Along with the chair, the board will also appoint a campaign committee, either separate from or a subcommittee of the project steering committee, to devote its efforts exclusively to fund-raising, special events, and public relations in support of fund-raising. The committee should include both board members and leading supporters of the museum. Besides the chair, committee members should be among the largest potential donors to the campaign. Similar to expectations of the project steering committee of the board, the campaign committee requires board and other members who are willing to devote time and energy over a long period—perhaps two to three years. They should also be prepared to assume leadership roles in various aspects of the campaign; for example, a well-connected member of the business community could take the lead in soliciting corporate contributions. The committee should begin its work with a charge from the board. The senior museum development officer will staff the campaign committee. In the absence of a museum administrator, the campaign consultant may fill this role. The director will also be an active participant in the committee's work.

Henceforth, the campaign staff must work closely with the architect and the design team as concepts for the building project are being developed. Nothing inspires and galvanizes donors like a rendering of the proposed project. Project details, especially those illustrating added amenities and enhancements to the visitor experience, should be available to the campaign as soon as enough decisions and funding are in place to ensure their delivery.

ETHICS OF GIVING AND RECEIVING

Before beginning a capital campaign, it is incumbent on the board of trustees to ensure that appropriate policies and procedures are in place with regard to sources of support. Some of these policies are procedural and some are more substantive, going to the heart of the museum's values. You and your board should be familiar with the 2000 update of the 1978 Code of Ethics by the American Association of Museums (AAM). It offers guidelines on governance, collections, and programs. Aware of increasingly complex relationships between donors and museums and between businesses and museums as well as increasingly sophisticated development strategies in the nonprofit sector, the AAM has also issued guidelines for developing and managing support from individual donors and businesses. *Guidelines for Museums on Developing and Managing Business Support* (November 2001) and *Guidelines for Museums on Developing and Managing Individual Donor Support* (November 2002) help museums develop policies and practices to address their relationships with businesses and donors respectively. The guidance document on individual donor support, for example, stresses:

> It is essential that each museum draft its own policies, appropriate to is mission and programs, regarding its relationship with individual donors. Policies provide a consistent position that can be articulated by trustees and staff and understood by the public and are vital to a museum's public accountability.[1]

Thus trustees should be sensitive to the appearance of conflicts of interest by trustees or staff when selecting architects and other consultants, and when awarding all contracts. Increasingly, trustees must also be alert to ensuring that donors, individual or businesses, do not exercise control over the content of programs, exhibits, or other museum activities. It should go without saying that museums will also comply with applicable laws governing nonprofits, including lobbying of public officials, and taxable income from unrelated business activities.

Other professional associations have also adopted statements of ethical principles that can also serve as useful guides. Among them are the Association of Art Museum Directors and the Association of Fundraising Professionals.[2] See the website and the Listserv of the Institute of Museum Ethics at Seton Hall University, funded in the fall of 2007 by the Institute for Museum and Library Services, for lively discussions among museum staff members for developing or revising their codes of ethics.[3]

The campaign committee is responsible for developing additional policies, as well as procedures and practices that flow from the board's policies associated with gifts. The committee will develop companion policies that spell out donor and museum obligations: staff behaviors and practices; the nature and timing of payments of gifts; what the donor can expect in the way of naming rights and other forms of donor recognition, length of time, and circumstances under which a name can remain associated with an event or space; museum acknowledgment of receipt of gifts that formalizes the transaction; and timely and accurate reporting by the museum.

Naming Opportunities

Of all the campaign policies and procedures, those associated with naming a building or parts of a building are the most critical. Gifts of any magnitude attract media attention. Both the museum and the donor must be prepared for intense scrutiny and comment. Therefore, before approaching major donors with naming opportunities, museums should have clear and current board-approved policies in place for naming of buildings, parts of buildings, and museum programs. Many publicly supported institutions must adhere to state or local government naming policies which may limit naming to individuals who are no longer living, or to individuals who have been citizens of the state or locality. Many universities now have policies that allow parts of buildings to be named (e.g., classroom, auditorium, or center) after meritorious faculty members while reserving the names of whole buildings for major donors who reach predetermined contribution levels. More and more museums are following suit. Where there are no externally imposed limitations, museums will want clearly defined board policies, including specifying the level of donation for each naming opportunity. For example, attaching a name to a new building may command a donation of several million dollars, while naming an auditorium, only a million or so dollars. When the museum's building project is in the early stages of design and all the major spaces have been identified, naming opportunities for various areas of the facility, excluding the name on the front, should be spelled out in the campaign literature. The museum leadership, campaign committee, and campaign staff, guided by the visibility and/or public impact of a space or program, will determine relative value of each to be presented to donors. The name on the front of the building is likely to have been decided in the early stages, although on occasion a major donor, such as Steven Udvar-Hazy, the major contributor to the Smithsonian's National Air and Space Museum's facility located at Dulles Airport, may appear unexpectedly from initial campaign appeals. The value of the gift associated with the name of the building is a matter of negotiation between the lead donor and the museum, which may take time to conclude.

Naming a building after a founder or an individual who has been the impetus behind the museum and the project's development may present its own challenge. In such cases the board would be wise to spell out donor benefits, including the extent of inclusion in project decision making, well before the campaign begins. Increasingly, organizations are asking donors to include sufficient funds to endow the maintenance and renewal of the named building or space as part of the gift, and donors are responding. No donor wants his or her name on a building that has fallen into disrepair, or chiseled off a facade because another donor will be funding a renovation.

Related Issues

Often the terms and timing of payment are an issue and several family members may be in the discussion. Thus the museum will wish to keep the gift confidential until all the terms are settled with all donors of a specific gift. At the same time, the campaign should have developed clear policies on the purpose for which the gift is intended as well as terms and schedules of pledge payments. It is also essential that the donor and the museum have terms of the agreement thoroughly reviewed by legal counsel. An interesting case occurred at the Smithsonian Institution several years ago when the secretary and a major donor easily came to an agreement on the terms of a generous, but rather unusual, gift that involved a naming opportunity. Both were comfortable with and confident that they understood the terms, but lawyers for both quickly perceived that future generations would need something more substantial in writing to avoid confusion as to the gift's intended purposes. The matter was handled with dispatch and the gift has brought pleasure to millions. Even with the best of intentions, however, there are numerous examples of gift agreements that did not end as happily. Friction between the museum's leadership and donors can occur for a variety of reasons: donors as founders disapprove of a museum's change in course, museums violate tacit donor expectations or formal agreements, donors' fortunes are unexpectedly depleted, and donors change their minds about honoring their pledges. While not all these unfortunate circumstances can be prevented, museums with clear board-approved policies have a much better chance of avoiding these publicly embarrassing, and costly, situations.

Staff and Volunteer Preparation and Support

The campaign committee is also responsible for ensuring that its members, trustees, staff, and volunteers are trained to successfully solicit gifts and well versed in following through with appropriate acknowledgments and record keeping. Training includes a thorough grounding in the above policies as well as in articulating the museum's mission, its vision for the future, the campaign goals, and how the prospect can participate. Who contacts whom must be clear at each phase of the campaign. Within the museum, the director will be heavily engaged and will lead or participate with the campaign chair and/or members of the board in all visits to major individual, foundation, or corporate prospects.

The committee cannot overlook the importance of good record keeping and systems to support the campaign. The donor database is an important tool for maintaining good ongoing relations, as well as for future planning. Accurate recording of gifts and terms of the gifts (e.g., lump sum, paid out over two years) are essential for the museum to remain in good standing as a nonprofit entity. They are also essential for predicting cash flow. There are good commercial software packages available for these purposes, but with today's sophisticated and easy to use applications, only museums with very large donor bases need to go beyond tools already available at little or no cost.

CAMPAIGN PLANNING AND IMPLEMENTATION

The first phase, called the quiet phase of the campaign, is an intensive planning period when the campaign committee along with museum staff and/or consultants drafts a case statement, develops and integrates a campaign communications plan with all other communications planning, develops prospect lists, identifies potential key donors, determines the amount the campaign needs to raise, prepares a budget, undergoes training, develops operational policies, and oversees preparation of campaign materials.

The key output of this period is the case statement—a brief (no more than seven or eight pages), compelling picture of the museum and its needs, its vision and reasons for undertaking the campaign, fund-raising targets for specific elements (bricks and mortar, endowment, exhibits, and other programs), naming opportunities, and the benefits that will flow to the museum and the community from the funds raised. A well-crafted statement should energize the campaign committee and generate excitement and enthusiasm among supporters and potential supporters. If the museum is also undertaking a business plan, many of the arguments for support are similar or the same in both documents. Developing narrative and data can be a shared effort so long as intended audience for each is reflected in the final products.

Communications Planning for Fund-raising and Marketing

All successful fund-raising campaigns have a strong communications component. Case statements, brochures, advertisements, and excellent design and photo documentation underlie these campaigns. Attractive concept drawings and other project-related materials, including digitally animated flythroughs, are strong complements to the case statement. Phrases and images from the case statement will become themes repeated throughout the campaign in its literature, its public presentations, and its public relations efforts. The communications piece is often closely related to the campaign leadership team. Who speaks on behalf of the museum? Which individuals have lent their names to the cause as honorary chairs? Are friends groups involved in serving as advocates or soliciting donations? Communications plans should have key messages, for example, "building civic pride," and short descriptions of goals, convey a sense of urgency (seizing a major opportunity) for the project, and, finally, assure that donors are given proper recognition.

The campaign communications plan should cover the following components: description of key capital improvements, any related program and endowment goals, and who will be responsible for donor development. Especially important also are the appointment of campaign spokespersons and clarification of the relationship of the capital campaign to the annual campaign, as well as delineation of staff and board responsibilities. How will board members be trained for their roles? What kinds of logos and graphic images will be developed? This information must appear consistently in all public materials: brochures, websites, exterior signage, press releases, and advertising. The plan will include a question and answer component that provides information that can be used as talking points in speeches and in meetings with potential donors. A schedule of public events should be developed, including presentations to public gatherings, talks at professional conferences, community service club meetings, and neighborhood association events. The campaign communications plans should also include a time line for implementation and opportunities for celebration of milestones achieved in the campaign.

Prospect Planning

Research about and development of prospects with values congruent with the museum's mission and its goals is an important component of campaign planning. Ideally, long-term relationships will evolve from these encounters and prospects will become sustaining contributors in the museum's future. Prospects seldom show up unannounced, however; nor do many of them have clear ideas about what to support. Campaign plans must lay the groundwork for finding and matching donors to specific campaign goals.

A gift table (figure 9.2), a companion piece to the case statement, is a key aid in prospect planning. It is a working document for the committee and staff that matches project and goals with potential gifts and grants. It expresses the amounts needed for each target area, for example, for design and construction of the building, reinstallation of exhibits, new exhibits, and endowment for building care and future renovations. It then projects the size and number of gifts needed to meet all the targets. Literature about fund-raising makes much of a giving pyramid, in which a small number of donors, appearing at the top of a pyramid, give the largest gifts and a large number of donors forming the base give smaller gifts. Some campaign watchers suggest that the top third of the gifts come from the top ten givers, the next third comes from the next hundred givers, and the remaining third from the small gifts of many. Be aware, however, that the giving community differs from museum to museum. Hence each museum has to determine its strategy by evaluating its own donor pool and its own capacity to attract the large gifts from the few or numerous small gifts from the many. Assuming the pyramid approach, a simple gift table for a $24 million campaign might look something like figure 9.2.

This example illustrates the number of donors needed at various levels to reach the target for the capital project. However, to reach the projected number of donors, the campaign will have to conduct research on and cultivate many more prospects to arrive at the desired number of donors. In a large campaign, the table may be further subdivided into specific parts of the campaign: for construction, endowment, exhibits, and the like. The table is also useful for tracking progress and for staging campaign phases and their implementation. Once the total campaign goals and donor pools are identified, a campaign budget can be developed into stages that match target amounts and dates of each campaign phase.

AMOUNT OF GIFT	NUMBER OF GIFTS	TOTAL
$ 2,000,000	1	$ 2,000,000
$ 1,000,000	3	$ 3,000,000
$ 500,000	6	$ 3,000,000
$ 400,000	5	$ 2,000,000
$ 300,000	5	$ 1,500,000
$ 150,000	10	$ 1,500,000
$ 50,000	40	$ 2,000,000
$ 25,000	40	$ 1,000,000
$ 100 - 24,000	5,000 +	$ 8,000,000
TOTAL...$ 24,000,000		

FIGURE 9.2
Example of a Gift Table

For example, during the quiet phase, only a few prospects will be cultivated. The largest investment will be donor research and time of the campaign chair, the director, and board members. During this quiet phase great care is given to planning the approach to major donors. A thorough understanding of what motivates individual giving provides an important context for conducting prospect research. Extensive research on the museum's prospects, their interests, and their past philanthropic activities will help the museum match its identified needs with donor interests and preferences. The most visible naming opportunities will likely be offered during this phase. Once the lead and other major donors are secured, they will be encouraged to join the campaign and assist in solicitations of their colleagues and acquaintances.

At some point the campaign committee will declare the quiet phase complete. Some sources advise that this should occur when 50 percent of the overall campaign goal has been pledged or reached. Others suggest reaching 80 percent before going public. A museum could also decide that reaching the design and construction goal is sufficient and the remainder of the targets can be met in a successive phase or phases. Each museum must determine for itself when it is ready to declare to the world that it is launching a campaign and has already secured a certain percentage of its total goal. As the campaign moves to a public phase and attention moves down the pyramid, a greater investment will be made in donor research, special events, and campaign materials to attract second- or third-tier givers who for the most part will be well acquainted with the museum. As the campaign moves down the pyramid and away from the museum's most likely candidates, more emphasis will be placed on materials that introduce the museum to the audience, with more direct mailing, more generalized events, phone and web-based solicitations used to explain why the museum is undertaking a campaign, its needs, and its importance to the community. At each successive phase, the campaign committee should announce the successful completion of one phase and the launch of another. Each phase should be celebrated and each new phase should be launched with a recognition event to mark the occasion. All phases must be fully delineated and carefully communicated to the media, to prospects, and to the general public.

As noted earlier, the campaign budget is an important component of the operating budget requirements in support of a capital project. At the same time museums must pay attention to keeping campaign expenses within reason. Donors wish to support programs, not fund-raisers. A rule of thumb is that at least 75 percent of the funds raised should be spent on programs. Several organizations, such as GuideStar and Charity Navigator, monitor nonprofit performance. Their websites are excellent sources for benchmarking and for keeping abreast of emerging philanthropic issues and topics.[4]

SOURCES OF FUNDING

The possibilities for project funding are limited only by a museum's creativity, boldness of strategies, and willingness to do extensive research. However, there is an A-list of types of funders who traditionally constitute the bulk of the resources for museum projects. While an array of fund sources exists, the museum must develop a strategy to prioritize how it will concentrate its resources and efforts, a strategy that seeks sources best aligned with its mission and goals, the funding patterns of its community, and the comfort zone of its leadership.

Board of Trustees

Begin at home! At the outset, members of the board of trustees must make the first commitment. Every member of the board must pledge something as part of the campaign launch and that something should be generous. If potential donors view the board's financial commitment as substantial, they are likely to follow suit. While each museum board will have members who are not individuals of means, they must make some contribution to demonstrate board solidarity and support. They can also assist by soliciting individuals who do have financial resources and by articulating the value of the museum to potential donors.

Longtime Members and Supporters; Other Individuals

A museum that has been preparing for the future will already have a successful annual giving program in place. Supporters who are annual givers have already signed on to the museum's goals. They may need additional encouragement to increase the level of their annual giving, but most can be easily persuaded to make a larger onetime gift to the campaign. Typically, they will raise the level of their annual giving thereafter. The annual giving program is generally the most fruitful source of individuals likely to make significant campaign gifts. The museum can identify other individuals who have not supported the museum in the past but, for reasons uncovered in careful prospect research, may be persuaded to give by the campaign chair, museum director, a longtime supporter, and/or a case statement that captures their imagination and/or resonates with their values.

Local Businesses

Businesses in the community like to be associated with winners. They also recognize that strong cultural institutions attract and hold a talented workforce as well as bring tourists who swell the local economy. A glance at the list of donors in the annual report of any sizable cultural institution illustrates that local businesses are major forces in sustaining them. They are strong candidates for significant onetime gifts as well.

Corporations

Corporations may have established foundations for distribution of grants, may make direct contributions to nonprofits, or contribute in-kind donations of goods or services. Large corporations make a point of contributing to organizations in communities where they have headquarters or major presence. Ever mindful of maintaining the goodwill of the community, they may be counted on for annual sustaining gifts and significant campaign gifts. In some instances, they may be candidates for naming opportunities. There is scarcely a sports arena in the United States now named after a beloved sports figure or local hero. Increasingly the name on the marquee is that of a major corporation. Museums allow corporate names as well, such as the General Motors Hall of Transportation at the Smithsonian National Museum of American History, for buildings, parts of buildings, special exhibits, or programs. The O. Orkin Insect Zoo inside the Smithsonian's National Museum of Natural History is a wry case in point.

Appropriations

Many state and local governments appropriate funds for cultural institutions, whether occasionally or as part of an ongoing program. The nature of such funding, and how it is administered, varies from state to state or locality to locality. Construction funds for cultural institutions regularly creep into federal and state appropriations as earmarks added by legislators for projects in their districts. The U.S. Congress has never hesitated to earmark funds for such purposes. Some museums hire legislative advocates assisting them in securing favorable funding. The periodic reauthorization of the federal highway transportation bill can generate a feeding frenzy by institutions in the know. The most recent reauthorization of the federal highway transportation act, signed by President George W. Bush in August 2005, had over six thousand earmarks for home district projects, with museums, and particularly their surrounding infrastructure, among them. *Regular* appropriations are worth exploring. Earmarks, while interesting to consider, cannot be assured and may get traded away in conference negotiations or removed under threat of a veto. They may invite public rancor if the earmark is only tangentially related to the intended purpose of the appropriation. They also require regular contact and close connections with one's member of Congress or legislator.

Foundations

Many well-known national foundations award grants for programs, exhibits, and other initiatives, but only one, the Michigan-based Kresge Foundation, awards grants for bricks and mortar as a matter of policy. It offers challenge grants for new construction, renovation, purchase of real estate or conservation easements, and major equipment. It has recently begun encouraging challenge grant applicants to consider green construction, signaling an expectation likely to be the wave of the future.[5] Many smaller local family foundations do provide funds for construction, as well as for initiatives and sustaining operations. These local foundations generally have simpler application procedures than larger ones and can respond more quickly to applications.

In general, foundations prefer supporting initiatives such as educational programs or exhibitions rather than ongoing operations, although some local foundations contribute regularly to programs within their communities. Numerous local and national foundations provide support for exhibits and other museum programs and initiatives. The best resource for information about foundations is the Foundation Center, based in New York, with branches in four other cities. With the most comprehensive database on grant makers, it operates research and training programs in its library centers at its five locations and a national network of over three hundred cooperating collections. Many of its resources are also accessible online and are free or available at reasonable prices. Another excellent source is the *Chronicle of Philanthropy* and its website with links to foundations and corporations.[6]

Government Agencies

Most museums are familiar with federal agencies that support museum programs. The Institute of Museum and Library Services, the National Endowment for the Arts, the National Endowment for the Humanities, and the National Science Foundation come immediately to mind. Securing funding from these agencies with regular grant-making programs takes time, planning, and adherence to strict application guidelines. Most state government agencies also have grant programs worth exploring. As a rule, they do not fund construction.

Special Events

Long a staple of fund-raising strategies, special events can range from small, intimate dinners with a guest artist, historian, or scientist to black-tie galas. Their primary purpose is to raise money for the museum and its programs and they are most often tied to a specific activity or event (e.g., opening of a new exhibit, acquisition of a significant addition to the collection, or celebration of a milestone). They also serve other purposes: to attract a variety of individuals, including newcomers, to the museum, provide an opportunity for the museum to showcase or preview its offerings or recognize major supporters, and give the museum favorable media coverage. Those attending leave with good feelings about the museum. On the other hand, special events require a considerable investment of staff time and money to produce. While there is a public expectation that such events will accompany campaigns and openings, museums should conduct a careful cost-benefit analysis before undertaking them.

Business Partnerships

Vendors scheduled to operate one or more business activities by long-term contract within the new facility may fund the cost of construction for build-out of the area they will occupy if the contract is structured to reflect that investment. Food and beverage operations, including catering rights in large museums as well as retail operations, are increasingly taking this approach. There are consultants with expertise in setting up these types of relationships who should work in conjunction with your staff to ensure the quality supports your brand and visitor experience as well as address other vendor obligations that may contribute to visitor experience. It is also an area that should be explored in more depth in the business plan.

IN SUMMARY

Campaigns should not be undertaken lightly. At the same time they can catapult a museum to another level of visibility in the community and onto a higher-level playing field. The old adage about success breeding success is certainly true in fund-raising. Most nonprofits have stories about donors who step up without being approached. New supporters attend fund-raising events and respond to direct mailings. In short, many individuals or organizations are waiting to be asked, but no one has offered a link to something that resonates with them. Donors like to be associated with winners. With proper care and cultivation, they will not only remain as supporters, but will bring other supporters along as well.

Do's and Don'ts

- Conduct a feasibility study early in the process.
- Have clear policies in place for donors and fund-raising staff.
- Select the consultant to conduct the feasibility study with care.
- Undertake cost analysis of major fund-raising strategies.

- Concentrate on fund-raising techniques or strategies with the highest yield for the least amount of time and resources.
- Do not move forward with the project if the feasibility study indicates either the community or the museum is not ready for a capital campaign unless an angel appears with a checkbook.
- Do not neglect donors once the gift is in hand. You want to keep them as friends. And they also have friends.

Red Flags
- The museum's purpose and intent are unclear to the public.
- Policies on relationships with donors and corporate sponsors are vague.
- The museum fails to acknowledge donors promptly.
- Donors direct content.
- The museum fails to meet its fund-raising goals.

NOTES

1. American Association of Museums, *Guidelines for Museums on Developing and Managing Individual Donor Support*, November 2002.

2. See www.AAM.org, www.AAMD.org, and www.adpnet.org for ethics statements.

3. See the Listserv of the IMLS-funded Institute of Museum Ethics at Seton Hall University for discussions of ethics codes development at www.museumethics.org.

4. See nonprofit report cards at www.charitywatch.org of the American Institute of Philanthropy, www.give.org of the Wise Giving Alliance of the Better Business Bureau, www.CharityNavigator.org of Charity Navigator, and www.guidestar.org of Guidestar. From Jacklyn P. Boice, "Getting Down to Business," *Advancing Philanthropy*, May 2005, 16–23.

5. See www.kresge.org.

6. See www.foundationcenter.org and http://philanthropy.com.

Communications Strategies

PLANNING FOR COMMUNICATIONS

From the very outset, your museum must develop a plan to keep internal and external stakeholders abreast of the building project. Communication with staff allows them to own the project and understand their role in the process. Timely and regular external communication before and during a building project keeps the public and external stakeholders aware of closings and project progress, and can build excitement and support for the project's completion and opening. After opening, your museum must continue to communicate effectively about the project and value to the community in supporting exhibits, programs, research, and the improved care it provides for your collections. Because the building will present a new experience for staff and public, the messages associated with external marketing and internal operations will be critical. The risks associated with inadequate communications are high: lack of support from donors or in the press, staff morale issues, and possibly turnover.

This chapter will address a variety of communications tools, including use of the Internet, project websites and web cams, virtual walkthroughs, news releases, annual reports, press briefings, and other media approaches before, during, and after construction. You will need to use these techniques as well as your museum intranet and regular staff or departmental meetings for keeping staff engaged throughout the project to ensure smooth sailing during planning and throughout the construction project. Finally, communications strategies are a fundamental part of fund-raising and marketing. Your strategy should be to align your communications with the case statement and justifications for your capital campaign.

Figure 10.1 outlines recommended approaches for effective communications.

Who Is Responsible?

Ultimately the museum's governing board is responsible for an effective communications strategy for the building project. Senior management, the museum project manager, and the public relations staff will be directly involved in crafting and implementing the plan. Because all staff members have a stake in the project, the museum needs to give them as much information as possible. In addition, curatorial or public programs staff can serve as advocates for the project and therefore can benefit from communications and public speaking training. A primary official spokesperson is important to ensure that messages are consistent. That person should be the museum's director. The board chair or capital campaign chair can also be a spokesperson, but for the sake of consistency, the public face of the museum needs to be the director. Other players are involved, including the museum's public affairs staff and outside media or marketing firms. These individuals are directly involved in crafting a communications plan, key messages for the public, and training museum staff.

INTERNAL	EXTERNAL
• Town Meetings	• Focus Groups
• Project Website	• Public Meetings
• Staff Media Training	• Public Events
• Task Force Planning	• Media Plans
• Walkthroughs	• Website

FIGURE 10.1
Communications Plans

During the construction phase the museum project manager should be tasked with the job of serving as a daily liaison between staff and construction team to ensure constant updates on the construction progress and warnings about hazards in the building, deliveries of supplies, and other day-to-day activities.

When Do You Create a Communications Plan?

Communication is continuous. As soon as your museum has decided to embark on a building project, the strategies for communication must be crafted. Even in advance of the decision to proceed, many stakeholders have been involved with the project. Community members, museum members, volunteers, potential or current donors, and staff are all a part of the museum's family of stakeholders. Throughout the process of planning and implementation each group must be kept informed. Because the building project is highly visible and involves enormous amounts of time and funding, there are significant milestone decisions which need to be communicated with care. These include

- Site selection
- Architect selection and building design
- Decisions to close or stay open
- Historical preservation concerns
- Capital campaign launch and major gifts
- Construction impacts
- Collections impacts
- Opening timing and events

As each of these decisions is reached and implemented, it is important that you keep your internal and external audiences informed and involved. For example, the selection of an architect will have major impact on the resulting design and cost as well as public support and visitor interest. Sharing information about the process, the qualifications, and the options associated with various architectural firms is fundamental to making responsible decisions. Anticipation is frequently high regarding the selection process. Staff are worried that the design will not work well operationally; the public may feel that it is inappropriate or unattractive; while the press may criticize the costs. Full accountability in weighing options is the best approach.

Equally important is the decision to stay open during construction or close partially or fully during the months or years of the project's implementation. Visiting public, donors, and members will need to know how the museum will continue to serve them while closed; and staff will need to know how they can continue business as usual through this disruptive period (see chapter 11 for an extensive discussion of this decision).

COMPONENTS OF A COMMUNICATIONS PLAN

Communication methods vary, and often the museum is not in complete control of the message. Internet websites, blogs, email, and the press are all ways in which information about the building project, whether negative or positive, can be disseminated with lightning speed. The traditional methods of internal and external communications through news articles, press briefings, paid advertising, and direct mail are a baseline expectation while many museums are employing technology to share information more widely, less expensively, and more quickly. Coordination with key media outlets is crucial in developing support and sharing your story with the public. You may wish to engage a media partner; often a radio/TV outlet to help publicize the museum's building project and grand opening.

The most important determinant of a successful communications plan is whether the museum can motivate stakeholders to align behind the project. Doing this involves a great deal of input from staff and key external parties. The use of focus groups can be extremely helpful as the museum begins its rollout of the building project. Not only will these intensive interview sessions allow for good feedback in the planning of the programs for the museum, but they will also incorporate ideas on design and ways in which the building may impact the local community. In addition, if your museum building project visually impacts the architectural character of the neighborhood or creates traffic congestion, you will need to work with neighborhood associations, preservation societies, and local government agencies.

Likewise, design decisions that may have impacts on collections, education, and exhibition staff will certainly require their early input. For example, architectural planners will do intensive staff interviewing about work process and future space needs during the design phase. Staff working group planning, a team-based approach, includes analyzing impacts on collections, recommending new exhibitions, ideas on building maintenance, or even suggesting ways to staff programs.

Communications Strategies

The following are all excellent ways to communicate about the planning and ongoing implementation of the building project:

- Town meetings with staff and outside groups
- Public presentations by board members and the director/CEO and often the architect
- Newsletters to members
- Museum websites including images
- Press conferences and media advisories
- Radio and television interviews
- Advertising in advance of opening and afterward
- Signage/banners at the site
- Murals on construction barriers created by artists or students
- Signage on highways and on public transportation
- Exhibitions at the museum about the project
- Traveling exhibitions that relate to the project
- Partners who will share information about the project
- Museum associations that feature the project in publications or conferences
- Events hosted at the museum for neighbors, tourism officials, hotels, and taxicab drivers
- Hard-hat tours during construction
- Opening receptions for members, donors, and other key supporters
- "See it now" tours before the museum closes for construction
- Articles in newspapers, television and radio ads, placement in travel publications
- Video histories of the project for broadcast

Using a variety of ways to communicate is critical. People are busy and seek a variety of options for getting information. Many people will not read the newspaper or a direct mail newsletter, but will learn about the museum from a web publication.

Your communications plan should include a regular series of updates to your public and staff. For example, a monthly newsletter can be sent to members or posted on the website. Key milestones such as the selection of the architect, the groundbreaking, topping off, or other interesting architectural accomplishments will need special attention, as well as the ribbon cutting and grand opening. This is also an opportunity to remind the public about funding needs as well as list any special programming the museum in conducting during construction. Your museum staff can also benefit from sharing project information on the office intranet.

The Message

Your museum needs to be clear about the project in all your communications. Timing is also important in that information should not be premature or incomplete. Make certain that what is shared with staff and the public is well thought out information. Building credibility and enthusiasm for the project is the goal. But, if there is a setback such as a change in the fundraising goal or an accident on the construction site, this information needs to be shared as quickly and honestly as possible.

Public opinion is a critical factor in museum construction. There will certainly be members of the public who are unhappy about the project. Some neighbors will not like a new building that may be an incursion into a favorite park or historic district. Members of the public may feel that money invested in your museum could be used for more worthy causes. This is bound to be an issue where public tax dollars are allocated to a building program. Careful work with community groups, government agencies, historic preservationists, museum members, and the press can make or break your building project's success.

Communications need to be included in the museum's project budget. The types of services will include web design, publications design and production, marketing, and advertising. Board and staff may need to work with media relations firms to learn about key messages and effective communications techniques. This can be of great assistance in the fund-raising phase of the project.

The Art Museum of Western Virginia (Taubman Museum of Art) in Roanoke, Virginia, has done a good job of communicating with the public. Randall Stout's $66 million, 18,000-square-foot project initially aroused controversy in the region. During the project's construction the museum's website contained a vast archive of material about the progress of the project, and a web cam tracked the construction over a three-year period from groundbreaking to opening. This museum has also provided some instructive ways of dealing with negative criticism. In response to derisive press, a positive and descriptive article was written by the museum education director and a board member involved in the project.[1]

Public Activities during Construction Projects

If your museum has closed during construction, the following practices can be very important in continuing to stay relevant. Collaborating with other local museums or libraries on exhibitions, traveling exhibitions of key objects circulating to regional or national venues can be a fine way to share collections during construction as well as to advertise the building project. Public events at the museum site, such as concerts, lectures, or other festive activities will allow the museum to stay in the public eye.

Probably one of the most successful approaches to communicating with the public is the Internet. Museum websites can provide details of the building project, including photographs, live web cams, flythroughs of the finished spaces, video or audio statements by the director and the architect, time lines, and donor acknowledgments. Press releases can be posted as well as newsletters that provide monthly progress updates. Excellent examples of using the web include the Museum Renovation section of the National Museum of American History with "sneak peek" features into the construction zone or the Fort Worth Museum of Science and History during its closure for a major building project. The website included a web cam, a digital time lapse sequence, FAQs, testimonials from community leaders, and links to giving. The Currier Museum of Art in Manchester, New Hampshire, a 30,000-square-foot expansion which opened in 2008, featured a countdown clock to opening, photo galleries of construction, and ways the museum stayed in touch with audiences during the shutdown. The California Academy of Sciences $450 million renovation used the web to feature information on the architect and project team, construction web cams, virtual walkthrough of new spaces, and behind the scenes information on movement of living collections.

BRAND MARKETING AND COMMUNICATIONS

An important component of the communications during a building project is creating a brand for the museum—creating an image in the mind of the public regarding your museum.[2] It is an effort to help you stand apart from others. Branding often includes a graphic design and tag line that are highly memorable. For example, the Detroit Institute of Arts campaign "Great Art New Start" and its tag line "let yourself go" gives a glimpse to visitors of something new in store for them. New York's Museum of Modern Art unveiled its 2004 expansion with a campaign that was tagged "Manhattan Is Modern Again."

Many museums under construction hire additional staff or contract with a consultant to help with marketing and rebranding efforts.[3] Working with a cultural arts marketing firm the Indianapolis Museum of Art (IMA) totally rebranded itself during the construction. Research showed that people viewed the museum as an old, off-putting, unwelcoming sort of institution. Playing with the museum's initials, the firm created an ad with the headline "I AM A NEW WORLD OF ART" and has used "It's My Art" in additional advertising, on its website, and throughout its publications. The new branding is a hit and was awarded two prizes in the 2006 Museum Publications Design competition (for its retail shopping bag and its "Contemporary Opening" ad campaign series).[4]

In addition to its logo and letterhead, the museum should think of the entire visitor experience as part of its brand. Therefore, a museum's brand includes:

- Previsit: website, advertising, publicity, outreach
- Getting there: approach, parking, entry
- Arrival: queuing, coat check, information, ticketing, restrooms
- Navigation: signage, way finding, amenities
- Programs: orientation, exhibitions, events, education
- Food and shopping experiences[5]

Because building projects often affect a majority of these experiences, the museum must carefully consider how the brand will and should change when the building (re)opens. The Milwaukee Art Museum actually turned its expansion into a new logo—a stylized depiction of the building's Burke Brise Soleil, a moveable, wing-like sunscreen unprecedented in American architecture.[6] Museums that chose to continue to host a substantial amount of programming off-site (e.g., the Walker Art Center and the Cleveland Museum of Art) developed a "traveling" identity.

Engaging marketing professionals to ensure that messages are clear, consistent, and compelling is critical to properly communicating the new museum to its audiences. A written marketing communications plan should include measurable goals, activities, and projected costs as well as address opportunities and threats.[7]

In addition to a marketing communications plan, the museum must think through its public relations activities. Of particular importance with a building project is a plan for crisis management. With deadlines for opening often slipping in the construction field, it is important to be prepared to manage and promote positive messages to the public through the press.

In order to get the message of the day out to the public, Margaret May recommends deploying a variety of methods, including publicity, promotional materials, packaging, outreach, alliances, and partnerships.[8] In its experience getting the message across, the Walker Art Center found it much more difficult to keep national audiences informed about temporary closings than local audiences. The Walker worked with travel agencies, hotels, airports, and local tourist associations to get the word out. Rack cards were created that described off-site programs and emphasized the fact that the main museum building was closed.[9] Bus tour operators, school tour coordinators, and the travel industry must all be informed about what is happening at the museum.

Additional public relations methods employed by museums include press briefings, ad placements, media training for staff, and hard-hat tours for members of the press. For example, the Walker Art Center helped staff members "tell the story" by providing them with talking points ("three-bullet elevator conversation points") in order to communicate the new brand to others. The National Museum of the American Indian, prior to opening its new building, supplied media training for senior staff, giving them the opportunity to practice in front of a camera and to improve their public speaking skills.[10] To be effective, museums must give the press what they need to produce the story, whether it be images of the museum and collections for broadcast networks to use with stories, answers to frequently asked questions, fact sheets, or high resolution images of architectural plans. Being proactive will allow the museum to shape the story and build excitement.

Public relations outlets should include traditional media (e.g., newspapers, television, radio, magazines, and travel publications) as well as newer ways to reach out to the public (e.g., blogs, social networking sites like Facebook, image-sharing sites like Flickr, video-sharing sites like YouTube). The museum's website and email newsletters should serve as a critical and cost-effective means of communicating with the press and other constituents.

IN SUMMARY

Museums face a daunting job when it comes to effective communication. Many options are available and all should be considered, keeping in mind the cost and the staff ability to manage the various approaches. Consider the following factors in developing your communications plans.

Do's and Don'ts

- Don't hide bad news, but be proactive in telling the truth.
- Fix problems quickly and inform everyone.
- Have one point of contact for communications.
- Consider branding strategies in marketing the project.
- Work closely with the architectural design team to ensure you have images and other illustrations available to share with the staff and public.

Red Flags

- Staff morale leads to slowdown in productivity, turnover.
- Staff members misinform each other or outsiders about the status of the project (e.g., talking about the lack of resources to complete the project on time).
- Media coverage focuses on controversy related to design or cost that is not responded to.
- Neighborhood criticism of construction impacts without developing a liaison to address concerns.

NOTES

1. B. Scott Crawford and John B. Williamson III, "Don't Judge a Museum by Its Cover," *Roanoke Times*, December 5, 2007.

2. Margot Wallace, *Museum Branding* (Lanham, MD: AltaMira, 2006), 151–59.

3. The following discussion is adapted from Dana Allen-Greil, "Closed to the Public" (paper produced for course requirement at George Washington University Museum Studies program, April 2006, Washington, D.C.), 14–18.

4. American Association of Museums, "2006 Museum Publications Design Competition Honorees," www.aam-us.org/getinvolved/nominate/oldpubcomp/pubcomp.cfm (accessed April 27, 2006).

5. Margaret L. May, "Museum Institute at Sagamore: Developing Audience Experiences and Marketing," 1–7, www.lord.ca/Media/Artcl_Audience%20Development-MMay.pdf (accessed May 5, 2008).

6. Milwaukee Art Museum. "The Building: Burke Brise Soleil (Wings),"
www.mam.org/thebuilding/burke_brise_soleil.htm (accessed April 4, 2008).

7. Hugh H. Genoways and Lynne M. Ireland, *Museum Administration:
An Introduction* (Walnut Creek, CA: AltaMira, 2003), 253.

8. May, "Museum Institute," 6.

9. Walker Art Center staff, interview by Dana Allen-Greil, August 3, 2005.

10. "Branding, Building, and Bashes: Capitalizing on Your Museum Expansion"
(session at the 2006 annual meeting of the American Association of Museums,
Boston, April 30, 2006).

11

Operations

The purpose of this chapter is to reinforce the museum's need for detailed operational plans prior to and during construction and at start-up. In the best of worlds, by opening day new exhibits will be installed, permanent ones reinstalled, collections will be relocated and properly stored, and staff members will be in their appropriately fitted out workspaces.

In reality the museum does not return to "normal" for a year or more after opening. In some instances museums lack funds to fit out parts of the museum completely and must wait months or years to fully realize the project that was designed. In other cases, collections stored off-site remain to be moved to the new location. Nonetheless, most museums manage a public opening that appears seamless to visitors while staff copes with completion behind the scenes.

Although this chapter appears near the end of the book, you must heed its message at the beginning of the project planning process. Once again we begin with planning: an effective operations plan depends on engagement of the full staff during its development and on a strong communications plan throughout the life of the project. Going from the planning of a museum construction project to occupancy and shakedown of the new space may take years. Players will come and go, loyalties will be tested, and much will be demanded of the museum's staff and supporters.

This chapter will cover each stage of the operations plan, focusing first on the technical aspects: timing, assignments, processes, and decisions, and concluding with observations of the impact on, and changes experienced by, the curatorial, collections, education, exhibit, administrative, food, and retail services staff who make it happen over that period of time. It assumes that fund-raising activities, likely to include a capital campaign, are moving in parallel and are well under way, and despite the fact that many goals will have been met before construction begins, the intensity level of the campaign will continue beyond opening events. The tasks and activities of the development/campaign, public relations, and special events staff are discussed in chapters 9–10.

PRECONSTRUCTION DECISIONS

This section focuses on the development of an operations plan covering the period leading up to and through project design, during construction, and opening. Maintaining effective operations throughout the process is challenging and requires careful consideration and planning. The operations plan itself, developed in close consultation with staff, should include a master schedule for all tasks and activities with responsibilities spelled out in advance for each, along with goals and objectives with clearly defined performance targets (time, cost, quality/impact of program and product), as well as a budget. There is a sample operations schedule/checklist at the end of this chapter that should be linked with the operations budget. The plan must also include a strong set of support mechanisms to facilitate decision making and help staff cope with change.

Staff Issues and Considerations: Anticipating Anxiety

Throughout the project process, you must pay attention to staff concerns. The museum's leaders, especially members of the steering committee, are often so caught up in the excitement of the project and the increased pace and workload that they fail to see that staff members are not as fully engaged as they are. In fact, staff may be slowing down the process in a variety of subtle and not so subtle ways. The much parodied motivational parable *Who Moved My Cheese?* addresses how human beings adapt to change.[1] Managers must be alert to the disruption and uncertainty the building project is creating. *Managing at the Speed of Change,* by Daryl Conner, provides a thoughtful guide for managers to cope with and lead staff through rapidly changing circumstances: "the single most important factor to managing change successfully is the degree to which people demonstrate *resilience*: the capacity to absorb high levels of change while displaying minimal dysfunctional behavior." Conner counsels leaders to view change not as a mysterious event but as "an understandable process that can be managed."[2]

Staff members' anxieties may spring from a pending increase in workload, job uncertainty, whether they will have a voice in decisions, whether the process will give them adequate direction, visibility, or credit. Many concerns can be alleviated by (1) engaging staff members upfront in developing the operations plan, (2) spelling out in advance their roles and responsibilities during the project (Rewriting job descriptions to reflect new and/or additional duties is a good step: it is a formal acknowledgment that all parties understand that daily work life will change.), and (3) keeping them informed about progress of the project and related activities, such as fund-raising and outreach initiatives, as well as bumps along the road, especially those that change the schedule. Chapter 10 suggests several communications strategies to inform and engage staff.

Open or Closed?

Well before project initiation, existing museums must decide whether to remain open, closed, or partially open during construction. The choice will have far-reaching consequences internally and in the community. All other operational planning will flow from this decision. Much depends on whether the museum is currently in facilities away from the construction site or whether it remains in the facility undergoing renovation and/or an addition. See chapter 7 for consideration of the physical framework for making this decision. Drivers of the decision include public visibility, access for the public and staff, operability of building systems, highly site-specific costs, overall project schedule, staff morale, and ability to deliver programs and exhibitions. There are no right or wrong answers. Each museum must weigh all factors to determine the best course of action for its particular circumstance. Each museum must seek input from all its stakeholders: staff, researchers, volunteers, vendors, members, trustees, school systems, local businesses and public officials, visitors and community, before making the final decision.

The following section, concluding with "Top Ten Critical Issues," is an excerpt from an unpublished paper by Dana Allen-Greil on the effects of closing during construction based on a series of interviews with staff members of museums that closed during construction.[3]

IMPACT OF CLOSING A MUSEUM DURING CONSTRUCTION

Renovation and expansion projects offer an opportunity to extend the museum's mission by increasing exhibition space or by adding and improving facilities for educational programming. A museum in the midst of a building project, however, must balance staying useful and open to the public, on the one hand, with completing the project in a safe, cost-effective, and timely manner on the other. This section will explore how and why museums make the decision to close their facilities during construction, focusing particularly on the impact the decision has on the museum and its audiences. Attention is paid to ways in which museums attempt to stay open to the public through alternate spaces, partnerships, and outreach activities.

Closing a museum facility impacts key stakeholders in significant ways. Visitors, members, researchers, staff, the board, volunteers, sponsors, partners, affiliates, and local schools and businesses are all affected. A museum must work diligently to minimize the negative impact of closing in order for its overall building project to be considered successful.

In order to successfully recover from closing a building, museums must carefully plan and orchestrate the work of the museum in the name of the mission. Feasibility studies and strategic planning help to keep the organization on track while a marketing communications plan nurtures the institution's ongoing relationship with its constituents. Special events to mark the closing and opening of the building generate buzz and create fund-raising opportunities.

Museums considering building projects can learn from the insight of other institutions that have recently completed similar projects. It is, therefore, to the benefit of all museums that institutions conduct and publish evaluations based on their experiences and suggest best practices to others in the field.

Deciding to Close

From the beginning, planning for a museum construction project should incorporate input from the board, director, staff, donors, and the community (including a formal feasibility study). The decision to build is often a popular one, benefiting from a collective sense of opportunity and the buzz of anticipation. The decision to close during construction, on the other hand, is met with resistance and should be informed by a careful analysis of the potential impacts of closing the facility.

Financial Implications

The financial implications of closing a museum building include the loss of earned income from admission, membership, shops, food service, and other amenities. (The bottom line is impacted even if a museum remains open during construction. As visitation drops, so does the museum's earned revenue stream.) Closing the museum often allows the construction project to be completed in less time, significantly reducing overall building costs. Additional savings in operations costs are sometimes realized in reduced utility bills, decreased security costs, and other operating costs that may be temporarily reduced or eliminated while closed to the public. Memberships tend to decrease during a construction project whether the museum closes or not (though the rate of decrease is lower for museums remaining open); however, they rise after a renovated or expanded building is reopened.

Closing a facility has financial implications beyond the museum itself, and thus the potential impact to the surrounding community must also be considered. Even if a cultural institution remains open, construction at a destination institution may impact tourism in the surrounding area. Open during construction of its $66 million Animal Planet Australia addition, the National Aquarium in Baltimore experienced a drop in attendance. Nearby Inner Harbor museums, restaurants, and hotels also suffered from decreased business due to the commotion of major construction on the waterfront and the subsequent decline in visitors to the area's anchor institution.[4]

Effects on Support Base

Changes in the way the museum serves its communities during construction impact the museum's ability to fulfill its core mission. When a museum is the only one in town or is the most significant cultural institution in its region, the public and other constituents often have objections to closing their beloved institution, even temporarily. Despite the sense of loss related to a facility closing, the museum must consider that many projects can be completed more quickly in a closed building than in one that remains open to the public. A faster time line can ultimately mean far less inconvenience for the community than a prolonged project in which entrance locations continually change and it is unclear which galleries are open at any given time.

Closed institutions risk losing members, donor enthusiasm, and the goodwill of the local community. Membership perks such as free admission or discounts at the shop and food services are not applicable without a facility. Corporate sponsors are looking for opportunities to promote their brand and will look elsewhere if the museum is not generating public attention. The museum must take steps to mitigate the potential negative impacts of a facility closure.

Impacts on Educational and Loan Programs

As the educational role of museums has increased in importance over the past several decades, museums have made strides in connecting with local school districts. A shuttered or partially closed facility can make serving this audience more difficult. The Detroit Institute of the Arts, for example, had to cut school groups drastically during construction because it was unable to fit large groups of children in the museum at one time. To combat decreased college attendance at the Minneapolis Institute of Arts, the most frequently requested objects by professors were placed in a single gallery to remain on view throughout the project.

Whenever possible, museums should attempt to maintain access for researchers and scholars to its collections, archives, and staff expertise during construction. If physical obstacles stand in the way to continued access, a concerted effort to digitize collections and create online access could assist in meeting the needs of this audience. Affiliated museums that rely on collections of large institutions for exhibitions will suffer from impaired access to the museum's collections. When museums are forced to impose loan moratoriums during construction, peer institutions will have to look elsewhere for resources. Object donors and exhibition sponsors may express concern when artifacts go off display and exhibitions close. While the needs of the museum must take precedence, steps should be taken wherever possible to alleviate the discontent of these long-term stakeholders.

Safety Concerns

Another consideration is the safety and protection of the collection and of people (staff and visitors) throughout the construction project. Many objects must be protected from vibration and dust as well as fluctuations in temperature and humidity. Fire safety, construction hazards, and other risks may require keeping people not related to construction away from work zones. In some cases the museum has no option but to close due to damage from earthquakes (e.g., de Young Museum sustained seismic damage in 1989), floods (e.g., Beauvoir, Jefferson Davis's Biloxi home, was damaged by Hurricane Katrina), and other natural hazards (e.g., snow collapsed a roof at the B & O Railroad Museum in Baltimore).

Variations on Closing

Once the decision to close a museum for construction has been made, the museum has several options beyond simply closing for the entirety of the construction process. The institution may choose to close only during key phases, to close only certain parts of the building during construction, or to utilize a temporary space. If the project is an expansion or a move to an entirely new building, the museum may only need to close for the duration of the move itself. Museums have come up with a variety of creative ways to continue to matter to their communities, balancing programming during construction with the need to concentrate on facilities work.[5]

Closing completely. Some museums choose to close completely in order to focus efforts on the new construction without the distraction of ongoing operations of an existing facility (e.g., Newseum and Capital Children's Museum, which will be reborn as the National Children's Museum). Other museums (e.g., de Young Museum in San Francisco, California Academy of Sciences, Fort Worth Museum of Science and History) needed to tear down their old buildings to make way for the new. During construction, the Fine Arts Museums of San Francisco (FAMSF), which runs the de Young, capitalized on space at the Legion of Honor, another museum under the organization's purview, to exhibit collections. The museum also rented a downtown storefront to run education programs, brought outreach activities into the public school system, and participated in partnerships with the nearby Yuerba Buena Center for the Arts.[6]

Museums that have closed (or plan to close) their facilities for extended periods of time during renovation or expansion include the Getty Villa (eight years, renovation/expansion), the Smithsonian American Art Museum and the National Portrait Gallery (six years, renovation), the Morgan Library and Museum (three years, renovation/expansion), the Akron Art Museum (two years, expansion), the Amon Carter Museum in Fort Worth (two years, expansion), the Currier Museum of Art in Manchester, New Hampshire (a year and a half, expansion), and the National Museum of American History (two years, renovation).

Short-term closings and phased gallery closings. Many museums look for an alternative to closing. Staff at the Detroit Institute of Arts felt it would be too much of a disservice to the public to close the only fine arts museum in metropolitan Detroit, also one of the largest in the state of Michigan and the Midwest. Staff at the Indianapolis Museum of Art, which is similarly positioned within the region, echoed these sentiments.[7] A museum may be able to remain open throughout most of the construction project by closing during key phases of the project or by phasing partial closures so that some of the galleries are always open to the public. Despite staying open, however, museums often experience a decrease in attendance and membership during the period of construction.

The Detroit Institute of Arts (DIA) closed twice (once in August 2005 for five weeks and again in May 2007 for several months) during its expansion in order to save nearly a year of additional construction time. When it announced the closing schedule, the DIA prepared itself for a public outcry. Because of careful messaging and advertising, however, the public was sympathetic about the need to close. A blockbuster exhibition after the first closed period and a press conference to update the public on the status of the renovation helped bring visitors back, although overall attendance was down compared with preconstruction figures.

Other museums that have used a combination of closing completely for short periods of time and phased closing of individual galleries include the Milwaukee Art Museum (five months, expansion), the Indianapolis Museum of Art (five months, expansion), and the Seattle Art Museum (one year, expansion). Other museums that have kept closing time to a minimum include the Asian Art Museum of San Francisco (a year and a half), the Peabody Essex Museum in Boston (six months, expansion), and the San Diego Natural History Museum (three months, expansion). Museums that remained open but used the phased approach to closing individual galleries during construction include the Louvre, the Denver Art Museum, the American Museum of Natural History, the Montreal Museum of Fine Arts, and the Minneapolis Institute of Arts.

Acquiring alternate locations. Museums can maintain a physical facility by renting or purchasing an alternative location during construction at its flagship facility. The most famous and comprehensive example of this approach was undertaken by the Museum of Modern Art (MoMA), during the redesign and renovation of its midtown Manhattan building. In May 2002, the museum closed its Manhattan facility; one month later MoMA QNS, a temporary home in Long Island City, opened to the public. The facility in Queens, a repurposed staple factory, served as the base of the exhibition program and operations through September 2004. Two months later, the renovated Manhattan location reopened and the museum began converting MoMA QNS into a study and storage center.

MoMA QNS proved successful at drawing crowds and maintaining the flagship museum's public profile and membership, although success came at a high price, totaling $55 million for acquisition, renovation, and moving costs.[8] By purchasing the space, MoMA avoided rental fees for temporary exhibition space, and was able to repurpose it to other mission-central functions; however, the multimillion-dollar price tag is out of the reach of most museums.

When MoMA QNS was opened as a temporary exhibition space, nearby museums in Queens (e.g., the P.S.1 Contemporary Art Center, Isamu Noguchi Garden Museum, and the Sculpture Center and the Museum for African Art) saw a steep rise in attendance. This increase in visitorship was especially apparent during record-breaking blockbuster exhibitions at MoMA QNS such as the Matisse Picasso in 2003.[9] Unfortunately, when attention turned back toward Manhattan, nearby shops, restaurants, and cultural institutions suffered the effects.

The Liberty Science Center in New Jersey followed a similar path but on a smaller scale. A renovated historic railroad terminal, dubbed the Riverside facility, was made available to the center through a partnership with Liberty State Park and the New Jersey Department of Environmental Protection.[10] The Golden Gate Park location for the California Academy of Sciences and Steinhart Aquarium closed while the institution built a new facility in its original location; an alternate location in downtown San Francisco featuring a museum and aquarium was open to the public during construction.

Maximizing partnerships. Museums can rent facilities or partner with organizations with appropriate spaces to continue programming. In the summer of 2004, the Walker Art Center in Minneapolis turned its building closure into an opportunity by hosting a series of Walker Without Walls events and exhibitions in its sculpture garden and surrounding grounds as well as throughout the Twin Cities metro area. Target Corporation, headquartered in

Minneapolis, provided millions of dollars' worth of in-kind marketing—including billboards, signs on public transportation, radio spots, and magazine ads. Outreach strategies such as this can help diminish overall loss of support due to closure.

The Newseum also maximized its partnerships to present programs in a strategic way to retain public recognition of the museum and its mission. Ongoing partnerships with the Smithsonian Associates meant the Newseum was able to sustain programs and courses for the local D.C. metro area. An existing partnership with the National Press Club enabled the museum to continue a series on major issues and trends in the news; these programs were routinely covered by C-SPAN and presented to a wide audience in their entirety. The museum also developed a partnership with the D.C. Public Library system to provide programs for elementary and middle school students, and used traveling exhibitions and online activities to reach out to a national audience.

Electronic and other outreach. A museum temporarily without a facility for visitors can look to established outreach techniques to connect with national and international audiences. Some or all of these techniques may already be in place at an institution, but the closed period provides an opportunity to increase the scale and intensity of outreach efforts.

A popular way to maintain public access to collections is to create a "greatest hits" show featuring the institution's best-loved objects. The exhibition can be located within the museum's open galleries in a phased gallery-closing approach or featured at a nearby location, for example, museum, convention center, or library, depending on the security and safety needs of the objects. The National Museum of American History, for example, developed a Treasures of American History exhibition featuring over 150 objects that was displayed at the nearby National Air and Space Museum. This approach, like many outreach activities, poses branding and marketing challenges: visitors may be confused about the source of the collections. Regardless, such efforts allow continuous public access to important cultural treasures. Increasing outgoing loans can also help put artifacts on display in other museums when they cannot be shown in their own home, bringing the collections to a wider audience who might not otherwise ever see them. Other opportunities include traveling educational kits for use in the classroom, publications, speaker bureaus, and conference presentations.

Increasingly, museums rely on electronic outreach to connect with their visitors, provide educational experiences, and offer information on their collections and exhibitions. Online exhibitions do not have to be tied to exhibitions that have ever come together in the physical world. The web offers museums the ability to provide immersive, interactive visits to its audiences in a cost-effective and far-reaching manner. Museums can webcast events to a wide audience or offer electronic field trips and web chats to engage students in the classroom. By producing engaging content for the web and offering ways for audiences to interact, the museum can maintain an important connection to its constituents. Museums such as the Walker Art Center have experimented with the use of cell phone audio tours to provide tours around the grounds of the closed museum facility as well as provide information about where to see traveling exhibitions or participate in other off-site events.

Museums and other cultural institutions have access to a wide array of tools for outreach during a facility closure. The only limits to maximizing these tools are the budget and the priority, per the museum's strategic plan, that outreach will take for staff who are busy with the other important tasks of a museum construction project.

Impact on staff and volunteers. Museums should not forget that staff and volunteers are on the front lines of the frenzy that accompanies such projects. Their efforts, workspaces, and habits are intruded upon during the upheaval, and museums must strive to keep morale up and motivation high in order to prevent institutional momentum from decelerating.

Museums may face any or all of the following challenges throughout the building project: staff cuts, increased workload, additional facilities to manage (e.g., off-site storage, off-site exhibition space, off-site event space), reduced amenities (e.g., food service, restrooms), construction noise, office moves, disrupted access to collections, as well as general confusion and disorder. Museums that close to the public for an extended period of time may need to release employees and contractors whose primary jobs are to interface with visitors. Docent programs may need to be suspended.

With cramped and makeshift office space, the construction at the Indianapolis Museum of Art impacted staff in a physical way. Messages were sent constantly by the person serving as liaison between staff and construction workers, with information about everything from where to find the staff entrance that day to how to navigate the construction zone.[11] The de Young Museum, for example, committed to keeping all staff directly employed by the museum. Because the museum did not fill vacant positions, however, remaining staff had to work harder. The Newseum offered staff a generous buyout program rather than imposing layoffs, and at least one staff member was retained in each department to continue research and development for the new museum. Staff reductions were supplemented by budgeting for contractors as needed and many former employees served as contract employees at one period of time or another.

The staffing challenges facing a museum do not end when the museum (re)opens its doors. Leonard Aube's "Smooth Passages: Tips for Surviving the Transition from Capital to Operating" includes creating a strategy to keep staff beyond the inaugural year. He writes, "Employees who guide major aspects of successful campaigns are prime targets for recruiters. When experienced personnel leave, they take institutional memory with them, and stakeholder relationships suffer setbacks—all at a time when the institution is attempting to find a solid, operating foundation."[12]

Docents and volunteers are important repositories of institutional memory and bridges to the community. In order to keep such dedicated teams active, museums should develop a plan for continuing the program during closure. At the National Museum of American History, some of the docents have been with the museum for nearly forty years, and many were called on to continue their service within the temporary Treasures exhibition during closure. Volunteer forces can also serve as friendly guides for visitors coming to a museum that is partially closed or visiting the new building for the first time.

Despite the many challenges facing volunteers and staff, opportunities also exist, such as testing new ideas and modes of working, team building, and celebrating milestones. Few staff members will have prior experience with a building project to help them cope. The best way to approach the construction endeavor is as a learning experience for everyone involved. Front of the house volunteers, who are knowledgeable about how the public interacts with objects and the building, should be drawn on to help design and plan the new space. At the Indianapolis Museum of Art, volunteers were frequently queried by staff about what information they needed in order to communicate effectively with visitors about the building project. Volunteers can also be a part of rethinking the institution's approach to visitors, joining frontline and guard staff in refreshing their customer service skills before (re)opening.

Special Events to Mark Closing Date

By hosting special events and celebrations to mark the closing of the building, the museum can create opportunities to generate buzz, honor milestones, and thank its constituents. While these special events can be costly, they can also be vehicles for raising funds and for generating donor enthusiasm about future projects. Museums often see a spike in attendance in the weeks prior to closing, particularly when the building will remain closed for an extended period of time. Some museums choose to honor the closing date by hosting special events or offering extended hours, while others decide not to highlight the closing date at all.

The Walker Art Center hosted an all-night party to mark its closing in February 2004. The Newseum also hosted a series of special events before permanently leaving its old facility in March 2002 and offered extended hours for several weeks prior to closing. The National Museum of American History, which did not plan any major public events for its closing in September 2006, marked the occasion through a press photo opportunity and a ceremonial taking-down of artifacts, including the flag that hung over the Pentagon after the September 11 attack.

IMPACT OF REMAINING OPEN DURING CONSTRUCTION

As noted above, the decision to remain open brings its own issues. If the contractor must work around staff and their programming and keep collections protected in place, the construction schedule will be lengthened, and project and operating costs will be higher. The collections are at increased risk if they remain on-site and staff becomes frustrated with constant shifting to accommodate construction and aggravated with the messiness created by construction activity. The public is likewise confused and annoyed with shifting and limiting of activities. There are varied approaches to remaining open during construction.

Remain Open at a Current Site Removed from the Construction Site

If remaining open during construction at the current "old" site (this variation assumes the museum is moving to a new facility), the museum may need to relocate its collections off-site in rented or borrowed space. Every effort must be made to protect collections in secure safe space with limited access, appropriate protections against theft, humidity, and temperature extremes, insect infestation, dust, and vibration.

Top 10 Critical Issues to Address When Closing a Museum

Decision making. Involve a broad base of constituents in your decision to close, carefully considering the financial implications, health and safety, public service ramifications, and effects on support base. Strong leadership is key.

Planning. Use the feasibility study and strategic plan to benchmark performance, guide changes to the intellectual program, and inform the marketing communications plan and any necessary rebranding efforts. Planning is critical to ensure your project meets your own and your audience's expectations.

Communication. Share, publicize, and connect effectively with constituents throughout the construction project using the cost-effective, creative, as well as traditional channels.

Ongoing evaluation. Know your audience and meet its needs. Plan to evaluate before, during, and after the facility closure with measures of success that speak to the mission, rely on verifiable data, and reveal the long-term health of the museum.

Learn from others. Find other museums that have gone through similar projects and contact them. Your museum colleagues are happy to speak frankly and reflectively about what they've learned.

Continue programs. To the extent possible, continue to serve your public through alternate facilities, partnerships, and electronic outreach. Use the opportunity to prototype new program formats and target new audiences.

Nurture staff. Care for your employees through a proactive approach to motivation and morale problems. Maximize any available downtime by giving staff the opportunity to research and test new ideas.

Celebrate (re)opening. Reengage audiences, donors, the board, and the staff. Give your thanks and use the opportunity to create new relationships within the community. Don't overdo it.

Research and development. Closing provides a unique opportunity to step back, evaluate, and plan for the future. Apply this time to thinking about processes, big ideas, and new or revised goals.

Share your experiences. Use the knowledge you've gained from your building project to help other museums following in your footsteps. Compile the results from your ongoing evaluations and publish them for colleagues along with your suggested best practices and lessons learned.

If staff remains at the old site, they must not only maintain engaging exhibitions and programs in order to retain the public interest, but also must plan and prepare for opening of the new space while located at the old site. Thus staff will be working for the most part from drawings and be unfamiliar with the new facility as it develops. They may feel isolated as management and development staff focuses on the new facility, often absent for long periods. Their responsibilities may also require frequent travel between the current and new sites.

On a positive note, this is likely to be the least costly option, not only from a construction schedule and logistical standpoint, but also for staff morale and public acceptance, provided staff have a reasonably comfortable working environment, continue to have access to the collections, and maintain uninterrupted public programming at the original site.

Remain Open at the Construction Site

Remaining open with ongoing construction on-site or inside the building is the most costly option and the most difficult one for the staff, who must contend with construction dust, debris, pest infestation, noise, odors, power interruptions, opening and closing of spaces, and construction and delivery crews inadvertently wandering into staff and collection storage areas. If the collections remain on-site, their security and maintenance of appropriate climate conditions will be of paramount concern to the staff. In addition, staff will be subject to frequent moves and interruptions and perhaps denied easy access to the collections, disconcerting at the least, disorienting and frustrating in most cases. Passageways, parking areas, loading docks, and elevators are often blocked or tied up by construction activities and staff may find their staging areas for changing exhibits, holding special events, or educational activities have been pared back significantly to accommodate construction staging. Visitors too will feel the change, often aggravated by the same dust, noise, and disruptions staff experience. In addition, amenities they have come to expect, such as a coat check area or food service, are likely to be curtailed or makeshift. They may also grow weary of the limited number of activities and the infrequent exhibit changes.

The working conditions and restrictions for the construction team on-site are governed by the specifications in the contract documents. If you remain open, make sure the specifications thoroughly capture your needs and are well understood by the construction workers so that they and the staff can coexist, accomplishing their work every day.

On a positive note, remaining open helps to ensure that the staff and volunteer complement remains intact. This fact, coupled with program continuity and access, may keep staff morale stable. Area retail activities that depend on museum-driven business will also be ensured continuity. Members and visitors can remain engaged, will appreciate continuity of operations, and can join in the anticipation of the promise of new spaces. At the same time, the museum will need to structure its messages to the community to focus on the future, not the current limitations of operating in a facility during construction.

OPERATIONS PLANNING

Once the open or closed decision is made, it must be communicated internally and externally, along with where collections, staff, and volunteers will be located and what the museum plans for ongoing programs and continuing engagement with the community. A myriad of other decisions flow from the close or stay open decision, including whether and how to phase the project. See Figure 11.1 at the end of the chapter summary for a sample of an operations schedule/checklist. Also see chapter 6 for a discussion on project phasing. The other decisions involve development of an overall strategy to minimize cost and aggravation, maintain staff and volunteer morale, and maximize public attention and engagement during construction. They include answering the following questions:

Collections

- If off-site: Where is safe, convenient storage, who handles relocation moves, will objects be conserved or rehoused before or after moving, how much will it cost, will staff access continue or be curtailed?
- If on-site: What safeguards are in place to ensure climate controls, protection from dust, debris, insects, construction activity, and staff access; who is responsible, how much will it cost?
- Will collections be loaned or traveled during construction? Who is responsible, what is the cost, and how will costs be recovered?

Staff and Volunteers

- Will there be staff and volunteer layoffs; where will they be located, what will their assignments be, and how will they remain engaged?

- How will the museum project manager keep staff informed?
- Will there be contract employees to assist in collections moves? For whom will they work?
- Will there be additional assistance for fund-raising, public relations, exhibit design and preparation?

Programs

- What level of programming will be maintained?
- Will there be alternate venues in the community? What will work? Where are appropriate venues? How much will they cost, and who will pay?
- Should there be increased web presence? Who is responsible, what is the content, and how much should be invested?

Overall Image and the Public

- Will there be an aggressive, ongoing communications program with a focused message? Who is responsible, what is the scope, how much will it cost, and how is it integrated with the museum's image and programs?
- Will there be continuation of special occasions, such as special recognition events? Who is responsible and how much will it cost?
- How is continuous engagement with donors and members sustained?
- Who is responsible, what are the strategies, and how much will they cost?

The operations planning process should consider all these major questions and assign responsibilities and develop budgets and time lines to address each of these areas.

PLAN IMPLEMENTATION DURING CONSTRUCTION

The start of construction brings relief to the staff—the waiting, which could have been for years, is over and a new or renovated facility will soon be a reality. Despite upheaval and a pending increase in workload, there is excitement. If the museum is closed for any length of time it can also give some staff members an opportunity to take inventory of their tasks, turn to conservation matters, or plan programs and exhibits without the daily pressure of business as usual. For others, especially those engaged in fund-raising, opening events, and opening exhibits, however, the fevered pace quickens as the countdown to opening begins. Reality for all sets in and staffers settle into their tasks. They will include some or all of the following:

Staying in the Public Eye

- Assisting the public relations and marketing staff in keeping the public engaged with the museum during closures, limited services, and/or schedule disruptions by:
  a. Maintaining appropriate contact with donors, members, and researchers about ongoing and future programs
  b. Working with schools and community groups to deliver educational programming in settings outside the museum
  c. Fielding traveling exhibits or loan programs
  d. Maintaining an active web presence
- Fostering anticipation for the opening among ongoing and new supporters through community contacts

Preparing for Opening Events

- Preparing objects for exhibits[13]
- Coordinating the exhibit development schedule for access to the new space and for special requirements such as climate controls with exhibit designers and the museum project manager, who in turn coordinates with the construction contractor
- Ordering supplies and equipment, fabricating displays, selecting technologies
- Preparing exhibit-related publications, posters, educational, and virtual materials
- Coordinating with retail services for exhibit-related products and offerings
- Assisting public relations in preparing public announcements and promotional materials
- Assisting public relations, special events, and development staff in developing exhibit-related and other opening events
- Hiring or contracting and training vendors, security, and maintenance personnel for opening events

Preparing for Ongoing Operations

- Planning staff realignments, such as retaining or releasing temporary staff, hiring new staff to fill and/or manage and care for the additional space, including maintenance and operations, security, program, and administrative staff

- Planning move in of staff, objects, equipment, and furnishings
- Planning staff orientation
- Training staff for operating new equipment, from building systems to telephones
- Planning move in and offerings of retail operations, including specialized offerings related to opening
- Developing operating procedures and schedules for new spaces

STAFF CONSIDERATIONS: MANAGING STRESS

During this period contract employees may augment staff to help move collections and develop exhibits. Whether on or off site during construction, the constant disruption to schedules will take its toll. The museum leadership is tending to donors, the press, and the board with less time for staff concerns. This period of time can be characterized at best as confusing, frustrating, and tiring. As project phases wax and wane, so does the visibility of individual staff or staff teams. Contract and temporary employees may be in the ascendancy as various projects come to the fore. Competition may give way to resentment or jealousy. The closer to opening day the higher the tension levels. Meetings become more frequent and tempers grow shorter, schedules slip, omissions crop up, and at time things simply go wrong. Often during this time, however, it is outside events that throw staff into disarray. As opening day approaches, donors or public officials may expect special accommodation, such as VIP tours. Worst of all, the construction schedule can slip! Managers need to reread Murphy's and related laws and expect most of them to apply. Make no mistake. Parts of the building will not be turned over to the staff as planned, electrical work to support an exhibit will not be finished, debris will be everywhere, and climate controls for special objects will be on back order. At the end of the construction process, it is the staff who must be flexible. The opening events are set and there is no other way to make up the lost time. The old museum space and the old ways don't look so bad anymore. Throughout the construction process, and especially as opening day draws near, the museum leadership must build in activities to mitigate staff anxiety and stress: some planned, some spontaneous. Celebrations of milestones, such as a topping off party, time to reflect on and say good-bye to the old workplace, massages, and occasional unscheduled R&R days will add greatly to their resilience.

MOVING IN AND OPENING UP

Opening day is only a few weeks away. Much remains to be done, but the end is in sight and staff is banking on a waning supply of adrenaline to save the day. The Construction Team has begun to turn over portions of the building to the staff for exhibition installation, move in, and dry runs. The pace quickens and there are a myriad of tasks to complete.

Moving In

- Staff, including security, housekeeping, maintenance, and technical personnel, tour new quarters, get oriented to the new space, trained, and move in, although unpacking may have to wait until opening activities are over.
- Staff and volunteers walk through and practice their assignments for opening, such as securing the loading dock, managing access to secure areas, and staffing coatrooms.
- Technical and exhibit support staff are being trained to operate new systems and equipment.
- Exhibit installation is ongoing and nearing completion
- Media and IT systems are programmed and brought online.
- Retail operations move in their products and supplies, orient and train their personnel, stock their service areas, train staff, and test menus (yum!).
- Caterers and other events specialists tour facilities to determine pathways and adequacy of spaces and support for their activities.
- The construction team is still in some spaces finishing or touching up.

Shakedown

At this point the work of the curators, educators, and exhibit designers is nearing completion. Programs are in place for execution and the special events staff takes charge of everyone's lives. Activities include:

- Caterers and events coordinators dashing about
- Behind the scenes, staff training of docents and volunteers to lead groups through the new exhibits, to assist in ticketing, way finding, crowd control, and what to do in emergencies
- Training staff to use new technologies, systems, and equipment
- School and community groups testing orientation strategies

- Members of the press touring the facility and the exhibits and conducting interviews with staff, senior management, and board members to prepare reviews just prior to opening
- Shops and food services testing their operations and menus with visiting groups
- Security, housekeeping, and maintenance staff completing their training, getting their assignments, and practicing their tasks
- Front of house staff testing ticketing and software and moving groups through the building
- Special individuals, including the trustees, longtime friends and retired staff, and donors getting preview tours
- Local tour operators and taxicab drivers are also getting previews
- The construction team is probably *still* in some spaces finishing or touching up

Soft Opening

As opening day approaches, the museum will likely schedule several days of carefully orchestrated special events, with each group being treated to a unique experience. Various groups of members and friends get a preview of the exhibits and the new space. The soft opening predates the public opening and serves as a dry run for the main event.

Soft openings also provide occasions for the staff to celebrate and for the museum leadership to thank all the teams—the staff members and their families, the design teams, the construction team and all the subcontractors and workers who brought the project to fruition—to give them the sneak peek they so richly deserve (if they are not *still* finishing or touching up).

Public Opening

The special events of the public opening may be spread over several days so that each constituency will feel special. Events range from ribbon-cutting ceremonies, to special blessings, to black and white tie by invitation-only galas, to face painting for children, clowns, dancing, and string quartets. The events are celebratory and designed to showcase both the new facility and the exhibits and programs the new facility now affords the museum and the community.

Invitation lists are extensive and as comprehensive as the museum and its sponsors can afford. They may include:

- The board of trustees and public officials; corporate sponsors; partners, special guests associated with the museum's design and construction, its history or its exhibits; major donors; and leading citizens of the community who have supported the museum in a variety of ways
- Members of the press
- Educational and community groups
- Scholars and researchers
- Local businesses, particularly in adjacent neighborhoods
- Staff members, families, and friends
- The public

Getting to Normal

In the weeks and days leading up to the opening, museum management would be wise to troubleshoot issues as they arise by appointing SWAT teams and providing them with additional funding to address the hundreds of small details needed to address those oops! moments on the spot, such as IT glitches, exhibition logistical problems, a missing sign, a door that won't open, or the wrong shade of blue. After opening, many tasks lie ahead before the museum can become fully operational. Those directly related to completion of the punch list (a list of open items to be completed or corrected by the construction team); commissioning, including training of facilities staff to operate the new building's systems; and receipt of documentation are covered in chapter 6. The remainder includes:

- Implementation of policies and procedures that heretofore were only abstractions
- Staff reorganization and transition to new locations, new assignments, and new alignments, including assimilation of new staff
- Releasing contract and temporary staff or retaining them on a temporary or permanent basis
- Mastering the way finding, for both staff and volunteers
- Caring for new exhibits
- Monitoring exhibits for technical, way finding, or labeling issues

- Monitoring retail activities for trends, visitor preferences
- Gathering feedback from visitors
- Evaluating the success of the project (the topic of chapter 12)
- Developing new programs to engage new publics
- Completing collections relocation if needed
- Maintaining new space
- Maintaining morale

Staff Issues and Considerations: Overcoming Letdown and Moving Forward

Fallout. There is growing evidence that the heavy workload and levels of stress for museum staff, particularly for those with the heaviest responsibility for the project's success, result in a high degree of burnout.[14] Exhaustion is cited as the primary cause. Directors and directors of development and membership are the most visible among those who depart weeks or months after project completion, but other staff members often leave in large numbers as well. Some have held off retirement to help realize a dream. But others not on the front line also depart, completely exhausted and let down after the high levels of excitement preceding opening.[15]

There is also evidence that some projects have met neither the goals nor the expectations put forward in initial planning. In several notable cases visitation projections have fallen short, forcing some museums to close and regroup before reopening with a changed focus, a temporary tenant, and/or scaled back staff and programming. In other cases problems with building systems have forced extensive and expensive rework and delays.

While museum staff is relieved to be beyond the opening, in addition to exhaustion, with actual building occupancy staff experiences another period of confusion. All the spaces, once only lines on a drawing, are now real and cannot possibly meet all the expectations that have been building for many years. The usual grumbling after move-in to a new facility ensues. Lines of authority are now redrawn, with different individuals in the ascendancy and others no longer in the spotlight. New staff doesn't fit in and some of the most highly regarded temporary and contract staff has been released. Even though planned, their departure rends teams that have worked together for months or even years. Having lived on a high for several weeks, staff morale now may plummet. Exhaustion and depression set in and discord reigns. Depending on the perceived public success of the new facility, the exhibits, and opening programs, staff searches to find fault. Much of this letdown is unavoidable, but the response can get out of control unless the museum leadership manages the morale and momentum and refocuses staff on organizing for the future.

Moving forward. Now is the time for praise, recognition, and celebration within the museum family. It is also time to put the past into perspective, to remember the good things about the old location, or before there was a facility or even a paid staff. Setting aside times to allow the "old" staff to share these memories with the new staff, preferably over a carryout meal or two, or a happy hour after closing, can smooth their integration into a cohesive whole. The work of the project and move-in teams should be publicly acknowledged and thanked. Then the museum leadership must move the focus to the present. With additional space, the museum will never be the same. This is a good time to list all the positive features of the new surroundings. The best medicine, of course, is to begin planning anew, reorganizing to take advantage of the new spaces and new amenities, engaging staff in discovering the possibilities the new facility offers—ideas not even thought of during project planning and construction. New staff can participate fully in future planning and continuing staff can be opened to new possibilities.

It will take many months, perhaps even years, to settle completely into new surroundings. Some museum leaders say it takes ten years before a major building project is fully integrated physically, operationally, and financially into the mainstream of the organization and into the community. Whether or not this is true for all museums is hard to say, but the process does take time. Museum leadership must stay alert to staff members' concerns while continuing to lead them to acceptance of change. In a few short years "new" will drop out as a modifier to "museum" and be replaced by "our." Only then will the project's goals and expectations be realized.

IN SUMMARY

This chapter focuses on the myriad elements that must be coordinated to survive a construction project, beginning with a detailed plan of tasks, responsibilities, and time frames. It explores the pitfalls, opportunities, and mitigation strategies of and for a museum's decision to remain open or closed during construction. It also stresses the importance of attending to morale and engagement of staff, volunteers, and the public throughout the process—accommodating stress and concerns without losing sight of the overall goal: moving the project forward.

Task	Who	Start	End	Targets	Issues Comments
Pre-Construction					
Develop project plan and performance measures	Director, senior managers in consultation with staff	Several months prior to construction			
Open or close decision	Steering Committee in consultation with appropriate staff (curators, public affairs, educators)	Several months prior to construction or more than a year			See discussion in text
Communicate decision to staff and public	Director, reinforced by trustees, implemented by director of communications	Several months or more than a year prior to construction			
Staff location and assignments	Director and senior managers	During design			Retention and assignments driven largely by decision to remain open or to close
Secure collections on or off site	Curator, collections manager	Several months prior to construction	When secure storage is available on site or at permanent location		Will staff have continuous or limited access during construction?
Volunteer location and assignments	Director and senior managers	During design			Retention and assignments driven largely by decision to remain open or to close
Decisions to travel collections, exhibits, offer programs in community venues	Director, reinforced by trustees, communicated by director of communications; implemented by program staff	Logistics under way several months or a year prior to construction			Staging area for exhibits or for offering programs must be obtained

FIGURE 11.1
Operations Schedule/Checklist

Task	Who	Start	End	Targets	Issues Comments
Planning the move to the new space, including securing on or off site staging space for storage and preparation of objects and related exhibits preparations needs	Director, Project Manager, program directors and staff, director of development	Prior to and during construction			Part of a master coordination schedule for move in, installation of exhibits and opening events/activities coordinated with Steering Committee through the project manager as part of the planning process
Planning reinstallation of permanent exhibits	Project Manager, staff and exhibit designers	Prior to and during construction			Included in master coordination schedule
Planning special opening exhibits	Project Manager, staff and exhibit designers	Prior to and during construction			Included in master coordination schedule
Planning special opening events	Director, director of development, key donors, members, and trustees	Prior to and during construction			Included in master coordination schedule
Opening Activities					
All staff and volunteers tour of new space; celebration	Director and Project Manager	When space becomes available; hard hat tours prior to acceptance			
Staff orientation	Project Manager, senior staff	When space becomes available			Focus on wayfinding, operational issues, assignments during opening events

FIGURE 11.1 continued

Task	Who	Start	End	Targets	Issues Comments
Building operations and maintenance staff training	Building commissioning contractors	During construction, and when space becomes available			Focus on how to operate new systems equipment
Move of collections if applicable	Curator and staff, contractors	When space becomes available			Part of master coordination schedule for logistics
Reinstallation of exhibits	Staff and exhibit designers	When space becomes available			
Installation of special opening exhibits	Staff and exhibit designers	When space becomes available			
Private tours for donors, trustees, business partners, public officials	Director, Project Manager and/or design team members	When space becomes available; or limited number of hard hat tours prior to acceptance			
Special events honoring various individuals and groups who helped on the project; staff and their families	Director, trustees, director of development, special events coordinators and contractors	Prior to and leading up to opening			Staged according to development plan
Special activities for families/school groups/community	Education staff, docents	Prior to and leading up to opening			Tours, orientation to new space, and celebratory activities
Post Occupancy					
Shakedown and implementation of evaluation	All, led by Director and Project Manager; formal evaluation by team designated for the task	When the excitement wears off	Within 3-4 months		What worked, what isn't working, easy fixes, solutions for long term corrective actions

FIGURE 11.1 continued

Do's and Don'ts

- In consultation with all staff, develop a master schedule coordinated with the construction schedule indicating responsibilities; keep staff apprised of all changes to the schedule.
- Take care of yourselves and each other by building into the schedule rest, celebration, appreciation, and reflection time.
- Engage with the immediate community at every point of contact possible, including area businesses and local organizations near old and new sites, keeping them informed of project progress.
- Hold frequent progress meetings of all those in key roles to ensure everyone knows everyone's business and no detail is overlooked.
- Have contingency plans for construction delays, bad weather during opening, exhibits that cannot be completed on time, unavoidable loss or prolonged absence of a major board or staff member.
- Don't overlook antagonism among development, program, and administrative staff.
- Don't forget that the board and major donors are also experiencing their own anxieties.

Red Flags

- Unforeseen risks to collections, staff, or visitors
- Disorientation of staff with disruption of routine
- Major construction delays
- Low staff morale during and after construction (à la postpartum depression)
- Disruption from loss of temporary staff—permanent staff feel both the loss and the burden of additional work

NOTES

1. Spencer Johnson, *Who Moved My Cheese?* (New York: Putnam, 1998).

2. Daryl L. Conner, *Managing at the Speed of Change* (New York: Villard, 1992), 6–7.

3. Dana Allen-Greil, "Closed to the Public" (paper, George Washington University Museums Studies Program, 2006).

4. Julekha Dash, "Aquarium Expansion Delayed," *Baltimore Business Journal*, October 8, 2004.

5. Martha Morris, "Planning for Collections during a Building Project," in *The Manual of Museum Planning*, ed. Gail Dexter and Barry Lord, 2nd ed. (Walnut Creek, CA: AltaMira, 2000).

6. Deborah G. Frieden, project director, New de Young Museum Project, interview by author, April 2006.

7. Indianapolis Museum of Art staff, interview by author, April 2006.

8. Barbara Pollack, "Moma Makes Its Move," *ArtNews Online*, June 2002.

9. Joseph Berger, "Queens Ponders Post-Modern Life," *New York Times*, May 16, 2003.

10. Liberty Science Center, press release, "Liberty Science Center Unveils Plans for Major Expansion," April 2, 2004.

11. Indianapolis Museum of Art staff, interview by author.

12. Leonard J. Aube, "Smooth Passages: Ten Tips for Surviving the Transition from Capital to Operating," *ASTC Dimensions*, May-June 2001.

13. The authors recognize that planning for opening exhibits, including activities such as procuring design firms or inviting guest designers, will have begun well in advance of construction initiation. Actual exhibit development will likely coincide with the construction schedule.

14. Dorothy Spears, "When the Final Touch Is the Exit Door," *New York Times*, March 12, 2008.

15. For a personal account of surviving a construction project, see Elaine Gurian, "Moving the Museum," in *Institutional Trauma: Major Change in Museums and Its Effect on Staff* (Washington, D.C.: American Association of Museums, 1995).

Evaluation

The purpose of this chapter is to consider what constitutes a successful building project and how museums can measure and evaluate success. While this is the last chapter in the book, it should also be viewed as the first new chapter for a museum that has just completed construction. At this point you can assess what you have accomplished and begin a new journey with new goals, new visions, and new targets for further improvements and further success. This section will describe how boards, funders, the media, audience, and staff evaluate success, who is involved in evaluation, when it is done, and key items to measure. It will suggest ways to benchmark, how to identity and adopt best practices, and how to include stakeholders in the process.

MEASURING PERFORMANCE

There is helpful literature on measuring performance. A comprehensive program takes time, effort, and thoughtful preparation.[1] While there is ample literature evaluating programs and exhibits, what information exists on the impact a new or renovated building has on a museum's success is largely anecdotal or taken from personal accounts about individual projects. There is little quantifiable information on the degree of success, how museums have managed disappointing results, how they have capitalized on success, or whether their marketing efforts during and after project completion met expectations. Where information exists, this chapter will identify efforts to evaluate the long-term impact of construction projects on a museum's success.

This account assumes museums approaching a major building project either have an ongoing process for data collection or have established one when developing the strategic and business plans described in earlier chapters. The museum's exhibit designers, educators, curators, and other managers who determine inputs, outputs, and outcomes related to museum goals should each have developed an ongoing evaluation program with a limited number of key performance indicators within the framework of the strategic plan. Thereafter, with oversight from each area staff and volunteers can track key data on simple spreadsheets. Much of the information typically collected by a museum is useful in evaluating the success of a building project.

Typical data that museums should be collecting prior to the project include attendance, overall operating costs, income sources, energy consumption, security and operation costs per square foot, cost to raise a dollar, visitor satisfaction, return on public relations efforts, and net funds raised by type of activity (e.g., special events, direct mail). You will also want to add measures unique to your project, its mission and project goals, its setting, programs, and collections. It is tempting to short-cut formalizing this evaluative portion of the project, given the allure and the workload of planning the project itself. Baselines are important, however, as they can be used to measure the impacts of changes or improvements before and after the project. The museum leadership can also use baseline data to determine follow-up efforts, such as surveys and benchmarking, to develop appropriate quality and effectiveness measures in operational and programmatic areas following occupancy. Additionally, performance measurement and regular data sharing during the course of the project are essential reminders and challenges

- To staff to maintain focus on the project goals and targets
- To the steering committee, campaign committee, and the project team to monitor project status (e.g., schedule and fund-raising)
- To the public to engage them in anticipation and to show them how the museum is delivering on the project

WHO CARES ABOUT PERFORMANCE?

Let us fast-forward for a moment. Your new exhibits are in place, the ribbon has been cut, and the celebration is over. It's time to sit back and rest for the first time in months. Not so fast. The morning paper has a review of the new space and the opening gala. The local schools are calling to schedule field trips. And, oh, the board meeting is coming up next week. The trustees are going to ask, how do you feel about the project? Is it what you wanted? How do you know if you accomplished your goals? Who cares?

The board of trustees cares. And so do the donors, and so does the staff, and so does the public. The trustees want to know if you have done the right thing and if you have done it well. All the financial backers—appropriators, donors, members, foundations, underwriters, business partners—want to know if their resources were used wisely and if the project will produce the results promised in the campaign literature. The staff members want to know whether their program goals are being met in the new facility. Are the collections safe, accessible, and in good climate controlled conditions? Are the public program spaces inviting and well equipped? Can staff be more effective and efficient in their new work spaces? Is the IT infrastructure sufficient to support exhibit and program needs into the future? Does everything work? Are the spaces easy to maintain? Can the facilities staff operate the new systems? Do sight lines in the galleries aid security? And the public wants to see if the new place is the same, but better than the old one they loved. Are there more amenities, are there welcoming public gathering spaces, ample places to sit, good food at reasonable prices; are the new exhibits exciting, accessible? Is this a place where they want to spend their free time, bring their families and friends, and return to again and again? And when the excitement dies down, the museum management will want to know how well it has allocated the project resources: staff, time, and dollars.

Among the criteria for success are:

Was the project completed on time?

Was the project completed within the planned budget?

Did the museum meet or exceed fund-raising goals?

Did the museum meet or exceed attendance goals in the first few weeks?

Has the museum attracted new members and new donors?

Since opening, has the museum attracted new business to the neighborhood or the community?

How well has the museum adjusted to its new success or its disappointing results?

Did the project fall short, meet, or exceed program expectations?

Did the museum fall short, meet, or exceed attendance goals after twelve to eighteen months?

HOW DO YOU MEASURE SUCCESS?

Answers to the first five questions above are straightforward. Whether the project meets the latter goals will take some time to answer: time for the staff to settle in and establish normal operating patterns; time for a critical mass of visitors to view exhibits and attend educational programs, and decide whether to return and encourage others to do the same. But there are deeper, longer-term questions to be asked and several methodologies for finding the answers.

The success of a construction project can be evaluated against predetermined targets developed in the planning process, against the museum's past performance, against the museum's competition, and against peers using benchmarking and best practices. It is particularly useful to measure performance over time.

Against Targets

During the planning process, and particularly during the development of the business plan and the case statement, the museum will articulate what it hopes to accomplish with its construction project. There will be multiple objectives. Among them might be a building that makes a design statement to the community; that brings collections, staff and programs together under one roof; that offers discrete spaces for public programming; that replaces and upgrades outmoded building and IT systems; that adds public gathering spaces, retail space, and other amenities; and that offers more and better space for collections research and care. Measures of attainment of these objectives may be qualitative or quantitative. In the case of a design statement, success might be in the eye of the beholder—the architecture critic of the local newspaper, the donor for whom the new space has been named, the facilities manager who has to maintain and operate the new spaces, and the exhibit designer who has to work around dramatic internal spaces and/or visitors. In some cases design success cannot be measured until years after project completion.

The Guggenheim museums are good examples—critics and the public will never agree on the success of their designs. Interestingly, a bad review may be better than no review at all. Another increasingly common measure is the extent to which a project is "green," using a benchmark system such as LEED.[2] Sustainable building design is discussed elsewhere and good publications on the topic are now appearing regularly, not only for design and construction professionals, but also for museum and general audiences. In a related vein, an inside the museum measurement the board will find interesting is energy consumption per square foot compared to consumption in the former spaces.

Against Oneself

Longitudinal studies of your own museum are the easiest to assemble. Museums collect data about visitors in a variety of ways: counting as they enter, collecting demographic profile data, tracking levels and frequency of participation in museum programs, collecting written and one-on-one surveys of visitors and nonvisitors, using focus groups, opinion surveys, and comment notebooks. They also accumulate other data: number and size of gifts and grants, percentage of restricted versus unrestricted gifts, size of and earnings on the endowment, size and composition of membership programs, numbers and ages of school groups, earnings from retail activities and rental of space. They should also be collecting feedback from staff on expectations, satisfaction with working conditions, their assessment of whether they have improved productivity, and what opportunities they are seeking for mentoring and growth. Ideally a museum will have been tracking these data over time, analyzing year-to-year growth, dips, and seasonal fluctuations to measure its current status against past performance. By the time a construction project is pending, you should have good baseline data.

Ideally, you should identify baseline data at the time you settle on the vision statement for the project. Those data, along with goals, objectives, and attendant performance targets established in the strategic plan and other projected related plans, should provide the framework for evaluating performance during and after the project. Allen-Greil noted in her study an important example of front end evaluation: the Detroit Institute of Arts queried visitors in considerable detail about their expectations of its planned building and exhibition revitalization program.[3] This kind of preproject effort sets the stage for an effective evaluation of a project's success. If a good data collection program has been in place for some time, analysis of data sets before, during, and after construction is not difficult and can be undertaken by each programmatic or functional area of the museum. Interns or volunteers can be taught to maintain the data and to do simple analysis. Little has been written about the impact a building project has on attendance or on other aftermath phenomena. In 2003, Amy Gilligan and Jan Allan conducted a study of science center projects, offering some interesting conclusions and cautions.[4] Among the cautions was a word about measuring attendance. On this particular indicator, the authors advise that measurement should be delayed until at least a year after opening. While a museum may expect a surge in attendance after opening for several weeks or even months, the novelty wears off. Thereafter, in most cases, visitation will drop off, and in some cases, dramatically, as was the case with the Guggenheim Soho, which was forced to close after several years of poor attendance.[5] There are stunning successes of course, among them the "Bilbao effect," the Guggenheim's museum in Barcelona (which recovered its initial investment of $183.8 million within the first six years of its operation, as well as the enormous impact it has had on tourism in the city),[6] the U.S. Holocaust Memorial Museum in Washington, D.C., and the Museum of Modern Art's 2004 expansion in New York.[7] Little formal study beyond that of Gilligan and Allan exists on this critical indicator, although anecdotal evidence is accumulating, some of it indicating overly optimistic projects or failure to market effectively during construction phase and after opening.[8] An additional study of the impact of an infusion of lottery funding for cultural institutions in England yielded mixed results.[9] Leonard Aube offers an interesting perspective on the dangers of ignoring first-year operating costs, including marketing, in the capital campaign as well as on the need to include additional operating funds to sustain the museum through a significant drop in income several months after opening.[10]

Against Competition

The marketing analysis section of the business plan should provide ample information about the competition, be it other museums in the community, a performing arts facility, a waterfront attraction, or a nearby theme park. The most obvious measure is annual visitation, but the more subtle and interesting measures include sources and amount of financial support for each. Most of this information is easily attainable through annual reports, press releases, and local economic development agencies. Certainly a renovated, new, or expanded facility can be justified in part as a counter to the competition, but you must also be realistic about projected increases in the size of the audience your project can attract.

Against Peers: Benchmarking and Best Practices

Benchmarking is commonly used by industry and government to improve productivity or effectiveness. Selected organizational processes are compared with the best-known practices internally or in an external organization. The comparison can yield important insights for improvement opportunities. Museums use benchmarks as aids to strategic planning, to understand their competition, learn new approaches, solve problems, continuously improve, and find partners with whom to share data and information for mutual improvement.

Good literature on benchmarking abounds.[11] Organizations of all types are finding this to be a useful tool and one that their boards are familiar with. Increasingly museum associations are leading benchmarking processes with their memberships. The process is straightforward, but comparing processes and practices across museums is not an exact science.[12] The steps are:

- Select similar museums or organizations
- Design questionnaire
- Conduct survey
- Evaluate results

A good benchmarking project takes time to determine what practices or processes you want to benchmark, select organizations with which to compare, design a clear and concise questionnaire, and conduct the follow-up. Typically organizations selected are asked to "partner," that is, agree to share their data and descriptions of their processes. All participants receive project findings, data are aggregated; information about individual organizations is not shared without permission. Museums look at similar organizations to ensure transferability of a practice. However, museums have also recognized that some of the best practices come from dissimilar organizations. Disney World with its management of long lines and Nordstrom with its pioneering approach to customer service have been widely emulated by vastly different organizations.

Design of the questionnaire takes considerable time and effort to determine exactly what the museum wants to learn. You may gather information by hard copy, email copy, online survey tools, phone interviews, and site visits. The latter is often cited as the heart of understanding a best practice: an on-site visit to understand history, context, and how a process actually works, explained by staff who developed it and use it. The visits often lead to ongoing dialogue and information sharing well beyond the duration of the project. Relevant topics covered in the 2002 benchmarking study of thirty-one museums engaged in construction projects conducted by the Smithsonian Institution's National Museum of American History included:

- Strategic planning relative to new building projects
- Project programs, selection of the architect, and budget development phases
- How projects were funded, as well as details of capital campaigns
- Decision to close or remain open
- Communications systems
- Project staffing

The study revealed that in museum expansions "the best programs have a clear link to organizational strategic planning, support the museum's vision, are keenly aware of the needs of their communities, and navigate the many challenges in funding and implementation. Successful characteristics include the development of master plans, feasibility studies and business plans, adept use of consultants, and intensive involvement of stakeholders throughout the process."[13]

Following analysis of findings, a museum engaged in benchmarking identifies practices it wishes to adopt, determines the gap and the changes it would have to make to meet the benchmark, and decides whether to rework its process or practice.

AN ONGOING EVALUATION PROCESS

Ideally, evaluation of your project's success does not end with gathering and analyzing data, interviewing the staff, or asking the public for its reaction to the new space. You can use all the information collected, whether qualitative or quantitative, to establish a new baseline for measuring future initiatives. Evaluating success can be messy and uneven. Hard data cannot always be teased out of a wealth of anecdotal evidence; comparisons are difficult even among seemingly like organizations. And some projects by most measures would be deemed failures. The City Museum of Washington opened in a beautifully renovated historic structure and closed within eighteen months for lack of sufficient attendance. And, like the Bellevue Arts Museum, it weathered a disappointing reception but rebounded several years later with deliberate repurposing. These and other cases of disappointing results highlight the need to ground, clarify, and manage expectations from the outset. A good evaluation process in the beginning, with regular measurements and open communications throughout the process, might have mitigated some of the disappointing impact.

In the end, findings of each evaluation method should be shared regularly and openly with staff and stakeholders. The aim of sharing should be to correct shortcomings or strengthen targeted areas (not find fault or assign blame) and, most importantly, look to the future.

IN SUMMARY

It is worth repeating the following observations to ensure successful evaluation programs:

- Staff must understand and buy into the system or it won't work.
- Measures must be clear within the context of organizational goals.
- Everyone must understand the organization's goals.
- Functional unit goals and tasks must be clearly linked to organizational goals.
- There must be a clear system for tracking progress.

Additionally, senior leadership must be fully committed to using performance metrics to guide decision making and promote a culture that does not look for blame but values accountability for results. Museum leaders who follow this practice will find they can reach successively higher goals with a highly motivated staff.

Do's and Don'ts
- Create a comprehensive strategic plan that includes a strong SWOT analysis and outlines key indicators of success or failure.

- Include the board in developing performance measures and setting the targets.
- Don't overlook the power of measurable targets and accountabilities in the building project plan and their use throughout the plan.
- Don't omit this step: It is important to learn from mistakes, celebrate successes, and lay the groundwork for measurement as a normal part of operating in the future.

Red Flags
- Projecting unrealistic goals for post opening success.
- Failure to establish clear measures at the outset—if the museum doesn't make these expectations explicit, the public and press will define them after opening.
- Failure to track measures during the project.
- Failure to use results of performance measures for self-assessment and future planning.
- Staff turnover, including loss of senior leadership.

A FINAL WORD

We have now traversed the strategic planning circuit, from environmental scanning through visioning, goal setting, planning, and implementation of a major building project as the top priority, through occupancy, shakedown, and evaluation of success.

To those of you who are in the midst of (or have recently completed) projects, for the past five years we coauthors have observed and listened to how you have undertaken the daunting task of renovating, adding to, or building new museums. We salute all of you for your courage, vision, persistence, and resilience. And we thank you for sharing your experiences with us.

For those of you who are beginning a building process, we encourage you to explore this book, share pertinent sections with your fellow staff, and call on those who have already taken this journey.

We welcome your comments on what we say in this book and invite you to add to the store of knowledge by attending future Mid-Atlantic Museum Association Building Museum symposia, and by sharing your experiences with your colleagues in museum journal articles and newsletters.

NOTES

1. Stephanie Bell-Rose, "Using Performance Metrics to Assess Impact," in *Generating and Sustaining Nonprofit Earned Income,* ed. Sharon M. Oster et al. (San Francisco: Jossey-Bass, 2004).

2. Increasingly, LEED certification for new construction projects is an expectation of funding organizations, most notably the Kresge Foundation. See its website: "Environmental conservation—sustainable building practices, environmental stewardship and sound land-use planning—a core value of the Kresge Foundation." www.kresge.org/content/displaycontent.aspx?CID=59.

3. Dana Allen-Greil, "Closed to the Public" (paper produced for course requirement at George Washington University Museum Studies program, April 2006, Washington, D.C.), p. 25.

4. Amy Gilligan and Jan Allan, "If We Build It, Will They Come? A Study of Attendance Change after Expansion," *Dimensions,* May-June 2003, 3–4, 6.

5. Motolo Rich, "Build Your Dream, Hold Your Breath," *New York Times,* August 6, 2006.

6. Beatriz Plaza, "The Bilboa Effect," *Museum News,* September-October 2007, 15; and Denny Lee, "Bilbao, 10 Years Later," *New York Times,* September 23, 2007.

7. Melena Z. Ryzik, "Directions: the Shock of the Queue," *New York Times,* June 19, 2005.

8. See Gilligan for predictors of attendance increases and Morris for museums that have overestimated attendance or revenues and faced closures or severe budget cutbacks. Martha Morris, "Building Boom or Bust?" *Journal of Museum Management and Curatorship,* June 2007. Gilligan and Allan, "If They Build It," 3–4, 6.

9. Sara Selwood and Maurice Davies, "Capital Costs: Lottery Funding in Britain and the Consequences for Museums," *Curator* 48, no. 4 (October 2005).

10. Leonard Aube, "Smooth Passages: Ten Tips for Surviving the Transition from Capital to Operating," *ASTC Dimensions,* May-June 2001, www.astc.org/pubs/dimensions/2001/may-june/smooth.htm.

11. See Robert C. Camp, *Benchmarking: The Search for Industry Best Practices That Lead to Superior Performance* (Milwaukee: ASQC Quality Press, 1989); and Christopher E. Bogan and Michael J. English, *Benchmarking for Best Practices* (New York: McGraw-Hill, 1994).

12. Morris, "Expansionism," *Museum News*, July-August 2004; Morris, 2002 study, "Strategic Planning and Renovation Programs," National Museum of American History Smithsonian Institution, February 2003. Both of these are accounts of benchmarking studies the author conducted while deputy director of the Smithsonian Institution's National Museum of American History.

13. "Managing in the New Organization," *Harvard Management Update*, July 1999, 1–2.

APPENDIXES

Appendix A

STRATEGIC PLANNING WORKSHEET EXAMPLE

STRATEGIC PLAN: AUDIENCES

Goal: Audiences – Use our collections and scholarship to provide our public with effective presentations, products and services. (Public Impact)

Objective – Transform and revitalize the museum's exhibition program.

STRATEGIES:

Establish a long-term interpretive strategy addressing the Museum's two educational goals (see "Vision").

<u>Lead Responsibility:</u>
Director, Curatorial Affairs:
Director, Public Programs
- Improve visitor experiences by providing comprehensive orientation and easily understood wayfinding.
- Improve visitor experiences by providing excellent amenities and services.

<u>Lead Responsibility:</u>
Director, Public Programs
- Create a coherent relationship among exhibitions consistent with established themes.
- Establish the Museum as a bright, exciting and welcoming place for learning, socializing and public gathering through long-term exhibits using leading-edge techniques.

TARGETS:
- Develop an interpretive plan – FY06/07.

- Develop landmark objects concept – FY05.
- Develop welcome center concept – FY05.
- Develop a strategic plan for visitor services – FY06.

- Review exhibit priorities and adjacencies within content of renovation – FY05.
- Develop and open priority exhibitions. See "Scholarship" goals. – **FY 2005 to 2007.**
  a. Our history, our icons.
  b. Dreams of freedom.

Appendix B

Appendix C

Appendix D

- Thorough description of project scope, including project budget and time frame for completion, including responsibilities such as who obtains the permits
- Museum contacts and identity of the design team
- Process and schedule for selection including date and time of site visit and whether it is mandatory
- Scope of services needed and type of contract the steering committee anticipates the construction team will sign
- Statutory limits or requirements, if any, for the hiring process
- References from similar projects
- Résumés of all staff and whether they worked on referenced projects
- Firm financial information
- Bonding capacity
- Current workload
- Fees and what is included in fees

Appendix E

CONSTRUCTION MANAGER: SAMPLE INTERVIEW QUESTIONS

- What are your thoughts regarding the project vision statement, museum program goals, and implementation?
- Describe your approach to the preconstruction process.
- Describe your experience with similar projects, by program similarities, size, and phasing requirements performed in the past three to five years. For each project, were the project executive, project manager, and project site superintendent the same as for our project?
- Would you consider the projects successful? If so, what was the worst thing that happened and how did you address it with the owner and design team?
- Explain the involvement and responsibility of the project executive, project manager, and project superintendent.
- Regarding the construction manager project manager: How long has she been with your firm and what was her involvement in similar projects?
- What is your approach to staff continuity?
- How will the preconstruction team differ from the construction team?
- Can the construction manager identify the construction team staff to be assigned at the start of the preconstruction process?
- How will the construction manager accomplish major subcontractor cost estimating during the preconstruction process? Will the construction manager involve preferred mechanical/electrical subcontractors during the preconstruction phase or do the estimating internally?

- How do you build an atmosphere of teamwork with the design team?
- How do you use value engineering?
- If applicable, describe how to reach the best guaranteed maximum price (GMP) number? (See chapter 6.)
- If applicable, describe your approach to shared savings. (See chapter 6.)
- How do you approach reconciling program and costs?
- Discuss scheduling and phasing challenges you anticipate.

Appendix F

TYPES OF MUSEUM SPACES

Public, with Collections Present
- Lobby
- Exhibit spaces
- Orientation experience with collections

Public, without Collections Present
- Entrance canopy
- Vestibule
- Security
- Ticketing/cash booth/information/visitor services
- Orientation experience
- Education center
- Study/resource center/library
- Performance venues and auditoriums
- Retail
- Food and beverage
- Coatrooms
- Restrooms

Support, with Collections

- Loading dock
- Collections holding (clean and dirty)
- Collections processing
- Conservation labs
- Collections management offices
- Collections research area/labs
- Crate storage
- Circulation
- Collections storage

Support, without Collections

- Security area
- Monitoring station
- Locker rooms
- Security staff restrooms
- Gun locker and radio charging
- Offices
- Storage
- Institutional archives
- Exhibition furniture
- Site maintenance equipment
- Janitors closet
- Mechanical, electrical, plumbing, IT/AV rooms/closets
- Staff restrooms
- Offices for administration and staff
- Meeting rooms
- Workshops
- Exhibit and mount making workrooms

Glossary

A/E: Short for *Architect and Engineer*, or *Architecture and Engineering*, in a single firm or with an architect hiring engineers under the architectural contract.

AAM: Short for *American Association of Museums*, the national professional association that serves the museum industry, publishes industry standards, and provides educational materials.

AIA: Short for *American Institute of Architects*, the national professional association that serves the architectural field, publishes industry standards, and provides educational materials.

architect: A professional specializing in all aspects of the design of new or renovated built space, its environment, systems, and facilities.

as-builts: Drawings that show a building and its systems as they are once constructed, whether or not that matches the original plans. Should be based on drawings kept by the contractor and drawn up by the A/E at the end of construction. No warranty of being exact is provided, so *as-builts* should be used as a starting point, not a definitive guide.

beneficial occupancy: Partial occupancy or use of a constructed facility by the owner before construction has been completed and the facility turned over to the owner.

bond counsel: An attorney or law firm retained to issue a legal opinion that an organization has met the requirements to issue a municipal bond. May assist in preparing documents prior to issuing a bond.

bridge loan: Money borrowed, usually from a financial institution, to cover shortfalls in construction costs. Often used while awaiting pledge payments. Usually covered by future pledges or revenue sources.

building codes: Regulations, ordinances, or statutory requirements enforced by a government entity, relating to building construction and occupancy, and generally adopted and administered for the protection of public health, safety, and welfare. May also cover energy efficiency or accessibility.

business plan: A document summarizing a project's product, market, and competition, and proposing a strategy to produce the project, maximizing market response with minimum cost. Used in a *capital campaign* to communicate the project and its financial soundness.

capital campaign: A nonprofit organizational strategy for, and period of time allotted to, raising capital.

capital costs: Onetime costs of acquiring a site and building or renovating a facility on a site previously acquired.

cash flow management: Oversight of income and expense that results in available cash sufficient to project needs and available at times those needs occur.

change order: Contract modification document, issued by the client to the *general contractor* or *construction manager*, authorizing an alteration in the original design or specifications for a building still under construction. Neither the alteration nor its impact was included in the original design or cost proposal.

CM: See *construction manager.*

commissioning: Third-party verification process that building system components have been completed and operate with the original design intent and efficiency. The commissioning agent is hired by the owner during early design and finishes work at project completion.

competitive bidding: Cost proposals submitted to the owner by various contractors for a scope of work specified in drawings and specifications. Depending on the situation, the owner may elect for the lowest bid or the bid with "best value," which takes into account other criteria such as experience in building type and so on.

conceptual design: The first of four design stages, in which the general character and design concepts of an exhibit or architectural design are developed to meet the client's project needs. Precedes *schematic design*, *design development*, and *construction documents.*

construction budget: The sum established by the owner as available for project construction *hard costs*, including contingencies for bidding to contractors and for changes during construction.

construction documents: Final design process work product of drawings and specifications created by architects, engineers, and their consulting team communicating detailed project requirements so that contractors can plan, price, and implement construction of the design. After signing a contract, these are often referred to as *contract documents*. Subsequent to *conceptual design, schematic design,* and *design development.*

construction manager (CM): A firm or person hired to manage the preconstruction and construction phase of a building project to provide services which include estimating, constructability review, procurement of bids, and management of the *general contractor* and/or subcontractors who actually build the project. This firm or person reports to the museum's *project manager.*

contract documents: Documents which include drawings, specifications, addenda, special owner requirements that form the basis for the executed contract agreement negotiated between owner and contractors. See *construction documents.*

contractor: Firm hired by the owner responsible for building according to a scope of work described on the contract documents prepared by the *design team* for a negotiated or competitively bid price based on a competitive bid. The contractor may in turn hire subcontractors to perform special work as necessary.

cost of money: The interest expense of money borrowed plus the virtual loss of earnings on money used for a project and thus unavailable for investment.

design-build: A contractor entity or contract methodology in which design, fabrication, and construction are awarded under a single contract to a single legal entity.

design development (DD): The third design phase, which advances technical design of a project to approximately 60 percent completion of design. Subsequent to *conceptual design* and *schematic design*; precedes *construction documents.*

design team: A team of building specialists, led by a prime contractor, usually an architect, which includes all design disciplines needed to technically develop *construction documents* for bidding.

estimate of probable costs: The estimates prepared during predesign and design phases by an independent cost estimator or *construction manager* tracking project costs.

feasibility study: An investigation to determine whether a project is realistic in financial, physical, market and/or legal terms.

FF&E: Short for *furnishings, fixtures and equipment,* the items going into a building which are loosely classified as independent of hard construction. This definition can be different on different projects and may include loose equipment such as furniture, electronic equipment, collections storage equipment, and decorative or track lighting. Sometimes carpeting and short-lived interior finishes are in this category.

fixed costs: *Operating costs* over which the museum client has little or no control that occur on a regular basis, such as utilities or ongoing contracts such as maintenance or IT (information technology).

gross area (or gross square feet): The total square footage of a structure, measured from the outside building surface. Definitions of how these are calculated are included in chapter 6.

hard costs: Also called construction costs. Includes site and building costs; excludes *FF&E* and *soft costs.*

HVAC: Short for *heating, ventilation, and air conditioning,* also known as the *mechanical systems.*

lien: Legal claim on property equivalent in value to an unpaid obligation, usually held by a contractor against client property.

mechanical systems: See *HVAC.*

net area (or net square feet): Useable interior square footage, excluding stairs, walls, and so on. Also called *net assignable area.*

net assignable area: See *net area.*

onetime costs: Costs incurred on a onetime basis, such as a collections purchase or the contract for an exhibit designer.

operating costs: Costs of keeping the organization functioning ("the doors open") from day to day, for example, staff costs, rent, utilities. Sum of *fixed costs* plus *variable costs.*

operating reserves: Funds accumulated to cover unexpected deficits. A rainy day fund that should be repaid or replenished as soon as possible after draw downs.

postoccupancy evaluation: A process of evaluating the success of a project, after completion against metrics established at project inception. A variety of methodologies can be used to collect the data.

project budget: An itemized list of all project-relevant activities and expenditures over a specified period. This is the same as *total project costs.*

project manager: A key role in a capital project. Manages implementation and coordination of the capital project schedules, costs, and contracts. This title is typically used by leaders of the museum, design, exhibit, and construction teams.

punch list: Prepared near the end of construction—first by the contractor, then by the *design team* with owner input—to communicate items still unfinished, or not meeting contract specifications, that must be completed before the contractor is considered to have fulfilled the contract and requirements.

retainage: Money withheld by the owner from payment for work installed by the *general contractor* or *construction manager* to ensure the contractor and subcontractors will complete all work required. Retainage is an agreed-on percentage which is reduced at *substantial completion* and paid at close out after delivery of *as-builts* and final project warranties.

schematic design: The second design phase (up to 20 percent design completion), during which the architect assimilates the client's needs and creates drawings sufficiently communicating the project and its scale, its basic spaces and spatial relationships, for the owner's approval. Subsequent to *conceptual design*; precedes *design development* and *construction documents.*

shop drawings: Submittals are product information or drawings sent by subcontractors, product fabricators, or the *general contractor/CM* for all building components. The specifications are used to assess conformance with contract requirements. Shop drawings are reviewed and approved by the *construction team* and *design team* as well as the owner for compliance with project specifications.

short-term credit line: Used to back up an organization's internal revolving fund—to smooth out cash flow fluctuations. Similar to a *bridge loan.*

soft costs: Fees, permits, special inspections, legal and other costs for services to complete a capital project. Supplemental to *hard* (construction) *costs.*

specifications: Along with the contract drawings, the written requirements of the *general contractor*'s work, including a description of all materials to be used, their quality, method of installation, and warranty.

substantial completion: The architect's certification that construction is at a stage of completion for the facility's occupation or other intended use by the museum client. Usually triggers the building certificate of occupancy and release to the contractor of some of the *retainage* being held by the owner.

technical specifications: See *specifications*.

third party: An individual or firm impacted by actions of a museum client or any contractor, though not themselves part of the executed contract prompting those actions.

third-party financing: Funding raised by investors in private capital markets on behalf of municipalities or government entities with the expectation that the investment will be repaid based on government guarantees.

tort: A legal term for the injury inflicted by not performing a contractual obligation to specified standards.

total project costs: All costs attributable to a capital or exhibit project that are not part of the owner's *operating costs*. Includes site costs, *hard* (construction) *costs*, *soft costs* for fees, *FF&E* costs, exhibit costs, staff costs to manage the project including development costs, collections moving, curation, swing space rental, contingencies, and *endowment to support*. See *project budget*.

value engineering: An examination, often with the input of an outside consultant or expert, of project design solutions. Results in recommendations for alternative solutions of equal or better quality often with the goal of saving money. Value engineering recommendations may or may not be used. Value engineering is not an exercise of cutting building scope or quality to meet a budget.

variable costs: *Operating costs* that fluctuate and so are the most controllable, such as travel and purchase of supplies.

working capital fund: An internal revolving loan fund used to smooth out cash flow. See *bridge loan*.

SOURCES FOR DEFINITIONS

American Institute of Architects. *The Architect's Handbook of Professional Practice.* 13th ed. New York: Wiley, 2001.

Waite, Phillip S. Glossary to *The Non-Architect's Guide to Major Capital Projects: Planning, Designing, and Delivering New Buildings.* Ann Arbor, MI: Society for College and University Planning, 2005.

Selected Bibliography

PUBLICATIONS

Allen-Greil, Dana. "Closed to the Public: The Impacts of Closing a Museum for Construction." Paper, George Washington University Museum Studies Program, 2006.

American Association of Museums. *National Standards and Best Practices for U.S. Museums.* Commentary by Elizabeth E. Merritt. Washington, D.C.: American Association of Museums, 2008.

American Institute of Architects. *The Architect's Handbook of Professional Practice,* 13th ed. New York: John Wiley, 2001.

American Institute for Conservation of Historic and Artistic Works. *New Orleans Charter for Joint Preservation of Historic Structures and Artifacts.* With Association for Preservation Technology International. Washington, D.C.: AIC, 1992.

Anderson, Gail. *Museum Mission Statements: Building a Distinct Identity.* Washington, D.C.: American Association of Museums, 1998.

Anderson, Robert G. W. *The Great Court and the British Museum.* Reprint. London: British Museum Press, 2001.

Arts and Economic Prosperity: The Economic Impact of Nonprofit Arts Organizations and Their Audiences. Washington, D.C.: Americans for the Arts, 2002. www .artsusa.org/information_services/research/services/economic_impact/default.asp (accessed May 5, 2008).

Association of Art Museum Directors. *State of North America's Art Museums Survey.* Annual surveys. New York: AAMD, 2006. www.aamd.org/newsroom (accessed May 5, 2008).

———. *Managing the Relationship between Art Museums and Corporate Sponsors.* New York: AAMD, 2007. www.aamd.org/papers/documents/CorporateSponsors _clean06-2007doc.pdf (accessed April 6, 2008).

Aube, Leonard. "Smooth Passages: Ten Tips for Surviving the Transition from Capital to Operating." *ASTC Dimensions,* May–June 2001.

Berry, Tim. *Hurdle: The Book on Business Planning.* Eugene, OR: Palo Alto Software, 2002.

Blue Spruce, Duane, ed. *Spirit of a Native Place: Building the National Museum of American Indian.* Washington, D.C.: Smithsonian Institution Press/National Museum of the American Indian/National Geographic, 2004.

Bogan, Christopher E., and Michael J. English. *Benchmarking for Best Practices.* New York: McGraw-Hill, 1994.

Boice, Jacklyn P. "Getting Down to Business." *Advancing Philanthropy,* May 2005, 16–23.

Brophy, Sarah S. *Is Your Museum Grant Ready? Assessing Your Organization's Potential for Funding.* Lanham, MD: AltaMira, 2005.

Brophy, Sarah S., and Elizabeth Wylie. *The Green Museum: A Primer on Environmental Practice.* Lanham, MD: AltaMira, 2008.

Buzas, Stefan, et al. *Four Museums: Carlo Scarpa: Museo Canoviano, Possagno; Frank O. Gehry: Guggenheim Bilbao Museoa; Rafael Moneo: The Audrey Jones Beck Building, MFAH; Heinz Tesar: Sammlung Essl, Klosterneuburg.* Stuttgart: Edition Axel Menges, 2004.

Camp, Robert C. *Benchmarking: The Search for Industry Best Practices That Lead to Superior Performance.* Milwaukee, WI: ASQC Quality Press, 1989.

Cassar, May. *Environmental Management: Guidelines for Museums and Galleries.* New York: Routledge, 1994.

Chicago Museum of Contemporary Art. *Collective Vision: Creating a Contemporary Art Museum.* Chicago: University of Chicago Press, 1996.

Collins, Jim, with Jerry Porras. *Built to Last: Successful Habits of Visionary Companies.* New York: HarperBusiness, 1994.

Conner, Daryl L. *Managing at the Speed of Change: How Resilient Managers Succeed and Prosper Where Others Fail.* New York: Villard, 1992.

Council for Museums, Libraries, and Archives. *Security in Museums, Archives and Libraries: A Practical Guide.* London: Resource, 2003. www.mla.gov.uk/resources/assets//S/security_manual_pdf_5900.pdf (accessed March 31, 2008).

Crosbie, Michael. *Designing the World's Best Museums and Art Galleries.* Mulgrave, Australia: Images Publishing Group, 2003.

Darragh, Joan, and James S. Snyder. *Museum Design: Planning and Building for Art.* New York: Oxford University Press, 1993.

Dees, J. Gregory, Jed Emerson, and Peter Economy. *Enterprising Nonprofits: A Toolkit for Social Entrepreneurs.* New York: John Wiley, 2001.

———. *Strategic Tools for Social Entrepreneurs: Enhancing Performance of Your Enterprising Nonprofit.* New York: John Wiley, 2002.

Dropkin, Murray, Jim Halpin, and Bill La Touche. *The Budget-Building Book for Nonprofits: A Step-by-Step Guide for Managers and Board.* 2nd ed. Nonprofit and Public Management Series. San Francisco: Jossey-Bass, 2007.

Duberly, Sara, ed. *Organizing Your Museum: The Essentials.* Washington, D.C.: American Association of Museums, 2001.

Ezell, Lin. *Building America's Hangar: The Design and Construction of the Steven F. Udvar-Hazy Center.* London: D. Giles, 2004.

Falk, John H., and Beverly K. Sheppard. *Thriving in the Knowledge Age: New Business Models for Museums and Other Cultural Institutions.* Lanham, MD: AltaMira, 2006.

Faul-Zeitler, Roberta. "Green Museum Design: Is it Good for Collections?" *Collections Journal* 2, no. 3 (February 2006): 188–94.

Fiby, Monika, and Carlyn Worstell. "Developing a Zoo Master Plan: Why Is Master Planning Particularly Important for Zoos?" *Zoolex,* March 2003. www.zoolex.org/publication/worstell/masterplan/masterplan.html (accessed October 17, 2007).

Florida, Richard. *The Rise of the Creative Class.* New York: Basics, 2002.

Gardner, James B., and Elizabeth Merritt. *The AAM Guide to Collections Planning.* Professional Education Series. Washington, D.C.: American Association of Museums, 2004.

Genoways, Hugh H., and Lynne M. Ireland. *Museum Administration: An Introduction.* Lanham, MD: AltaMira, 2003.

George, Gerald, and Cindy Sherrell-Leo. *Starting Right: A Basic Guide to Museum Planning.* 2nd ed. Nashville: American Association for State and Local History, 2004.

Gillette, Vicki, and Susan Christian. *Planning to Succeed: Preparing a Business Plan for Your Nonprofit Organization.* Washington, D.C.: National Trust for Historic Preservation, 2000.

Gilligan, Amy, and Jan Allan. "If We Build It, Will They Come? A Study of Attendance Change after Expansion." *ASTC Dimensions,* May–June 2003, 3–4, 6.

Gurian, Elaine Heumann, ed. *Institutional Trauma: Major Change in Museums and Its Effect on Staff.* Washington, D.C.: American Association of Museums, 1995.

Hislop, Richard D. *Construction Site Safety: A Guide for Managing Contractors.* Boca Raton, FL: CRC Press, 1999.

Hopkins, Bruce R. *Starting and Managing a Nonprofit Organization: A Legal Guide.* New York: John Wiley, 2004.

Hopkins, Karen Brooks, and Carolyn Stopler Friedman. *Successful Fundraising for Arts and Cultural Organizations.* Phoenix, AZ: Oryx, 1997.

Howe, Fisher. *Welcome to the Board: Your Guide to Effective Participation.* San Francisco: Jossey-Bass, 1995.

Huberman, Martin. *Transformation: Building the Rubin Museum of Art.* DVD. VideoArt Productions, 2005–2006.

Institute of Museum and Library Services. *Museum Data Collection Report and Analysis.* Prepared by L. Carole Wharton, McManis and Monsalve Associates. Washington, D.C.: Institute of Museum and Library Services, 2005.

Integrity, Civility, Ingenuity: A Reflection of George Washington; The Making of the Ford Orientation Center and the Donald W. Reynolds Museum and Education Center at Mount Vernon. GWWO/Architects and the Mount Vernon Ladies Association. Baltimore, MD: Creo, 2007.

Jensen, James. "Putting the Training Wheels On." *Exhibitionist,* Spring 2007, 42–49.

Johnson, Spencer. *Who Moved My Cheese? An Amazing Way to Deal with Change in Your Work and in Your Life.* New York: Putnam, 1998.

Kociolek, Patrick. "A Sustainable Academy." *Museums and Social Issues,* Fall 2006. www.lcoastpress.com/journal.php?id=4 (accessed April 10, 2008).

Libeskind, Daniel. *Breaking Ground: Adventures in Life and Architecture.* With Sarah Crichton. New York: Riverhead, 2004.

———. "Designing Soul." *Museum News,* March–April 2005, 45.

Liston, David. *Museum Security and Protection: A Handbook for Cultural Heritage Institutions.* Paris: Taylor & Francis, 2007. MobiPocket e-book.

Lord, Barry. "Is It Time to Call In an Architect? Perhaps Not Yet." *International Journal of Arts Management* 7, no. 1 (Fall 2004): 4–8.

Lord, Barry, and Gail Dexter Lord. *The Manual of Museum Management.* Lanham, MD: AltaMira, 2001.

Lord, Barry, and Gail Dexter Lord, eds. *The Manual of Museum Exhibitions.* Lanham, MD: AltaMira, 2001.

———. *The Manual of Museum Planning,* 2nd ed. Walnut Creek, CA: AltaMira, 2000.

Lord, Gail Dexter, and Kate Markert. *The Manual of Strategic Planning for Museums.* Lanham, MD: AltaMira, 2007.

MacLeod, Suzanne, ed. *Reshaping Museum Space: Architecture, Design, Exhibition.* London: Routledge, 2005.

Maher, Mary. *Collective Vision: Starting and Sustaining a Children's Museum; A Comprehensive Guide for New and Existing Institutions.* Washington, D.C.: Association of Youth Museums, 1997.

Malaro, Marie C. *Museum Governance: Mission, Ethics, Policy.* Washington, D.C.: Smithsonian Institution Press, 1994.

Massarsky, Cynthia W. *A Brief Tutorial on Business Planning for Nonprofit Enterprise.* Yale School of Management, The Goldman Sachs Foundation Partnership on Nonprofit Ventures. www.ventures.yale.edu/docs/brieftutorial.pdf (accessed April 16, 2008).

Massarsky, Cynthia W., and Samantha L. Beinhacker. *Enterprising Nonprofits: Revenue Generation in the Nonprofit Sector.* Yale School of Management, The Goldman Sachs Foundation Partnership on Nonprofit Ventures. New Haven: Yale University Press, 2002.

Merritt, Elizabeth E. *Covering Your Assets.* Washington, D.C.: American Association of Museums, 2006.

Merritt, Elizabeth E., ed. *2006 Museum Financial Information.* Washington, D.C.: American Association of Museums, 2006.

Merritt, Elizabeth E., and Victoria Garvin, eds. *Secrets of Institutional Planning.* Professional Education Series. Washington, D.C.: American Association of Museums, 2007.

Milwaukee Art Museum. *Building a Masterpiece: Milwaukee Art Museum.* With introduction by Russell Bowman and essay by Franz Schulze. New York: Hudson Hills, 2001.

Morris, Martha. "Building Boom or Bust?" *Journal of Museum Management and Curatorship,* June 2007.

———. "Expansionism." *Museum News.* July–August 2004.

Naredi-Rainer, Paul von. *Museum Buildings: A Design Manual.* Oxford: Birkhauser, 2004.

Nelson, Lee H. "Architectural Character: Identifying the Visual Aspects of Historic Buildings as an Aid to Preserving Their Character." *Preservation Brief* 17. www.nps.gov/history/hps/tps/briefs/brief17.htm (accessed March 31, 2008).

Newhouse, Victoria. *Towards a New Museum.* Exp. ed. New York: Monacelli, 2006.

Oster, Sharon. *Strategic Management for Nonprofit Organizations: Theory and Cases.* New York: Oxford University Press, 1995.

Oster, Sharon, Cynthia W. Massarsky, and Samantha L. Beinhacker, eds. *Generating and Sustaining Nonprofit Earned Income: A Guide to Successful Enterprise Strategies,* 269–80. Yale School of Management, The Goldman Sachs Foundation Partnership on Nonprofit Ventures. San Francisco: Jossey-Bass, 2004.

Park, Sharon C. "Heating, Ventilating, and Cooling Historic Buildings: Problems and Recommended Approaches." *Preservation Brief* 24. www.nps.gov/history/hps/tps/briefs/brief24.htm (accessed March 31, 2008).

Pine, B. Joseph II, and James H. Gilmore. *The Experience Economy: Work Is Theatre & Every Business a Stage.* Boston: Harvard Business School Press, 1999.

A Public Trust at Risk: The Heritage Health Index Report on the State of America's Collections. Washington, D.C.: Heritage Preservation, The National Institute for Conservation, 2005. www.heritagepreservation.org/HHI/execsummary.html (accessed March 18, 2008).

Ralph, Larry J. "Contracts." *Exhibitionist,* Spring 2007, 70–78.

Robinson, Franklin. "No More Buildings!" *Museum News* 81, no. 6 (November–December 2002): 28–29.

Roper, Kathy O., and Jeffery Beard. "Strategic Facility Planning for Museums." *Museum Management and Curatorship* 20, no. 1 (January 2001): 57–68.

Rose, Carolyn L., Catharine A. Hawks, and Hugh H. Genoways, eds. *Storage of Natural History Collections: A Preventive Conservation Approach.* Iowa City: Society for the Preservation of Natural History Collections, 1995.

Rosenblatt, Arthur. *Building Type Basics for Museums.* New York: John Wiley, 2001.

Salmen, John P. S. *Everyone's Welcome: The Americans with Disabilities Act and Museums.* Washington, D.C.: American Association of Museums, 1998.

Saul, Jason. *Benchmarking for Nonprofits: How to Measure, Manage, and Improve Performance.* St. Paul, MN: Fieldstone Alliance, 2004.

Seligson, Joelle. "Setting up CAMP." *Museum,* January–February 2008, 33.

Selwood, Sara, and Maurice Davies. "Capital Costs: Lottery Funding in Britain and the Consequences for Museums." *Curator* 48, no. 4 (October 2005): 439–65.

Silber, John. *Architecture of the Absurd.* New York: Quantuck, 2007.

Skramstad, Harold, and Susan Skramstad. *Handbook for Museum Trustees.* Washington, D.C.: American Association of Museums, 2003.

Trulove, James Grayson. *Designing the New Museum: Building a Destination.* Gloucester, MA: Rockport, 2000.

U.S. Department of the Interior. *The Preservation of Historic Architecture: The U.S. Government's Official Guidelines for Preserving Historic Homes.* Guilford, CT: Lyons, 2004.

U.S. Department of the Interior, National Park Service. *Secretary of the Interior's Standards and Guidelines for Archeology and Historic Preservation.* Washington, D.C.: U.S. Department of the Interior, 1983. www.nps.gov/history/local-law/arch_stnds_0.htm (accessed May 6, 2008).

Waite, Phillip S. *The Non-Architect's Guide to Major Capital Projects: Planning, Designing, and Delivering New Buildings.* Ann Arbor, MI: Society for College and University Planning, 2005. See the glossary.

Wallace, Margot. *Museum Branding: How to Create and Maintain Image, Loyalty, and Support.* Lanham, MD: AltaMira, 2006.

Weil, Stephen E. *Making Museums Matter.* Washington, D.C.: Smithsonian Institution Press, 2002.

Weintraub, Steven. "Museum Environment." *Collections Journal,* February 2006.

Whelchel, Harriet. *Caring for Your Historic House.* New York: Harry N. Abrams, 1998.

Wireman, Peggy. *Partnerships for Prosperity: Museums and Economic Development.* Washington, D.C.: American Association of Museums, 1997.

Woodward, Jeannette. *Countdown to a New Library: Managing the Building Project.* Chicago: American Library Association, 2000.

Yao, Cynthia, et al., eds. *Handbook for Small Science Centers.* Lanham, MD: AltaMira, 2006.

Young, Dennis R., ed. *Financing Nonprofits: Putting Theory into Practice,* 33–44; 157–81; 243–68. Lanham, MD: AltaMira, 2007.

Zeiger, Mimi. *New Museum Architecture: Innovative Buildings from Around the World.* New York: Thames & Hudson, 2005.

WEBSITES

American Institute of Architects. www.aia.org (accessed May 6, 2008).

American Institute of Philanthropy. www.charitywatch.org (accessed May 5, 2008).

ASTM International. www.astm.org (accessed May 6, 2008). Formerly American Society for Testing and Materials.

American Society of Landscape Architects. www.asla.org (accessed May 6, 2008).

Association for Preservation Technology International. www.apti.org (accessed May 6, 2008).

Association of College & University Museums & Galleries. www.acumg.org (accessed May 6, 2008).

BBB (Better Business Bureau) Wise Giving Alliance. *For Charities and Donors.* www.give.org; http://us.bbb.org/WWWRoot/SitePage.aspx?site=113&id= 4ef08b14-37cb-4974-a385-7f41f63b16b0 (accessed May 5, 2008).

BuildingGreen, Inc. www.buildinggreen.com (accessed May 6, 2008).

Chronicle of Philanthropy. http://philanthropy.com (accessed May 6, 2008).

Construction Industry Institute. www.construction-institute.org (accessed May 6, 2008).

Construction Management Association of America. www.cmaanet.org (accessed May 6, 2008).

Duke University, Fuqua School of Business. *Center for the Advancement of Social Entrepreneurship.* www.fuqua.duke.edu/centers/case/about (accessed April 5, 2008).

Foundation Center. http://foundationcenter.org (accessed April 5, 2008).

Greener World Media. *Greener Buildings.* www.greenerbuildings.com (accessed May 6, 2008).

International Association of Museum Facility Administrators. www.iamfa.org (accessed May 6, 2008).

International Code Council. www.iccsafe.org (accessed May 6, 2008). Construction codes for safety and fire protection.

Massachusetts Institute of Technology. MIT Enterprise Forum. *Business Plans and Financing.* http://enterprise.mit.edu/mindshare/planning (accessed April 5, 2008).

McGraw Hill Construction. *Sweets Network.* www.products.construction.com/portal/server.pt (accessed May 6, 2008).

Museum Design Magazine. www.musenews.net (accessed April 5, 2008).

National Conference on Cultural Property Protection. www.natconf.si.edu (accessed May 6, 2008).

National Fire Protection Association. www.nfpa.org (accessed May 6, 2008).

National Trust for Historic Preservation. www.preservationnation.org (accessed May 6, 2008).

Social Returns, Inc. www.socialreturns.org (accessed May 12, 2008).

Society for College and University Planning. www.scup.org/pubs/books/n-agmcp .html (accessed April 5, 2008).

U.S. Department of Energy. www.energy.gov (accessed May 6, 2008).

U.S. Department of the Interior, National Park Service. Technical Preservation Services. www.nps.gov/history/hps/tps/publications.htm (accessed March 31, 2008).

Index

About the Authors

Walter L. Crimm, AIA, LEED AP, is a planner and architect with thirty years of experience; he directs the Cultural Design Group at EwingCole in Philadelphia. His experience includes working with art, history, and natural history musems, and science centers throughout the United States on new, expansion, and renovation projects. He has written, lectured, and conducted workshops on the topic of museum planning, design, and construction with an emphasis on providing the tools necessary for navigating the building process.

Martha Morris is associate professor of museum studies at the George Washington University. She has thirty-eight years of experience in museums as a manager and leader. She began her career in collections management and most recently served as deputy director of the National Museum of American History, where she led strategic planning efforts and oversaw a variety of facilities projects. She has served as program chair of the Mid-Atlantic Association of Museums' Building Museums symposium since its inception and has published several articles on the topic of museum construction programs. Her courses include museum project management, leadership, administration, and building museums. She has directed student research and internship projects on the topic of museum building. Over the course of her career she has served as an AAM peer reviewer and has consulted with museums worldwide.

Martha has designed and conducted workshops on museum leadership and management and published several articles on this topic. She has BA and MA degrees in art history and an MBA.

L. Carole Wharton is the former president of the Society of University Planning and has extensive background in facilities planning and construction, budgeting, finance, and strategic planning. She has led facilities planning at a multicampus university and headed budget and planning at the Smithsonian Institution for a decade. She serves as a consultant to museums, colleges and universities, government agencies, and nonprofits and has conducted numerous workshops on planning, budgeting, and performance measurement. She holds an MA in English and an EdD in higher education administration. Carole is cochair of the Building Museums symposium.